Letters
from
Nicaragua

Some portions of this book have appeared in slightly different form in *Lesbian Contradiction: A Journal of Irreverent Feminism* (584 Castro Street #263, San Francisco, CA 94114).

First Edition
10-9-8-7-6-5-4-3-2-1

Spinsters/Aunt Lute Book Company
P.O. Box 410687
San Francisco, CA 94141

Cover and Text Design: Pamela Wilson Design Studio
Typesetting: Sally Goldin and Comp-Type, Fort Bragg, CA
Production: Bridget Boylan, Susan Buie, Martha Davis, Debra DeBondt, Jennifer Krebs, Jean Swallow, Sukey Wilder

Printed in the U.S.A.
Library of Congress Catalog Card Number: 86-62136
ISBN: 0-933216-22-X

Letters from Nicaragua

Rebecca Gordon

Foreword by
Barbara Smith

spinsters*/aunt lute*

SAN FRANCISCO

Acknowledgements

I would not have had the extraordinary privilege of working in Nicaragua, nor of writing this book, without the generosity of many people:

My *compañeras*, Betty Johanna, Jane Meyerding and Jan Adams, of *Lesbian Contradiction: a Journal of Irreverent Feminism* granted me a six month leave of absence and sustained me with their love and letters. Lynn Witt and Kate Sefton, friends who specialize in reconstruction of bruised psyches, worked their magic on mine. Both my parents put aside their fears for my safety more generously than I can imagine being able to do myself, in order to support this piece of work. Douglas Spence, "Joaquín," became a trusted friend and fellow traveler. Every member of the Witness for Peace long-term team brought a special grace and grit to our work, and I'm grateful for the opportunity to have worked with each of them. Barbara Smith agreed, in the midst of other compelling work, to write a foreword.

Jean Swallow brought me into the 1980's with the generous loan of a computer. Sherry Thomas and Joan Pinkvoss of Spinsters Ink/Aunt Lute provided emotional—and logistical—support beyond what any author can expect of her publishers. Without Joan's editorial vision, this would have been a much less complete book.

My partner, Jan Adams, definitely got the bad end of this deal. I hope that should—Goddess forbid—her work require the same kind of sacrifice from me, I can answer that call with the heart, honesty and faith she offered me.

Without the faith and passion and hunger for justice of the people of Nicaragua, there would have been no Nicaraguan revolution. To them, and in particular to Chilo Herrera of Jalapa, I dedicate this book.

Spring, 1986

Nicaragua

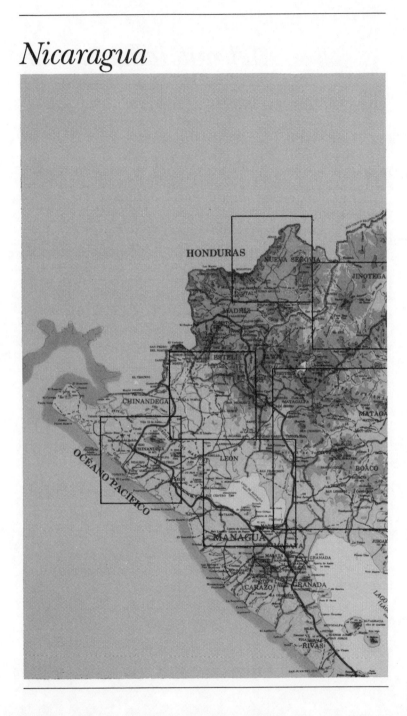

Nicaragua

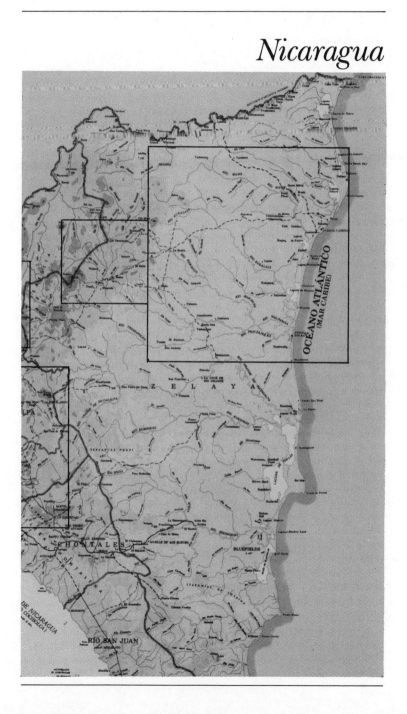

Nights in Siuna

If I sit out all night alone
watch Orion slowly shift his weight,
wait for the rifle fire to begin
again, or another mortar land;
If *me toca vigilancia*—the watching
touches me—and only my own
teeth talk to me, and hairs
rise up along my spine

Isn't this traitor fear of mine
the poem I send you?

And if you walk a picket line,
cold in the grey city, and rain
winds down your back like mercury,
the black print on the leaflets running,
and you are running down some back
street with some fifty others
fingers numbing and the Tac' Squad
coming on behind, too near

Isn't that traitor fear of yours
the poem you send me?

And if I wake in Nicaragua
sudden with the signal shots,
sweat gathering between my breasts
like troops that mass tonight outside Siuna;
and if this silent ache for you,
massing like a mine between
my breasts, explodes at a step
of memory: shock waves through flesh

This, then, is the poem that we make
between us, and the covenant:
Faith, hope and strength for the work
we've taken on together.

And revolution? That we'll also make
the night we find our hearts can spin
free between our breasts at last
and I rest in the solace of your skin.

Introduction

I had lived four months in Nicaragua the day I walked into the Sisters' house in Siuna and saw the map of the world on the wall. For four months I had been immersed in the internal life of Nicaragua, a country struggling to carry out its revolutionary project in the midst of war. For four months I had lived inside that struggle, following the political debates, documenting the achievements of that revolution and hearing the testimony of victims of that war. What news I got of events outside Nicaragua I had begun to interpret in reference to possible effects inside Nicaragua. Elections were coming up in November—*Nicaraguan* elections. When I thought about the U.S. elections scheduled for two days later, thought about the effects of a victory for Ronald Reagan, it was in the context of that victory's effect on Nicaragua.

So I lost my breath for a moment staring at the Sisters' Rand-McNally map of the world. The map made two things very clear: Nicaragua sits smack in the center of the world. And Nicaragua is a tiny country.

Now, the earth is a roundish ball floating in space. It has no top or bottom, except as these have been defined on maps through a particular collection of historical and political forces. It's no accident, for example, that the maps we know in the United States all follow the north-top, south-bottom convention, or that, following Mercator's projection, Greenland dwarfs South Africa, which is really nine times its size. My seeing Nicaragua at the center of the world on that map was the result of a particular collection of historical and political forces that have placed the United States on top, Central and South America on the bottom, and Nicaragua, for a moment in history, right in the middle of the struggle of the poor and dispossessed of the world.

Nicaragua is a tiny country of three million people. Looking at that map I remembered for the first time in months how small was the scale of death and destruction I'd witnessed. I remembered South Africa. I remembered Chile. I remembered the Philippines. I remembered East Oakland, California, and all the places where people are living and dying to birth something that looks like freedom. Nicaragua is just one of those places, but it is one that has caught the imagination of the world.

I spent May through December of 1984 working in Nicaragua with Witness for Peace, traveling in the war zones, hearing and recording the testimony of people who had suffered the effects of the U.S. government-backed *contra* war. During that time I wrote a series of letters to a group of friends and family members back home. And I wrote almost daily to my partner, Jan Adams. This book is a compilation of those letters. It is not a scholarly study of the Nicaraguan revolution. It is not a feminist critique of the Nicaraguan revolution. It is not even a sound history of the *contra* war. It's the record of what happened when one particular white lesbian feminist from the United States brought her own collection of questions, biases, skills and failings to Nicaragua at a particular time in its history, and had the privilege of living for six months inside that history.

This is a love story, about a revolution and a marriage. Did I fall in love with the Nicaraguan revolution? I hope not, because the kind of love revolutionaries need is harder than romance. I came to love the Nicaraguan revolution, even though there are things about it I dislike very much. And I came to believe that there is a great deal U.S. feminists can learn from that revolution—without attempting to transplant it whole to the very different political and economic soil of the United States.

And what about the marriage? These letters were written to a particular individual, the woman who has been my friend for twenty years, and lover for more than six. What we call our marriage is a partnership that enables each of us to do her work more deeply, more effectively. We try to keep each other honest. When I first thought about going to Nicaragua, it wasn't as if we didn't already have a full set of commitments and work at home. Two years before, we'd begun to publish a paper, *Lesbian Contradiction: a Journal of Irreverent Feminism.* While not as demanding as child-rearing, putting *LesCon* out quarterly requires fairly unremitting attention. I was proposing to abandon the project for at least two, and probably three, issues.

Beyond that particular project, I was proposing to abandon my share of the responsibility for keeping our little economic unit afloat. Our landlord had just informed us that our house was up for sale; we had to find a new place to live. If I went to Nicaragua, finding that place, and moving our household into it, would fall on Jan alone. We talked for many hours about these things. I remember Jan saying that if I went, there would probably be times when she would be very angry with me. In fact, in October, after she'd finally moved everything to the new apartment, I got a letter. "This is one of those times!" she wrote.

We talked about how hard it would be to maintain real contact with each other. For most of our friendship we have not lived in the same city, so the mere idea of carrying on through letters didn't bother us. But the time lapse did. Sometimes we'd get responses to each other's questions a month or two after they were asked. "I got a letter from you yesterday," she wrote me once. "It is very strange. They just sort of drop out of the sky." Some of our letters never arrived at all. Jan wrote me as often as I did her, letters that reflected the tremendous difficulty of this separation. Almost every one contained leaflets collected at some demonstration or other, along with Jan's acerbic and funny observations on the event. She sent running commentaries on the 1984 Olympics, and the Democratic National Convention, which San Francisco politicos re-named the "1984 Summer Games."

It may seem that there's not much passion in these letters, apart from an obvious sexual connection. A reader looking for romance may think I've edited it all out. The truth is I've removed very little; the passion is one we share for the fascinating details of the world, and for a politics that makes sense to us. This urge to talk, talk, talk to each other *is* what the relationship is about. And it is passionate.

So for months before I went to Nicaragua, we would run through Golden Gate Park after work, and talk—about the separation, about whether we'd be able to put it back together when I got back. "I'm afraid," she said, "that you'll grow beyond me somehow, that everyone here will seem childish to you after you've been where there's a war." We talked about the wars that go on here, too, and how no place is any more real than another.

And of course we talked about the small, but real possibility that I might not come back at all. Shortly after I left, Jan wrote to me, "You remember you said to me at the airport that if you got killed, you hoped I wouldn't hate the Goddess. Well the next morning I was running and feeling the grief and thinking that if you got hurt, the forces of the Right in this country would have made a killer out of me. Then I remembered what you said, and prayed about it, and one can't know of course, but I doubt that would happen. But don't you get hurt if you can help it."

The first two letters of this collection are different from the rest because they represent the distillation of all those months of talk. Jan and I wrote them for publication in *Lesbian Contradiction*, as a dialogue on the issues raised for U.S. feminists by the revolution in Nicaragua and by U.S. attempts to overthrow it.

I took a lot of political questions with me to Nicaragua. I wanted to know what this revolution had to teach the feminists of my own country. I wanted to know what a left revolution, or a Christian revolution, could offer women—and what it might threaten as well. I wanted to know about vanguard parties. Having seen a lot of hopefuls come and go in the United States, I wanted to see what happened when one actually won—and got a chance to put its program into practice.

I took a lot of personal questions with me as well. Would my relationship with Jan survive this separation? Did I have the courage for this work? Would I have the personal resources to withstand being lonely, afraid and inept in a far away place? The answer Nicaragua provided to those questions has been the greatest gift, the greatest privilege of my life. Because in Nicaragua I learned some things about history and community that shifted the whole focus of my attention away from my individual survival or "performance."

WITNESS FOR PEACE

In a way, the hardest thing for Jan—and my feminist friends—to understand, was not that I wanted to go to Nicaragua, but that I wanted to go with a church group.

Witness for Peace is a faith-based, nonviolent, grass-roots organization that places U.S. citizens in the war zones of Nicaragua, in order to share in some small way the danger created for Nicaraguans by U.S.-directed aggression, and to document the human effects of that aggression. WFP began when residents of the town of Jalapa, near the Honduran border, noticed a marked decrease in contra activity during a visit of North American church people in July 1983. From that experience grew the idea that a North American presence in border towns might provide a kind of "shield of love" (as WFP publications described it) for the Nicaraguans living in danger of contra attack. In November 1983, the first long-term WFP volunteers arrived in Jalapa.

I found the idea of U.S. citizens providing a "shield" for a presumably inert mass of Nicaraguans to be a pretty disgusting piece of arrogance when I first heard about it. But something about the project seemed profoundly right: if U.S. money is buying the supplies, the training, and even the soldiers to wage war against these people, then people from the U.S. ought to be there to share the effects of that war. The fact that WFP understood its work to be based in religious faith also seemed right to me, especially in the Nicaraguan context. Nicaragua is a deeply Christian, primarily Catholic, country, and its revolution has been informed by the theory and practice of liberation theology—which alone makes it something new under the sun.

I knew I wanted to be part of WFP. Convincing them they wanted me wasn't so easy, especially as I was not prepared to work intimately for six months in conditions of some danger without telling the whole truth about who I am. I was not prepared for WFP to treat Jan as anything less than my full partner. And WFP wasn't sure it wanted a lesbian—and a Jewish one at that—along on this Christian project. How might my being a lesbian look to the press? After all, one interviewer explained to me, WFP's constituency is ordinary church people, "and in the United States, that means white and middle class." To its great credit, WFP was able to examine its racism and homophobia, and decide it could not in conscience be working for justice in Nicaragua while perpetuating injustice at home. This was not an easy decision for some members of the WFP Steering Committee, who genuinely believed that the way I love is an affront to their God. Again, WFP's response to a Jewish applicant was not a reflex assumption that there was no conflict in inviting Jews to participate in a Christian project. After painful months of waiting, I was asked to serve as a long-term volunteer.

Two years later, I'm proud to have worked with WFP, proud of the work they continue to do in Nicaragua. In the time since I left, WFP has expanded its activities, providing a permanent presence in parts of the country we only dreamed of visiting when we were just fifteen people. WFP reports of contra atrocities have served as the basis for depositions presented by Nicaragua at the World Court. They have been used by the Washington Office on Latin America in compiling its highly respected reports on the contra war. WFP continues to be the only North American organization that systematically documents the direct and brutal effects of U.S. military policy on the Nicaraguan people. I used to wonder sometimes whether I had the right to ask someone to relive the horror of a contra attack, just so I could record one more story of torture and mutilation. But I have come to believe that it matters that the names of the victims—and of those who fought back—be recorded for history. That work WFP continues to do to this day.

Unlike our war against Vietnam, the U.S. war against Central America is happening very close to home. A few hours on a plane, a few more on a bus, or standing in the back of a pickup truck, and you can see for yourself what Nicaragua is—and what kind of war we're conducting there. WFP has made that possible for more than 2,000 North Americans. Many of these folks consider their two week trips to Nicaragua to have been the first political acts of their lives. Many of them come home changed, and ready to make change. I sometimes think WFP's biggest contribution happens here in the United States, in challenging the murderous ignorance our nation cultivates in its people.

A LITTLE NICARAGUAN HISTORY

On July 19, 1979, the government of Anastasio Somoza Debayle collapsed in Nicaragua, with the surrender of the National Guard to the Sandinista National Liberation Front (FSLN). Somoza's regime had been one of the bloodiest dictatorships in Latin America, and at the time of the triumph of the FSLN, not one sector of Nicaraguan society still supported him. Everyone—business interests, church people, workers, and the vast majority of Nicaraguans, poor *campesinos*—agreed that Somoza had to go. There was no national consensus, however, about how Nicaragua should be run in his absence.

Internationally as well, Somoza had lost what support he had. When he ordered attacks on his own cities, including the month-long bombing of Estelí, even the United States, Somoza's best friend and protector, was forced to withdraw military and economic support. No longer propped up by the country that had created and sustained the Somoza family's virtual sole proprietorship of Nicaragua, the dictatorship collapsed. Somoza's personal army, the Nicaraguan National Guard, dispersed and was permitted to flee north to Honduras, where a year later it became the nucleus of what would be called the *contrarrevolución*—the contra. In 1981, after the election of Ronald Reagan, the contra, funded, trained and directed by the United States, began their attacks on Nicaragua.

Current U.S. use of the contra in an attempt to bring down Nicaragua's government is not the first time the United States has interfered in the internal affairs of that country. The history of Nicaragua is largely a history of U.S. intervention and aggression. It begins in 1855 with one William Walker, a U.S. citizen who conquered Nicaragua with a private army. The next year he declared himself "President." His first official act in office was the re-legalization of slavery, and his presidency was immediately recognized by the U.S. government. Walker was thrown out a year later by a combination of forces, including the British and U.S. governments and various corporations, whose interests he had ceased to serve.

The U.S. next intervened militarily in Nicaragua when the Marines landed in 1909 to support a Conservative rebellion against Liberal José Santos Zelaya's presidency. The struggle between Conservatives and Liberals represented a conflict between the old landholding families and the newer bourgeoisie, and developed into a civil war, which was quashed by the U.S. Marines in 1912. Further civil war brought on another landing of U.S. Marines in 1926. They remained in Nicaragua this time until they were driven out in 1933 by General Augusto Cesar Sandino—but not before the United States had reorganized the National Guard under its own direction, and appointed Anastasio Somoza García as its commander. In 1934 the National Guard assassinated Sandino at Somoza's direction, and the Somoza family ruled Nicaragua for the next 45 years with the full support of the United States.

Somoza García, and later his sons Luís and Anastasio Somoza Debayle, treated Nicaragua as their private hacienda. The family and its associates owned twenty per cent of all Nicaragua's land, and a quarter of its industry. They allowed U.S. and Canadian companies to exploit the resources of the country, plundering the lumber, minerals, fish and fruit at the expense of its citizens. Almost half of Nicaragua's population was illiterate, most of these illiterates *campesina* women. (When asked about education in his country, as Penny Lernoux reports in *Cry of the People*, Anastasio Somoza Debayle replied something like, "Education? What for? I don't need people who can read. I need oxen!") Malnutrition and infant mortality were the worst in Central America. And the Somozas maintained their grip on Nicaragua through the terror, torture and massacres that were the methods of the hated National Guard.

In 1961, three men founded the FSLN, taking their party's name from the memory of Augusto Cesar Sandino, the leader who had driven the Marines out of Nicaragua in 1933. The history of the FSLN itself is long and complicated, but the program it put forth was relatively simple and straightforward, a particularly Nicaraguan combination of the ideas of Sandino, Marx, and Latin American revolutionary movements. The program included: access to education and health care for all; land reform, which makes land ownership possible for Nicaragua's majority, the rural poor; a mixed economy, combining state, cooperative, and private ownership of agriculture and industry; a foreign policy stressing non-alignment with any superpower; and popular participation in decision making at all levels, through mass organizations and eventually through elections as well.

The achievements of the Nicaraguan revolution are well known and well documented: the Literacy Campaign; the extension of health care to people who had never seen a medical worker; the institution of price supports to make basic necessities affordable for even the poorest families; agrarian reform; construction of housing, roads, water, and electric lines; and Nicaragua's first free elections, held November 4, 1984. Seven political parties participated, and the FSLN took 62 per cent of the vote.

The contras' atrocities are also well documented: the attacks on unarmed civilians and economic targets like hospitals and granaries; the torture and mutilations; the campaign of terror against workers in health care, education, communications and land reform. If Somoza was a bloody tyrant, and if Nicaragua has progressed so much since the Triumph, why then does the United States support the counter-revolution? Why has the United States initiated and maintained this war?

The U.S. has long had financial and strategic interests in Central America. Unlike other Central American countries, Nicaragua was never a *major* site for investment by corporations like the United Fruit Company. However, because of its proximity to countries where there has been heavy U.S. investment, control of the Nicaraguan government remains important to U.S. business interests. Nicaragua's location in the center of Central America makes its internal affairs of strategic interest to the U.S. as well. For instance, Nicaragua was the first site considered for the canal eventually built in Panama. Treaty difficulties and physical problems (the present canal is inadequate for modern supertankers) have generated a new interest in U.S. construction of a "Nicaragua Canal."

Since the promulgation of the Monroe Doctrine, the United States has asserted its right to dominate the Americas. A free Nicaragua poses serious dangers to U.S. control in the region. The United States continues to contend, without proof, that Nicaragua is "exporting revolution" to her neighbors. While U.S. claims about Nicaraguan arms shipments appear to be pure fabrication—Nicaragua needs all the arms its poorly supplied army can gather to defend its own territory—there is a sense in which these U.S. claims reflect the truth. Nicaragua is exporting something much more dangerous than arms: an example to other revolutionary movements. *"Si Nicaragua venció, El Salvador vencerá"* goes the slogan. "If Nicaragua has won, El Salvador will win." And that, the United States cannot abide.

A few words here about the expressions Nicaraguans use to describe changes going on in their country: The moment in July 1979 when Somoza's dictatorship fell was not the "Revolution," but the "Triumph," the culmination of eighteen years of organizing and struggle. The "Revolution"—also called the "Process"—denotes the ongoing work of building a new Nicaraguan society.

A CHRISTIAN REVOLUTION?

Many Nicaraguans describe theirs as a "Christian" revolution, meaning that in constructing a new society in Nicaragua, they are participating in the construction of the Reign of God—a community of peace and justice. As a feminist and the daughter of a Jewish father and "non-aligned" mother, I found the idea of a revolution based on Christianity as I have known it a little frightening. Still, I knew that the church in recent years has served as a vehicle for liberation in Latin America, and in my own country as well. Many Nicaraguans told me that it was the church that first taught them they were human beings, made in God's image, and therefore called to work for justice.

I studied Christian theology in college. There was a time in my life when my mouth was full of words for talking about God, when a Christian understanding was the best grid I'd yet found to place on the world. And then came marxism and feminism. And I had to rethink the significance, the cynical use through history, of the central symbol of Christianity—that man hanging on a cross. I saw how dangerous that symbol, with its invitation to imitate that sacrifice of self, had been to women and to other oppressed people. The call to imitate Christ I saw for the first time as what it has been for centuries: the call to the poor of the world to accept as the will of God their continued submergence in poverty and slavery. The call to the women of the world to accept male dominance. Christianity, I decided, was a great religion for rich white men. Let *them* go hang on a tree; it would do them good.

Feminism was a great gift in my life, but it left me with no way to talk about God, no way to acknowledge that my political work had a spiritual as well as a material base. So it was no accident that I chose to go to Nicaragua with a religious group, in spite of my deep suspicions of Christian theology and practice. Feminist readers may be disturbed by all the talk about God in these letters, and that instinct is probably right. But I wouldn't be telling the whole truth if I didn't talk about what sustained me when I was afraid—of failing, or of dying.

WOMEN AND REVOLUTION

As a feminist, I went to Nicaragua with a special interest in the revolution's effects on women's lives, and in discovering what women in the U.S. might learn from Nicaraguan feminists.

Nicaraguan women address their concerns, as women, most directly through their mass organization, AMNLAE. AMNLAE's initials stand for The Nicaraguan Women's Association, "Luisa Amanda Espinoza," named for the first woman militant of the FSLN to die in the insurrection. Until the November 1984 elections, AMNLAE had representation, along with other mass organizations, unions and political parties, in the Nicaraguan Council of State. (The National Assembly, elected in 1984, provides Nicaraguans with *geographical* representation by political party, rather than through organizations based on common interests. It will be interesting to see how this change in direct representation affects women's concerns.)

While committed to the *proceso*, the process of building a new Nicaragua, AMNLAE continues to actively pursue *reinvindicaciones*—restoration of rights—for women, often challenging government statements and practices in the process. Naturally, I wanted to know these women's views.

The women of AMNLAE spoke very clearly to me about the future of women in their country. "Look, *compañera*," said Susana, a woman in San Juan de Limay, "the history that is happening in Nicaragua today is the history of the revolutionary process. Women must inject ourselves into every aspect of that process. That is our best hope for enlarging the role of women in the new Nicaragua." Susana knew what she was talking about. She also knew that the time might come when AMNLAE might have to agitate more directly for women's rights.

There is a huge area of endeavor in which the interests of women and the interests of the revolution are clearly co-extensive. All the improvements of life brought about since the Triumph, the literacy campaign, health care, reduction of infant mortality, provision of price supports for basic products, granting of land titles, access to electricity and running water, have naturally affected women disproportionately. In Nicaragua as elsewhere, women were the poorest of the poor, and any revolution benefitting poor people makes great changes in the lives of women.

Nonetheless, the revolution alone has not created in Nicaragua the ideal feminist state. "We still have the problem of machismo," women told me, which manifests itself in domestic violence, abandonment of women and children, domination of men in the political process, and discrepancies in earning power between women and men. Want-ads in Nicaraguan newspapers still advertise for "Help Wanted—Male." (The number of people who actually find their employment through ads in the newspapers remains minute. Most of these, whether male or female, are middle-class Managuans.) AMNLAE has recently challenged the government's own sex-segregated want-ads, in letters appearing in the pages of the pro-government paper, *Nuevo Diario*.

Nicaragua has passed several celebrated laws aimed at creating women's equality: a law prohibiting the use of women's bodies to sell products; a law requiring fathers to help support their children; a law providing for equal pay for equal work. Laws are one thing, and social reality is another. Many women, for example, are afraid to enforce the family support law, for fear that men will require domestic or sexual services from them, in return for paying child support.

Six months in Nicaragua left me as convinced as ever of women's need for an autonomous feminism. The Nicaraguan revolution has begun to redistribute that country's wealth, and that equalization has improved the lives of many women. Like women in this country, Nicaraguan women still have far to go, however.

Nevertheless, I think U.S. feminists have a great deal to learn from the Nicaraguan revolution. In the Afterword, I sketch out some of the ideas and values emerging from that process, which we in the United States may find useful in our own work and lives. That's the beauty of a truly global feminism: the ways we strengthen each other.

MAKING CONNECTIONS

Since my return to the United States, people I knew in Nicaragua have already died in the war. Through a series of aggressive actions, the Reagan administration has continued to escalate that war, providing new financing to the contra and imposing a trade embargo. Nicaragua Libre may not survive the onslaught of U.S. intervention, I know. But history is long, and hope is a revolutionary virtue.

As this book goes to press in the summer of 1986, the struggle against apartheid intensifies in South Africa. The people of Chile have entered their fourteenth year since the U.S.-backed coup against Salvador Allende. The Philippines holds its breath to see what will come of Corazón Aquino's victory over an abandoned Ferdinand Marcos. In Philadelphia, Pennsylvania, a community rebuilds after a military-style police attack on Move, Inc. that destroyed sixty-one Black families' homes and murdered 11 people. And everywhere people are struggling in this moment in history to give birth to freedom, they find hope in the example of a tiny country called Nicaragua and its deeply imperfect, but precious revolution.

Foreword

In the week just past the United States Congress has approved one hundred million dollars in aid to the contras and given the C.I.A. official permission to wage war against the people of Nicaragua. The Supreme Court has ruled that state laws forbidding "sodomy" are constitutional, an opinion that directly attacks the right of Lesbians and gay men to exist. Because of these actions, the lives of the people who are the focus of this book are in a great deal more danger now than when these letters were written.

These travesties of justice, perpetrated by the legislative and judicial branches with the full collusion of Reagan's executive arm, occur on the eve of a frenzied celebration of "liberty" by those segments of the U.S. population who are privileged enough to feel that they have reason to celebrate. One of the sailing ships that will participate in the spectacle, despite protests, is the Esmerelda, which was used as a prison and torture center following the military coup in Chile in 1973.

This would seem like a perfect time to question what our side—the left progressive movements in this country—is accomplishing. It is certainly a time to feel a great deal of hopelessness, not to mention fear. Re-reading Rebecca Gordon's *Letters from Nicaragua* during these days has at the very least reminded me of our capacity to keep faith in the struggle despite all. In a letter dated November 12, 1984, Rebecca describes the immediate increase of U.S. military harassment in Nicaragua following Reagan's re-election. She writes:

> I should be discouraged, but I don't seem to be able to manage it, any more than I've managed to sleep much in the last week. . . I should be discouraged, but I can't quite manage it, when no one around me seems ever to have heard of despair.

These words embody the rare spirit of this book, the spirit of the Nicaraguans and of the writer who chose to spend six months in a war zone that her country helped create.

These letters, of course, provide first hand information about life inside the Nicaraguan revolution, information generally unavailable in the North American media. What makes this work so compelling, however, is not merely the facts that the letters convey, but the ethical, political, and spiritual framework from which they are written. This book demonstrates the very meaning of what it is to be an activist, to spend a life consciously committed to working for freedom. Rebecca's insights, a number of which she gains from witnessing the Nicaraguans' steadfast devotion to their struggle, have implications for people working in a variety of movements, not only on anti-intervention and feminist concerns. What Rebecca shares is the best of what activism can be.

Briefly, this is what I value about *Letters from Nicaragua*:
• The author fully believes in the necessity for revolution, not just in other people's countries, but inside our own.
• She indicates the kind of constant hard work it will take for that revolution to occur.
• She understands that any revolution worthy of the name must be committed simultaneously to eliminating sexual, racial, and class oppression.
• She understands that this is a long struggle, that if we do not see it succeed within our lifetimes, "someone will."
• She goes to Nicaragua with an attitude of humility, not to pass judgment upon the Nicaraguan people, especially in regard to gay and women's issues, but to try to find out how a totally different history affects a people's relationship to everything, including sexual politics.
• She believes that there are spiritual forces and resources which can help us to accomplish our goals and she does not hide her belief. Spirituality is at bottom about the power of transformation. So-called miracles—the phoenix rising from its ashes—are no more miraculous

than the transformation, for example, of slavery into freedom.

• She writes about all of the above as an out Lesbian feminist, demonstrating the essential ideological and ethical contributions of a movement and way of life that have often been dismissed as narrow, irrelevant, or just plain wrong.

• She openly shares her love for her partner, Jan Adams, to whom most of these letters are written, and shows how their life together has made her time in Nicaragua possible.

• She has a sense of humor.

• She has such reserves of hope.

When reading these letters, I urge people to think, as I often did, about how the U.S. government's malevolent treatment of Third World countries, including Nicaragua, is connected to the system of racism here. It is no coincidence that the U.S.' most extreme and violent foreign policies are visited upon nations inhabited by people of color. The fact that people of color are the majority of the world's population and that white people are a distinct minority also undoubtedly affects the U.S. attitude about life outside its borders.

In a recent speech in Washington, D.C. the Reverend Allan Boesak of South Africa makes this point quite clearly. He states:

"I have come to the conclusion that if it were white children who got tortured and killed the way our children get treated, the U.S. would long ago have gone in to change the situation, even if it had to be with air strikes or other violence. They would never have tolerated this," he maintained.*

The very same could be said of the U.S. government's support of the contras' murder of children in Nicaragua. Similarly, the invasion of Grenada occurred not merely because it was a tiny island where a socialist revolution had occurred, but a country occupied by Black English-speaking people whose example might well have been inspiring to Black Americans. Beginning with the annihilation of the American Indians, this country has always defined people of color as dispensable, justifiable targets of violence. Note that all of the nations Reagan has branded as terrorist just happen to be populated by people of color, including Nicaragua. Yet South Africa's verifiably terrorist white apartheid régime is never labeled or punished as such.

It is also essential to remember that there are people of color in the U.S. who live under conditions that we would only associate with life in "developing" nations. It is much easier to romanticize the situation of people who are suffering somewhere else, because that romanticization entails far less individual and collective accountability.

Rebecca raises this issue in one of her letters:

I'm going to have to come back to Central America someday, Jan. Is this seduction? Is it just that it's easier to identify with the poor of another culture? Maybe. Will you help me to remember the poor women of my own country? The longer I am here, the more I understand why what we have to work for in the U.S. is a genuine revolution. Nothing less will shift the power in the world. But a feminist revolution. And do I even know what that means anymore?

Those who think that any comparison between the situation of poor people of color here and people of color in Third World countries is exaggerated know nothing about infant and maternal mortality rates among U.S. women of color or the abysmal level of health care, education, and housing available in both rural areas and urban slums. In short they are oblivious to the reality of poverty and racism in their own country. A friend who also visited Nicaragua in 1984 shared with me a blatant example of the parallels between the situation of internally colonized people of color in the U.S. and that of people in Third World countries. While she was there she met a Nicaraguan health worker whose specialty was the prevention and treatment of tuberculosis, a disease which has not been considered a major health problem in the richest country in the world for decades. The "Third World" country where the Nicaraguan woman received her training in tuberculosis care was Harlem.

I raise these considerations about the significance of race not to make invidious comparisons or to rank levels of oppression. Since I have also had the opportunity to travel to Third World countries I certainly recognize the great difference in the *general* economic situation of the U.S. and that of other nations. It is important, however, for North Americans to address the complexities of our relationship to the rest of the globe, which we can only do by taking responsibility for the atrocities enacted by our government in our names, both inside and outside our country.

This is the kind of responsibility Rebecca took in going to and coming back from Nicaragua. It is these complexities, contradictions, and ethical questions which she faces in the pages of this book and in her life. Her own words best summarize the beauty and strength of *Letters from Nicaragua*.

Peggy Healy, a Maryknoller who has lived 11 years in a poor Managua barrio says that for U.S. citizens Nicaragua is for the weak—the U.S. is for the strong. She's right, and I know it folks. I may be scared sometimes, but my work here is easy compared to the constant effort of staving off despair that immersion in U.S. politics can be. I'm beginning to have a little faith in Nicaraguan patience. *"Esa es la guerra prolongada,"*— this is the long war. We may not live long enough to see the end of it. But someone will.

Barbara Smith
July, 1986

* The Guardian, June 18, 1986, p. 10

San Francisco

February, 1984
Dear Jan,
   This letter is my attempt to explain to you why I am volunteering for the Witness for Peace in Nicaragua. I feel as if I've explained it so many times now—to friends, to strangers—that I'm not sure that any of the power compelling me towards this action is left in me, but I'll try.

   After the United States invaded Grenada, something let go in me. I began to feel as if we were living in a special time, a crisis time. I'm afraid that for the people of Grenada the crisis is over; whatever their revolution may have been about, it will be years before there's any hope of its resurrection. But in Nicaragua there's a lot of hope. If, that is, the interests controlling the U.S. government's actions can be prevented from subverting this revolution, there's a lot of hope.

   You know what the idea behind the Witness for Peace is—that the presence of North Americans on the border between Nicaragua and Honduras seems to reduce the activities of the contra. Just how much effect this North American presence really has, I don't know. I have noticed that the contra waited to start their latest offensive until the last batch of WFP folks had left Jalapa (a little town on the border). My rational mind tells me that, as dedicated as the U.S. is to overthrowing the Sandinista revolution through the contra, ultimately the presence of a few U.S. citizens is not going to stop them. But it may buy some time for the Nicaraguans living in those border towns—time for pressure from within the U.S. to do some good. And really—all I have is myself. If I can't stop my government, maybe I can try to place myself between its agents and its targets.

All of which sounds very grandiose, as if I expected single-handedly to protect the Nicaraguan revolution from the U.S. government. The truth is that I expect to benefit much more than the Nicaraguans from my six months there. I want to know what this revolution is—and what it is for women in particular. I've always insisted that feminism must be an autonomous movement of women. I've been wary of leaping into "peoples' struggles," because so often "the people" turns out to mean "the *men*." I want to know whether the feminism attributed to the Sandinistas in books I've read translates into genuine improvement in the lives of women. I want to know what the women of AMNLAE think women have gained from the revolution—and what is still to be won. I want to know if it is possible to be a lesbian. Or whether it is possible to obtain birth control, or an abortion.

I know there's a great deal I can learn about Nicaragua through reading—certainly enough to have an informed opinion about U.S. policy there. But there are other things I can only know from my own senses, and from the heart, by being there.

I think that if by the Goddess' grace we survive the threat of nuclear war for a few more years, history is on the side of the poor in Central America. Fifty thousand died to free Nicaragua. I cannot imagine how many will die in all of South and Central America before the U.S. is finally driven out, the dictatorships finally destroyed, but I do think (as opposed to feeling or hoping) that it will happen, given the grace of enough time. I'd like to feel I was a very small part of that history.

There's a lot that appeals to me about the Sandinista government—its decentralization, its explicit commitment to women's participation in the revolution, its commitment to creating a literate, participating population. I'm sure there are things about it I would (or will) dislike, perhaps hate. I don't know enough to know. But I want to.

You know that sometimes I am terrified. I don't want to die in Nicaragua. And you know that I give myself a good 95 percent chance of coming back whole, if not unchanged. There's something strange to me about being able to drop for six months into the danger the people of Nicaragua live with their whole lives. But there's something even stranger about remaining completely insulated from that danger. It was created by my own government, and over the years I have benefitted materially from the danger in which other people live, whether I chose to or not.

I haven't worked much with peace activists in the past. Hope I can stand them. Hope they can stand me. We do have in common that our politics arise out of our spiritual lives. Whether we can recognize that in each other is another question. Most of the other participants will be Christians. How they're going to deal with having a nice Jewish girl (however familiar with Christian theology) in their midst, I don't know. What I do know is that in Nicaragua, as in much of Latin America, Christian faith has produced and sustained many genuine revolutionaries. Strange to think of reading the Bible as a revolutionary act. Strange, too, to know that so many who call themselves Christians in the U.S. are the abiding enemies of the justice which so many Christians in Nicaragua are working to achieve.

So that's the story. I want to go to Nicaragua because the historical moment seems to require something beyond my ordinary level of political involvement. I wish to God you could go with me. I hope you know that you are always in my heart, and that it's due in large part to our friendship and its content over many years that I find myself now with this ridiculous, inconvenient, frightening vocation.

◼ *So much love, Rebecca*

February, 1984
Dear Rebecca,

As I listen to reports on alternative radio that three thousand contras have infiltrated Nicaragua in the last week, I'm thinking about my answer to your letter about joining Witness for Peace. Oh hell—I DON'T WANT YOU TO GO!

Partly, realistically, I am afraid for your safety. There's a war going on down there, and you propose to inject yourself into it in a most defenseless manner. However, I know I am unable to assess accurately how much danger you are going into. And I know that whatever danger you are going to, the Nicaraguans live it without any choice in the matter. Thinking about the danger just muddles my head.

Anyway, mostly I don't want you to go because your going will disrupt the (relatively) comfortable, orderly pattern of the lives we've built together. I am used to having you around. Our partnership enables us to do so much more than either of us could do alone. I've gotten accustomed to our trying to write at the same time in our offices at either end of the apartment. You, too, are willing to trudge off to dreary but necessary little demonstrations for the myriad causes a progressive lesbian feminist needs to support. The idea of carrying on with the San Francisco end of *LesCon* by myself is daunting. It doesn't help, either, that just at this time the speculative real estate ferment here is threatening to get us evicted from our apartment.

But when I am brave, I know all of that just adds up to an assumption that it is possible, normal, for any of us here to live lives determined by our private priorities. And I know that assumption is bullshit, a false understanding of the time and place in which we live. I don't really think those of us in this country who have any energy left over from survival struggles (physical and psychic) can retreat into purely private concerns. If we really have anything left over, we have a moral obligation to give of our surplus in some way. But shit—we also have an urgent *self*-interest in turning around the way the world works (though this is liable to reduce our personal privilege).

I am glad you mentioned the Bomb. None of our attempts to understand this world (whether as feminists or anti-imperialists or what-have-you) makes any sense if we leave it out. The prospect of species extinction, possibly of planetary extinction, changes whatever rules we thought the game had. That the elites currently in power command the Bomb is the curse of our time. As Alice Walker has written, "Only justice can stop a curse." It is not enough to struggle against the Bomb by advocating disarmament or peace; only the rule of justice, in as many ways as possible, will remove the incentive to risk the extinction of our enemies and ourselves. If any of us want to go on living, we'd better work for justice (and maybe try not to fight too hard with others who are working for justice in ways we would not have chosen.)

It is in this context that I understand your wanting to stop the blatant injustice of U.S. support for counter-revolution in Nicaragua. Here are the Nicaraguans celebrating their victory over a particularly vicious dictator, teaching people to read, establishing clinics in areas where no doctor has ever been seen before. And some politicians in that big country up north, who hardly even know where Nicaragua is, want to stop the revolution—all to show the U.S. electorate they didn't lose a country to godless Communism. As if it were any of their business! It is obscene. There is tremendous justice in wanting to stand beside the Nicaraguans.

I have a lot more reservations about Witness for Peace than I do about the Nicaraguan revolution. My exposure to the Catholic pacifism of Dorothy Day, and to the Catholic Worker movement she founded, was responsible for changing my *sentiment* in favor of justice into a *commitment* to work for the long haul (often in areas Dorothy would hardly recognize). But I sure didn't find working with peace people easy. Too often they just erase from their thoughts the different experiences of people of color, women, lesbians (even when, as is often the case, they fall into one or more of those categories themselves). Too often they use moral righteousness as a bludgeon in intramural struggles. (Guess lots of feminists do that too.) Anyway, I just hope that set down in the context of a real revolution in Nicaragua, the peace folks will find better things to do than act out their frustration.

I know that when I worked with peace groups supporting the United Farm Workers Union, the peace folks seemed to get a lot out of exposure to *that* nonviolent grassroots struggle.

It seems to me that your going to Nicaragua is fully consistent with your commitment to feminism. Though I believe that in the end, it will have to be women who assert and promote women's interests (even revolutionary men are not going to do it for us), I also believe that progress for women needs to go along with general progress towards justice. Certainly in the Third World, where most people are barely surviving (and where women and children survive even less well than men) a redistributive revolution which spreads around money, education, access to medical care, etc., has got to benefit most women. Women in these countries will still have to fight the specifically patriarchal aspects of their oppression. They, especially, will have to secure control of their bodies through chosen birth control and abortion and will have to win employment opportunities which do not depend on connections to husbands or fathers.

I'm sure some women here will especially want to know the answer to your question about whether it is possible to be a lesbian in Nicaragua (and whether the revolution makes it easier or harder). I can't help speculating on the first part of that question—of course there are lesbians in Nicaragua. There are always lesbians or rather, there are always strong, self-directed women who are drawn to loving those who will return their love both passionately and respectfully. Under our variant of patriarchy, "respectfully" tends to mean that their lovers will also be women. But that doesn't mean that lesbians everywhere will look or think like lesbians here. Nor does it mean that strong, self-directed women are always lesbians. It does imply, however, that there will be more lesbians when the cultural context permits (or even suggests) lesbianism. And that is probably not the case in Nicaragua or any Third World country. Still, I'm sure the Nicaraguan revolution has unleased tremendous creative energy among women there—and women who would be lesbians here are running schools, clinics and army platoons. They are also probably enthusiastically becoming mothers, delighted to bring new life into a society being built anew. When you go, you'll have to draw some conclusions on this for me.

A lot of me wishes I could go, too. But I don't have the urgent call you feel to this; my urgent call at the moment is to the work we have underway, especially to *LesCon*. However, I serve notice: I am not your wife—I get to do the next mad but necessary adventure which life serves up for us. Who knows, maybe we'll get to do one together one day. ◘ *All my love, Jan*

◘ ◘ ◘

Managua

After weeks of preparation, the day finally came when Jan drove me to the San Francisco Airport and put me on a plane to Miami. There I was to meet up with the rest of WFP's new long-term team and fly with them to Managua. During a six hour layover in Miami, I succumbed to the temptation to call Jan for a few more words before I left the United States.

◼ ◼ ◼

Sunday, May 20
Dear heart,
   Still an hour to go till boarding. All my luggage is checked, my ticket okayed. I should be bubbling madly, but I can't seem to get past this cold, hard knot in my feelings. Suddenly, I'm terrified by the enormity of what I'm doing. Even the two men at the Aeronica Airlines counter are different from their American analogues. How will it be in Nicaragua? Suddenly, too, I'm absurdly lonely. I know I have to cry now and get past it, or I won't find my delight again for days.

I seem to have little appetite and to be wide awake. Life is good, though, and the joy will come back, I know. When you told me a few minutes ago on the phone how small I looked going down the ramp, I was able to see myself, too. I wanted to reach an arm around that brave, silly little woman. Is that really what I'm like? I think I love that little woman.

I haven't been this scared since I came out. And I think this adventure is going to change me at least as much. But I'll keep faith with you.

So much for high words and sentiments. I'd trade them all for the touch of you. So we make a world where we can have that.

Vaya con la Diosa, star-in-my-heart. God, I'm sentimental today!   ◘   *All my love*

Sunday night, May 20
Dear Jan,

Augusto Cesar Sandino Airport is small, sports "Welcome to Nicaragua Libre" signs and others celebrating the fiftieth anniversary of Sandino's death. Also signs in English touting the merits of two or three hotels and a rent-a-car place. It was almost dark by the time we got through Customs. I was the last, and the poor guy took one look at my knapsack and waved me through. Managua seems to be flat—though mountains, and one smoking volcano are visible from the airport. We put everything and everyone into WFP's king cab Toyota pickup, with four of us perched on top of a heap of luggage in back. "Don't go over any bumps!" I said. "This is Nicaragua," answered Arnold, the Managua Coordinator, and we headed off for WFP's house on the western edge of Managua.

In fact the road was new and smooth, a four-lane divided highway with a footpath down the median strip, on which many people were walking. We passed several billboards— some advertising auto repairs, one for the newspaper *La Prensa*, and others with revolutionary slogans. We drove through what was once downtown Managua and is now flat, empty land with a few unfinished four or five-storey buildings scattered around. The sun was setting behind these skeleton buildings which were begun before the 1972 earth-quake and never completed. As you know, that earthquake devastated Managua. Afterwards, funds to relieve its victims poured in from all over the world—and right into Somoza's pockets. Managua was never rebuilt.

It was hot, windy, dry. Apparently the rains are a little late this year. Palm trees, deciduous trees. Nicaragua seemed surprisingly brown from the air. Along the highway, groups of people waited for buses. We passed a few open air *cantinas* like ones I saw years ago in Mexico.

I had a good talk in Miami with Josefina, our WFP coordinator in the United States. That's one smart lady. She's working on a paper comparing the Puerto Rican and Nicaraguan economic models. (Puerto Rico: production using foreign capital and materials for export to foreign countries. Nicaragua: primarily agricultural production for home consumption.) Josefina believes that as the standard of living within Nicaragua rises, so will demand for U.S. imports. She believes it's to the benefit of U.S. business in the long run to allow Nicaragua's economy to develop into a genuine market for U.S. goods, something Puerto Rico has not done. Capitalist economics, but interesting.

Tomorrow we begin our two weeks of WFP training. We'll be learning more about Nicaraguan history and the various forces at work in the country today. They seem to go in for role-playing here, so I guess we'll practice meeting the contra as well. ■ *All love*

Monday, May 21
Dear Jan,

In answer to the all-important question, "Are there cats in Nicaragua?" I can provide a definite "Yes!" I know because last night as I was laying out my mat on the porch, two of them raced in full battle across the floor! Not so well man-nered here as ours is.

The WFP Managua house is big and empty, very clean. It has tile floors, concrete walls, and wiring that would make you blanch. Also two indoor toilets—one functional. The cleanliness is thanks to *Doña* Ana Luisa, who cooks and cleans for the short-term delegations. Ana Luisa has seven children and seventeen grandchildren. She's great friends with her husband's other wife. Ana Luisa's daughter, Blanca, studies at the University, and has a son, Leonardo, who is three and a half. Leonardo sings the Sandinista anthem and knows how to shout *"¡Patria Libre o Morir!"* ("A Free Country or Death!")

I took half an hour off from meetings to take a walk with a few of the others from the group. We walked about a mile up from the house towards a large hill with "FSLN" picked out on it in white (like the "South San Francisco, the Industrial City" that you can see driving back from the airport at home). This neighborhood is very mixed: several doctors' houses with two or three cars parked out front and up the hill from those, shacks of a room or two. On our street everyone has water and electricity, but up above us only some houses do. We saw flyers tacked up on a bulletin board, reminding folks to get their vaccinations on May 12th. At one house a woman was doing her laundry in an outdoor sink. Her kids were running and playing in the dirt yard. The electric line went right over her house, but there was no connection. I doubt she's on the water line, either, and I wonder where the water she uses comes from.

◼ *Mi mano y corazón*

◼ ◼ ◼

I spent my first two weeks in Nicaragua sitting in a circle on the floor of some WFP house or other—either in Managua, San Juan del Sur, or Jalapa. All of us new long-termers began to wonder if we'd ever stop talking and start working. For days we told each other our life stories, then for days longer absorbed information about Nicaragua—church politics, national politics. From Sharon, who had lived ten years in Nicaragua, we got important lessons in how to wave, how to signal "come here!" (reverse the actions we use in the U.S.) and how to point in the Nicaraguan style (lift your chin and purse your lips in the direction of the object or person indicated). I practiced dropping the s's from my tentative and undistinguished Spanish, and wondered how I was going to get along with this strange aggregation of people. Long-termers who had already been working in Nicaragua included:

Mary C., already a friend in the United States. WFP materials always described her as "a 57-year-old Gold Star Mother and grandmother." She'd lost a son in the Vietnam war, thereby acquiring the Gold Star, along with a new view of the actions of her government in that war. The November before my arrival, she'd left her community at the Catholic Worker Farm in Calaveras to work in Nicaragua and had been in Jalapa ever since. We hoped to work together in Somotillo, after the endless orientation was over, but as it turned out, the June 1st attack on Ocotal intervened, and after the first month or so, we rarely saw each other.

Peggy, from the New York City Catholic Worker. Small, dark and intense, Peggy had the journalist's habit of holding on to facts. She also had been in Nicaragua since November, and was suffering from hepatitis when my group arrived. The disease exhausted her, but it didn't keep her from talking in quick, organized paragraphs about what she had seen and learned in Nicaragua.

Arnold, Linda and their four children. Arnold coordinated WFP in Nicaragua. A church historian and college professor before joining WFP, he grew up in Puerto Rico, and so is bilingual. Linda also had hepatitis when we arrived, so I didn't meet her for a few days. Later, we got to be good friends. I admired her spiritual sense—and her biceps, the latter being the result of doing, by hand, all the laundry produced by a family of six. Carrie, Christian, Cliff and baby Carl became friends, too. They had adopted Nicaragua as their own country. Months later, when the U.S. threatened invasion after the 1984 elections, and a U.S. warship sat offshore near the port of Corinto, the four dug out their own "Corinto" in the mud yard behind their house. They equipped the town with a number of defenses the real Corinto would have loved to own, including hidden anti-aircraft guns. They sank the U.S. ship. But being the children of good pacifists they explained to me, "Don't worry. All the crew were rescued."

Peter, who plays the mandolin like my brother. And also like my brother he rescues valuable things from dumpsters. Peter has an extraordinary habit of easy cheerfulness which makes him much loved, if not easily known. He loves to cook. When I lived in Managua, we made many strange desserts together, like *pitaya* cream pie—made of a fruit so purple it's hard to believe it wasn't created in some laboratory. The most terrifying moments I spent in Nicaragua, the times I was most sure that death was imminent, were passed on the back of the WFP motorcycle Peter and I rode out to Xiloá for early morning swims. The wretched machine had only one footrest, so I had to wrap my right foot around Peter's—making it difficult to brake suddenly. We had only one helmet, which I insisted we take turns wearing.

Mary D., another Catholic Worker, and an attorney from St. Louis. She is still in Nicaragua, documenting the contra war for the Washington Office on Latin America. When I arrived, she was living in Jalapa with Mary C. She's tough and firm, a staunch feminist. I remember listening to her argue with the political secretary of the FSLN in Jalapa, pushing her yellow hair away from her face as she proposed nonviolence as a military strategy for Nicaragua!

Jean, a Sister of St. Joseph, also from St. Louis. Jean is wise about things of the heart and the spirit, cheerful, and sometimes a little overwhelmed by happenings on a material plane. We got along great.

Doug S., whom we called Joaquín. He and I were to spend many weeks traveling together. To the new recruit, Joaquín was a terrifying apparition—tall and spare with a thin mustache laid along his upper lip. He spoke rapidly when imparting information in English, as if to prevent any wandering of his listener's attention until the last detail was outlined. In Spanish, his personality softened, his speech slowed, and his face reflected a different patience. Joaquín turned out to have a hidden talent for amateur theatrics, along with a dry and bitter sense of humor.

Besides these old hands, there were eight of us new long-termers—a strange crew—all white, ranging in age from twenties to mid-forties.

Sharon came up from Costa Rica where she had been teaching Spanish to U.S. college students. She had first come to Nicaragua when she was eighteen, knowing little Spanish and no medicine—to work in a clinic in the "department" or state of Nueva Guinea. Three days on mule back had brought her to La Esperanza where, within a couple of months, she was delivering babies. I liked her immediately for her obvious identification with Nicaragua and her frank feminism. By the time I left Nicaragua, she'd become Assistant Coordinator with WFP—a very smart move on their part.

Gray, from Atlanta, was one of our two pastors. In his forties, tall and soft-spoken, with a mass of hair the color his name suggests, he'd recently married for the first time.

Stuart was our other preacher, a Presbyterian. Stuart is half theologian, half college sophomore. The second half tends to dominate in social situations, and sooner or later most of us became recipients of one of his "moons."

Larry grew up in a missionary family in Africa. Like Arnold, Linda and Sharon, he is a Mennonite—a member of one of the group of five traditional peace churches, which also includes the Quakers. Larry could always be counted on for calm in chaos—and an occasional dry imitation of the more flamboyant members of short-term delegations.

Doug I., now living in Texas, had done Sanctuary work before joining WFP. He was the first of us to acquire intestinal parasites—a condition he compared to having 10,000 contra committing sabotage in his gut. Both he and Gray had worked with the Peace Corps in the past.

Jenny and I only worked together once. We accompanied a short-term delegation of North Americans whose obsession with non-violence tried the patience of both of us. I appreciated her willingness to be a partisan for Nicaragua, when circumstances demanded it.

Miranda had lived ten years as a housewife in Mexico. I remember watching her float in her gauzy Indian cottons through the streets of Jalapa like a red and pink hibiscus bloom. She could say anything she wanted to in Spanish— always with the most astonishing British accent. Her English parents raised her on an Arizona chicken farm where they taught her, among other things, that a family should be able to entertain itself without recourse to television. Miranda had an endless supply of games she'd learned as a child. Joaquín's acting talents first surfaced during a version of charades she taught us. "I'm a democrat with a small 'd'," Miranda told me, meaning, in part, that she was disinclined to take orders from anyone—a sentiment I certainly shared. She teaches English as a second language in the U.S., and easily found herself doing the same thing in Jalapa. I found it odd, in the midst of a war directed against them by the United States, that so many revolutionaries wanted to learn English. But the hard truth is that many books on technical subjects are still written only in that language.

During the two weeks of training, the nature of WFP's project in Nicaragua became clearer to me. We really had two jobs: accompanying two-week delegations from all over the United States, as they visited Managua and the *campo*; and documenting the human effects of the contra war, which often meant traveling to places too isolated to accommodate entire delegations. In the end, I did much more of the latter, while other long-termers spent most of their time preparing for and hosting short-term groups. Because our work was largely reactive—responding to the actions of the contra—it was hard to plan very far in advance. Often long-termers didn't know where they would be from one week to the next. I thought, for example, that I would be living in Jalapa and I left most of my belongings there in early June, expecting to return after a short trip to Managua. It wasn't until months later, after I had traveled to Matagalpa and Jinotega, that I reclaimed those things.

◼ ◼ ◼

Wednesday, May 23
Dear Jan,
    If I had written this letter last night, as I had originally intended, I think I would have written, "I am going to die in Nicaragua." WFP was invited to a reception for delegates to a conference on human rights. Afterwards everyone went to eat at a strange and fancy hotel. With us was Sixto Ulloa of

CEPAD (a Protestant organization devoted to poverty relief and economic development in Nicaragua), which organized the conference. He sat with us and, in between some not too funny dirty jokes (all of which I got, including a pun), told us about his trip that day to Somotillo. He said, "Never in my life have I been afraid to drive on the roads, but today I was afraid. There were forty kilometers when I didn't see another human being." He went on to say that the people of Somotillo were preparing for a land invasion, that they all had trenches in their yards, that people were being killed in the countryside all the time. It seemed clear to me that to go to Somotillo, from his description of the situation, would be to court near-certain death.

That conversation, combined with talk earlier in the day about "interposition," had the heat running up and down my spine. We'd talked earlier about whether it makes sense in the context of an actual attack for WFP members to attempt to interpose ourselves between the contra and their intended victims. Apparently the WFP Steering Committee is split on the issue, but we are not *enjoined* from doing this. To the Committee's credit, they also know there are genuine questions, political and moral, about the validity of that kind of action. Should we do something that Nicaraguans themselves wouldn't do, for example? Let me assure you that interposition looks to me like men engaging in Gandhian grandstanding. I do not believe I'm called to die that way, but that may just be cowardice. I'm also not convinced the choice would present itself nearly as clearly as our speculations make it seem. In any event, each town here has Civil Defense teams and there are three distinct non-combat tasks they perform during attacks: first aid, firefighting, and care of children and old people. I'm willing to do any of these and if I stay in one place long enough, I'll try, as WFP folks have done in Jalapa, to get myself on one or another team.

I think it's likely that Sixto was exaggerating a bit the danger, to WFP folks in particular. But it certainly is real enough. I began to wonder whether I would really have the courage for this calling. No one else here seems to share my fears.

Today's a little different. I lay on my pad last night and realized that in order to go any farther with this project I had to get my fear under some kind of management. And I realized I had forgotten the promise I got the day I walked out in the woods alone in Calaveras County. That She hadn't said I wouldn't die, but that She wouldn't leave me. How quickly I forgot. But I think remembering it last night will stay with me now. I feel at much greater peace with that part of my destiny. I also think that the government and the Frente will do everything they can to prevent the death of *any* North Americans in Nicaragua and of WFP members in particular. They just won't let us go to places of greatest danger. Of course that doesn't prevent said danger from coming to us.

At last night's event, I shook hands with Dr. Rafael Cordoba Rivas, a member of the Junta; with a leading Moravian minister from Bluefields; with the woman who is the head of AMNLAE in Zelaya (Eastern Nicaragua) and with many other important and gracious persons. (The Junta's full name is the Junta del Gobierno de Reconstrucción Nacional. Its members make up the executive branch of the Nicaraguan government. *Junta* is a Spanish word for "board" or "council.")

Then off for this fancy meal in the huge, dark garden of what would look like a rather nice motel in the United States. It felt strange to me to have so many people waiting on us. It's not exactly that I don't think there will still be restaurants, come the Revolution, but just that a culture in which so many people are servants of one sort or another is still strange to me. For example, this morning we gave an interview in the Hotel Intercontinental to Hondur-Press (a wire service that appears to consist of one woman and one man). One of our folks happened to drop a plate, which immediately broke apart on the tile floor. A waiter immediately scooped up the pieces, and the WFP guy who had dropped it had no interaction with him at all. Odd.

This morning, Jenny, Miranda and I took a walk in our neighborhood. We came on a group of houses under construction: one room, maybe twenty feet by twenty feet, slant roof of corrugated metal, one vertical pole (a 3" x 3") in the center. The foundation interested me especially: as high as my waist, and made of stone two feet square and four inches deep. A young man was working on one unfinished house and we asked him a few questions. He bought all the materials for the house himself, although the stone was cut by a machine that belongs to the state. It cost him about 35,000 *cordobas*—$1,000 at the current exchange rate—to build. It's taken about a month, mostly because he had to buy the materials as he could afford them. He has a fine view of the FSLN hill from behind his house, which he took us out back to see.

The lumber was roughly milled and looked like older dimensional lumber at home—you know, two-by-fours that are really 2″ x 4″! Thought you'd appreciate those construction details, my carpenter friend.

People live in shacks here. Mostly wood, not cardboard, but shacks so tiny they look like toy houses. (I knew this, but the eye is still startled.) Shacks sit right next to big houses with three or four cars parked out front. The women stand on the dirt in front of their houses, cooking over charcoal burners made from 55 gallon drums and scrubbing their clothes at makeshift *pilas* (sinks).

Sometimes I'm very lonely here, as when the talk turns to Israel's involvement in Central America. I know it's true that Israel was the only country still supplying arms to Somoza in the last month he held power. I know that Israel serves as a U.S. proxy in shipping arms to the contra, and to the government of Guatemala. But because I'm a Jew, my response to the actions of Israel cannot be easy or simple, which I find difficult to explain sometimes. ◼ *All love*

Friday, May 25
Dear Janny,

I find myself frustrated trying to tell you about Nicaragua. What to say about Managua? First of all, the air always smells a little—of burning corn, or trash, or diesel. Then, it's noisy. Many vehicles have inadequate—or non-existent—mufflers. There's a lot of traffic, or rather, even a little traffic sounds like a lot, especially because people drive so fast. Besides the traffic, there are the insects and birds, all of whom have a great deal to say. In the yard here I see iguanas, like little dinosaurs. Makes me want to have spiny projections down my own back.

Much of Managua is open spaces. The *barrios* are probably not too different from the ones you saw in Tijuana. We've seen so many pictures of them in one country or another, but it's something to see them with slogans painted all over: *"¡A 50 años, Sandino vive!"* ("Fifty years later, Sandino still lives!") Today we visited the first housing project built in Managua after the Triumph. The houses were small, two or three rooms built of square clay bricks, sturdy. Each had electricity and water. The roads were dirt and I imagine they get pretty muddy during the rainy season.

Last night, Peter, Mary, Jean and I went to talk to Peggy Healy, a Maryknoll Sister who had just gotten back from a stint in the United States. She'd spent an hour talking with Tip O'Neill, apparently providing him with most of the language he used to denounce the contra in a recent speech. Oh, Jan, what a woman that is! Tall, bony, fierce, and what an intelligence. She said, "Nicaragua is for the weak; the strong are in Washington." Meaning that it is so much easier being here in Nicaragua than dealing with U.S. citizens and members of Congress. She said some other things I don't want to risk repeating in a letter, about plans for response in the U.S.—and by U.S. citizens in Nicaragua—in the event of an invasion in Central America. She said that everything she heard in Washington makes her believe that an invasion is almost inevitable, whether before or after the election. She hoped it can be deterred within the U.S. but says we have to be prepared to live and work beyond that time. She also talked about what it will take to get church people in the U.S. moving. As the government begins to repress church activities, like the Sanctuary movement, people will begin to see their personal stake in stopping intervention. She may be right, you know, that it's church people who are going to feel most threatened and personally limited in this one. In any event, it was an honor to meet this woman of fire.

Last night I sat up talking to Doug I., one of the other new long-termers. We talked about how hard it's been for us to leave our lovers to come to Nicaragua, and about how hard it may be to leave Nicaragua. (Don't worry about me, dear one; I'm coming home.) I was able to tell him some of my despair, the feeling I have some days that most women in the world will never be more than the slaves of slaves. And about how hard it is for me to decide whether I'm abandoning women's struggles by coming here. ◼ *All love*

◼   ◻   ◼

Only Doug I., Gray and I had left behind partners in the United States. It was hard for us to suppress the pain of those separations in order to be present to the work at hand. Very quickly though, I was faced with decisions they didn't have to make, decisions about just what I was willing to say to whom about my being a lesbian.

Although I knew that I had no intention of hiding my lesbianism from any North Americans connected with WFP, I was a good deal less sure what I would say to Nicaraguans. The second night I was in Nicaragua, I found out. We'd been invited to the opening ceremonies of a conference on human rights. At the reception I wrote about to Jan, I sat with a group of WFP folks and Sixto Ulloa, a leader of CEPAD, one of the organizations which invited WFP to Nicaragua. (CEPAD began as a Protestant church response to Somoza's failure to provide for the victims of the 1972 Managua earthquake. In pre-revolutionary times, the establishment of such an organization was an act of defiance, implying criticism of Somoza's relief program—a program designed primarily to relieve Somoza's personal financial concern. CEPAD's constituency is the abstemious Protestant churches of Nicaragua, many of them fundamentalist imports from the U.S., like the Assembly of God.)

We sat around this table in the courtyard of a hotel, listening to Sixto describe his trip to the town of Somotillo that day. Suddenly, I discovered that the subject had changed and that he was asking me a question. *"¿Y usted, Rebecca, está casada?"* (And you, Rebecca, are you married?) A few moments before, our table had been full of conversation. Now I felt the collective intake of breath as my WFP *compañeros* wondered, "What's she going to say?" So I took a breath myself and told my first lie in Nicaragua. "No, I'm not married." Everyone breathed out again, and the conversation rolled on.

Later, a number of WFP folks said they hoped I knew that they would have backed me up, no matter how I'd answered. But I knew I'd made a decision in that moment about how and to whom I would be open about my lesbianism in Nicaragua. WFP was invited to Nicaragua not by the government but by Nicaraguan churches. Our major partner there was CEPAD. I decided I did not have the right to jeopardize the entire program by making shocking declarations about my sexuality.

Homophobia was something I wouldn't tolerate from North Americans—no matter how tiny and isolated the place they might have come from—and all the short-term delegations I worked with knew I was a lesbian. But I went to Nicaragua to look and listen, to learn about Nicaraguan liberation, hoping not to impose my own priorities on the people of a place very different from my home. My job was to record the results of my country's war against Nicaragua. The *campesina* woman who leaned toward me across a table and told me about how her husband had been hacked to pieces by the contra was not the appropriate recipient for confidences about—or challenges to accept—*my* sexual orientation.

A few words here about what I think lesbianism—or gayness—*is*. I don't doubt that there are women in most cultures, including Nicaragua, who have close emotional and even, when it is possible, sexual connections with other women. But I am not convinced that every woman who has such connections is what we in the United States would call a *lesbian*. The existence of "lesbianism" as a cultural *identity* requires some material prerequisites—a certain level of consumption and urbanization. When, for example, people are living ten to a two-room house, sexuality can't mean what it does for people who have some possibility of privacy in lovemaking. When all personal efforts are directed toward simple survival, it doesn't make sense to ask, "Where are the lesbians?"

Lesbian and gay identities as we know them in the U.S. and Europe are actually a relatively recent historical phenomenon. (In saying that homosexual or gay identity is a recent, culturally conditioned phenomenon, I do not mean that lesbians and gay men are not *real*. I am very deeply a lesbian, and concealing that fact hurt me deeply. But I am able to be a lesbian precisely because such a thing existed in the time and place where I was born.) Homosexual identity simply does not exist in the same way in rural Latin America. Where it does exist in Latin American cities, it is usually as a cultural import from Europe and the United States. This places homosexuality in a genuinely mixed bag of other cultural imports—from tractors to dictatorships—to which Latin Americans understandably have mixed reactions.

In pre-revolutionary Cuba, for example, many people perceived male homosexuality as intimately connected to prostitution, in a market created by U.S. dollars and U.S. tourists. That revolutionary Cubans saw such prostitution as a part of U.S. exploitation of their country does not excuse the oppression of gays and lesbians in Cuba. (Nor does it begin to address the complicated feminist issues surrounding prostitution—issues which I found being discussed by women in Nicaragua.) But it does suggest explanations for the suspicion and mistrust of gays in Cuba.

The only recognizably lesbian women *I* saw in Nicaragua were also prostitutes, a butch-femme couple working in the port city of Corinto. But other North American visitors have made contact with Nicaraguan lesbians in Managua—many of whom support the revolutionary changes happening in their country. I sometimes wonder whether there was an element of cowardice as well as cultural sensitivity in my decision to remain closeted to Nicaraguans. And sometimes I wonder how closeted I really was; I spoke constantly about my *compañera* the carpenter and the work she was doing at home.

During those first two weeks in Nicaragua, I learned about another cultural import—U.S. Christian fundamentalism. Eighty-five per cent of Nicaragua's population is Roman Catholic. Most of the remaining 15 per cent are members of one Protestant denomination or other. Except along the Atlantic coast, the word for "protestant" is *"evangelico"*—evangelical Christians proselytized by missionaries from the United States.

All over Central America, representatives of conservative fundamentalist U.S. churches have carried their particular bag of hardline theology and right-wing politics. The theology concentrates on development of a personal, individual relationship with Jesus Christ, along with a reward in heaven for patient endurance of trials on earth. This is the Christianity that for centuries has been so useful to the owners and exploiters of the earth, offering the rest of the world "pie in the sky when you die." The politics are the usual melange of virulent anti-communism, support for the U.S., and woman-hatred. In Nicaragua, the politics involve an extra twist: these churches, which have never advocated pacifism in the U.S.—and which never did so under Somoza—today are teaching a very opportune nonviolence and are encouraging draft resistance.

Many *evangelico* churches have strict rules of personal behavior: no member may drink alcohol, smoke, dance or go to the movies. Women must not cut their hair short and must submit to their fathers' and husbands' authority. Young people may not date or marry outside the church.

Evangelico churches are growing in Nicaragua, and throughout Central America, partly because of vigorous work by missionaries. The services are well-attended by enthusiastic people, and feature fiery preaching and a great deal of singing, often accompanied by electric guitars and a rock-and-roll beat.

Protestantism takes a different form on the Atlantic coast, where most Miskito people are members of the Moravian church, a sect which originated in 16th century Germany. Unlike other *evangelico* denominations, the Moravian church has a genuine tradition of pacifism, similar to the Peace Testimony of the Society of Friends (Quakers). Moravians have strong ties as well with the Mennonite church, another "Peace Church" with German roots.

A handful of Jews also live in Nicaragua. Some who had close ties to Somoza left after the Triumph, but others have remained to build the new Nicaragua.

Catholic theology, politics and religious observance differ from their *evangelico* counterparts in a number of ways. While it has *evangelico* proponents, in Latin America liberation theology is primarily a Catholic movement focusing on the elevation of the poor and the creation of a just community on earth. Salvation in liberation theology is something achieved less by individuals than by an entire community. It is not at all surprising that the existing religion of an agricultural society should place emphasis on community—nor that the Protestant import from an industrialized, capitalist country should emphasize personal achievement, even in one's relations with God. It is surprising—and perhaps ultimately contradictory—that the idea of liberation should arise in the midst of so deeply authoritarian an institution as the Catholic church.

Nicaraguan Catholicism tends to be much gentler than the *evangelicos* in its judgments of the behavior of its people. Not only are more things permitted to Catholics, but there is a greater tendency to wink at their pecadilloes, a tendency that may seem unfamiliar to some North American Catholics. A church marriage, for example, is an expensive thing and relatively few Nicaraguan couples have had one. In spite of efforts by church officials to instill some, there is very little opprobrium attached to an unmarried woman having a child. Recently, Nicaraguan President Daniel Ortega and his wife Rosario Murillo appeared on "The Phil Donahue Show." Donahue spent a long time trying to get them to rebut his assertion that Ortega could not expect the support of the Catholic masses because he had not married in the church. His efforts were met with polite incomprehension on the part of the Nicaraguans. Finally, Murillo told him she didn't understand the question. All her children were baptized, she said, what was the problem?

The political and theological differences between *evangelicos* and Catholics affect their support for the Nicaraguan revolution, but in a complex and contradictory way. Most *evangelico* laypeople are hostile or indifferent to the revolution, while ordinary poor Catholics, many parish priests and Catholic lay leaders tend to be supportive. In church leadership, these positions tend to be reversed. Among *evangelico* leaders and church officials, there is qualified support for the revolution. And the Catholic hierarchy, led by once-Archbishop and now Cardinal Miguel Obando y Bravo is more than hostile. During the time I was there, church officials were implicated in efforts at anti-government organizing in Managua, for example, using films and other materials and money supplied by the W. R. Grace Company (a U.S. shipping and agribusiness conglomerate). These same films had been supplied to anti-Allende forces before the 1973 coup in Chile.

The presence of Catholic priests in the Nicaraguan government illustrates the complexities of church-state relations there: These include Miguel D'Escoto, Foreign Minister (the equivalent of our Secretary of State); Ernesto Cardenal, Minister of Culture; and Fernando Cardenal, Minister of Education. Since I left Nicaragua, Fernando Cardenal, a Jesuit, has been asked by his order to choose between the priesthood and the government. Photographs of the scolding administered to Ernesto Cardenal by Pope John Paul II are world-famous. The presence of active priests in government certainly does have its effects. It is hard to imagine Secretary of State George Shultz subjecting himself to a two-month fast in order to spark an "evangelical revolution" of nonviolent resistance to U.S. aggression, as Miguel D'Escoto did during the summer of 1985. The government's choice of Fernando Cardenal to serve as Minister of Education represents a genuine willingness to address the church's fears of anti-religious propaganda in public school curricula.

After days of presentations and process, and a quick trip to the southern resort town of San Juan del Sur, the long-term team arrived in Jalapa, just before a major contra attack on the city of Ocotal. Before we left Managua, I received a first batch of letters from Jan. She wrote about driving from Seattle to San Francisco: "On the way home I drove under Mt. Shasta for some hours, as one must, and it proved to be the occasion of the best prayer I'd had since you left. I was able to go deep into all the love I have for this country and feel the rage that feeling the love brings up and get to where I could pray. And I finally felt enough courage in myself to pray to carry some of your fear—after all, it is a damn sight less burdensome to me here than it must be to you there. Altogether, this was the first inkling I've had since you left that She was with me and there really is purpose in all this—just like what I go around telling people all the time."

Jalapa and Ocotal

Wednesday, May 30
Dear Janny,

We got into Jalapa yesterday at about five. The country around here is a lot like the country around the Catholic Worker Farm in Calaveras County—red earth, some pines, some deciduous trees. Of course, they don't have mangos in Calaveras. . . . The town is laid out in blocks beside a stream. Streets are dirt and rock, buildings adobe or concrete, many with running water, but *servicios* are strictly latrines. The WFP house is big, with eight or nine rooms arranged around two courtyards, like a capital "E" turned on its side. Not many vehicles in town, and many folks get around on horses.

WFP rents its house here from a woman who lives across the street. It's quite large for Jalapa and before the elections the National Guard used it as their headquarters. We have a mango tree in one courtyard and a coffee bush in the other. Mary C. says that Doña Isabel, our landlady, comes by to collect the mangos occasionally, but I plan to eat what I can before she gets to them!

Mary and I went around the corner in search of some instant coffee for breakfast tomorrow. The store didn't carry it, and the Tienda Popular (state-run store) was closed. A woman shopping in the first store told us she had a jar at home and invited us to come with her to get it. She introduced herself as Mercedes, recently arrived from Guatemala, where she worked with the Maryknoll Sisters. I gathered that her leaving Guatemala was not entirely voluntary. We walked several blocks, crossed a small stream and entered a little barrio of raw new houses. Mercedes led us into her house (more cut stone and rough boards) and found the jar of coffee. We sat down and talked for a while. She became very warm when she understood what WFP is doing in Nicaragua. We spoke a little more, mostly about what people here call *"la situación"*—the possibility of contra attack—thanked her for the coffee and took our leave.

The only failing of our huge house is that it really has no kitchen—just a sort of pantry and a hot plate plugged into a hanging outlet with a light bulb. So we won't be cooking much here. Instead, we eat at *Comedor Reyna*, where we have an arrangement to pay by the month. (Even though I don't much like our gigantic spiders I really can't consider them a failing of this house, since they live all over. Gloria, a friend of the household, says, "Oh, they don't do anything. They just keep your house clean,"—of other bugs, that is.)

On the way to dinner we ran into an old woman, a friend of Mary's. The first time she'd ever seen me, and she kissed me on the cheek. Good male friends also kiss each other on the cheek (once, not a Gallic embrace). Everyone in this town is friendly; that's culture shock.

I'll be going down to a couple of towns near Ocotal next week, in order to photograph destruction and take testimony. These towns were burned to the ground and 800 people displaced. Tomorrow night the local political secretary of the Frente is coming over to speak to us, so Doug and I will try to get a written introduction to make the job easier. Then, on to Managua at the end of next week to set things up for that part of the Rocky Mountains Delegation's stay. Then to Somotillo and the smaller town of Santo Tomás and Santa Teresa. When I mentioned to Mercedes where we're going, she said "Somotillo? That's the border." I protested that Jalapa is also near the border, but she says Somotillo is very different. In any event, we'll be three or four days in Somotillo setting up things for the delegation's stay. Then back to Managua to meet the delegation.

My permanent base for the time being will be Jalapa. It looks as though I may spend about one week a month in Managua to help put together a newsletter and work on a financial report. I guess they're really going to take advantage of my office skills. For a little while there, I was afraid I was going to be asked to work in the Managua office full time, which is not what I came to Nicaragua to do. Fortunately (in this instance) my Spanish isn't good enough to do the work of setting up appointments for delegations, and that's a big part of the job. I'm enclosing the words to a song from the *Misa Campesina* that I really love, *"él Diós de los Pobres"*:

Vos sos el Diós de los pobres,	You are the poor people's God
el Diós humano y sencillo,	the God who is human and simple,
el Diós que suda en la calle,	the God who sweats in the street,
el Diós de rostro curtido,	the God with the weatherbeaten face,
por eso es que te hablo yo	and that's why I talk to you
Así como habla mi pueblo	the same way my own people speak
porque sos el Diós obrero	because you are the worker God,
el Criso trabajador.	the Christ who labors.
Vos vas de la mano con mi gente,	You go hand-in-hand with my people,
luchas en el campo y la ciudad,	struggle in the countryside and the city,
Hacés fila allá en el campamento	You get in line in the camp
para que te pagen tu jornal.	so they can pay you your wages.
Vos comes raspado allá en el parque	You eat snow cones out in the park
con Eusebio, Pancho y Juan José	with Eusebio, Pancho and Juan José
y hasta portestás por el cirope	and you even complain about the syrup
cuando no te lo echan mucha miel.	when they don't use enough honey.
Yo te he visto en una pulpería	I've seen you in a juice stand
instalado en un caramanchel	sitting in a booth
te he visto vendiendo lotería	I've seen you selling the lottery
sin que te avergüence ese papel	without being ashamed of that little paper
yo te he visto en las gasolineras	I've seen you in the gas stations

chequeando las llantas de un camión	checking the tires of a truck
y hasta patroleando carreteras	and even patrolling the highways
con guantes de cuero y overól.	in leather gloves and overalls.

(By Carlos Mejía Godoy)

The Nicaraguan National Anthem is harder to sing than "The Star Spangled Banner," but the FSLN's anthem is easy. It goes like this:

Adelante, marchemos, compañeros	Onward, let's march, comrades
avancemos a la Revolución;	move on towards Revolution.
nuestro Pueblo es el dueño de su historia	Our people are the masters of their own history,
arquitecto de su liberación.	architects of their liberation.
Combatientes del Frente Sandinista,	Fighters of the Sandinista Front
adelante, que es nuestro el porvenir;	onward, for ours is the future
rojinegra bandera nos cobija	the red and black banner covers us
¡patria libre, vencer o morir!	a free country, victory or death!

The first verse goes like this:

Los hijos de Sandino	The children of Sandino
ni se venden ni se rinden—¡jamas!	will neither sell out nor surrender—never!
luchamos contra Yanqui	We struggle against the Yankee,
enemigo de la humanidad.	humanity's enemy.

Every time the Nicaraguans sing this song in front of North Americans, they're very careful to explain that they don't mean that *we*, the people of the U.S. are the enemy of humanity, but that our government is exactly that.

Last night, some of us participated in *vigilancia*, patrolling the night streets (unarmed of course, in WFP's case), looking out for any suspicious activity. We stopped at the house of some *campesinos*, a very pro-Process family. They asked me if I wasn't afraid to be here in Jalapa. I said, of course, weren't they? They agreed that they, too, were a little afraid. I said I figured since it was my government putting them in danger that I had a responsibility to be here. All in broken Spanish, of course. Sounds very grand, doesn't it? But the truth is that I'm feeling so helpless here, Jan. I know the contra couldn't last out the month without U.S. support, but my God, what hope is there of cutting that support? I really do believe that a million of these people are ready to die, including ones who, in the U.S., would be too young to know what dying is.

Mary C. says that if we're invaded she can't be sure she won't be on the front line loading ammunition. She knows that in real life her chances of getting there are slim, but I think her commitment to nonviolence ends with an invasion. On the other hand, she also believes that nonviolence is the only sane response to a genuine invasion.

Enclosed my first letter for the mailing list. ◘ *All love*

Saturday, June 2
Dear friends,

Now I know what a Nicaraguan funeral is like. Yesterday in the fighting at Ocotal a young man of Jalapa was killed, and this afternoon they buried him here.

The grave is cut deep and rectangular out of the ground. Once the casket has been lowered to the bottom and covered with earth, a platform made of ten or twelve boards is placed about six inches from the top. A rebar frame sits on this platform. Then the concrete, mixed with shovels beside the grave, forms a slab to cover the whole thing. The procession leaves the plaza in front of the church and reaches the cemetery within a couple of minutes. In this case we waited half an hour in the plaza for the grave to be dug. While we waited, we chanted the same series of calls again and again, led by the young women of the Sandinista Youth organization, and by other women a bit older. Always we began by shouting the man's name, then *"¡Presente! ¡Presente! ¡Presente!"*

At the grave, more shouting. These young women are serious as death, but laugh and giggle with each other; always their hands around each other's waist, or over shoulders, or holding another's hand. At the grave a woman—I think the dead man's mother—fainted and was carried away. In our house right now is the younger sister of another who died yesterday at Ocotal—the third in her family to be killed.

Ocotal is not far from here, a matter of two or three hours over dirt roads. Yesterday at 4:00 in the morning, something like 500 contra attacked the city. They were repulsed by the local militia, but not without casualties. An unconfirmed report says that one who died was the local director of IRENA, the reforestation agency. (All the hills around here were cleared—cut during Somoza's times.) Witness for Peace has friends in Ocotal. Many members of WFP delegations have stayed in the homes of people there. It's very close to us, physically and in spirit.

Since last night the telephone and telegraph lines have been out. Until this morning, Jalapa was cut off from the rest of the country. The highway opened today, and seven of the Witness for Peace people left for Managua or Ocotal.

In Ocotal, the contras' objectives were pretty clear: the radio station, the office of the reforestation project, the office of the Sandinista Youth. But the real objective in Nueva Segovia province is Jalapa, because this is the center of production—primarily agricultural—for the region.

Roberto Chavez, a planner for the Nicaraguan government, explained to us in Managua how the folks on the *asentamientos* (settlements) are really the first line of defense of Nicaragua. There are not enough troops in all the country to defend each town and settlement, but they are organized to defend themselves. In the region of Jalapa, most of these *asentamientos* belong to *campesinos* driven in from the mountains by the contra. Used to living in tiny towns, or as single families, these people are now living in groups of 250 or more, constructing houses, dining halls, laundry facilities. At Escambray, where I visited yesterday, the men attend to coffee production, and women and children work in a big communal garden. One of their favorite new crops is kohlrabi, brought by some *norte-americanos*. In the garden, and in the coffee, it's common to work with a gun slung over one shoulder. Everyone takes a turn at *vigilancia*, and they have fought off more than one attack in the past.

At Escambray, I also met Julia, eleven years a Delegate of the Word (a Catholic lay leader) and now the *responsable* for the garden. Like many women here, she has very few teeth, but much hope. "With faith in God and the strength of the people," she asks, "how could we be afraid?" She was standing outside the new *comedor infantil*, the community kitchen, where once a day the children of Escambray receive a free hot meal.

The meaning of the term *"responsable"* becomes gradually clearer to me. A *responsable* is the leader responsible for a particular area of work within some organization, like a cooperative. It's the *responsable's* job to make sure the work gets done, if not to do it herself. But *responsables* are not bosses; they are responsible both to the work itself and to the people who have chosen them, and they can be removed by the same people. A good *responsable* facilitates the work; she does not command it.

Because of the attack on Ocotal, Jalapa is on alert. Last night I did *vigilancia* with a woman named Estela, the *responsable* for the local CDS—*Comité de Defensa Sandinista*. Besides serving civil defense functions, the CDS is a form of community organization, assisting in the Literacy Campaign, for example. CDS's existed as a grassroots organization before the Triumph, and although today there is a national office in Managua, the basic unit is still the block committee.

With Estela and another woman of Jalapa, four of us spent two hours last night walking all over Jalapa, informing people of the attack on Ocotal and encouraging them to be alert. I myself think there's a good chance Jalapa will be attacked soon, although Estela believes the town is too well organized, and the contra will pick another target. It was soothing, in a way, to walk through the dark, warm streets feeling for once as if I were doing something.

Today I visited a *vivero*, a nursery where half-a-million seedling trees are waiting to be planted—part of the region's reforestation project. Pine for the hills and eucalyptus and citrus for the *asentamientos*. All must be planted during *invierno*, the rainy season we are just entering. But so many people who could be planting are fighting instead. In Jalapa it is the planting season, and the contra know it.

Dear friends, so far I'm well and healthy. As I said to Mary C., my Witness for Peace *compañera*, my problem is that it is hard to be in this country without wanting to cry every five minutes. Partly it's that I miss the people I love, but more it's that there is so much hope here, and so much heart, and so much pain. ◼ *All good struggles*

Sunday, June 3
Dear Jan,
   Everyone is out of the house for a few hours. This is the first time I have really been alone since I came to Nicaragua. I've made a vegetable soup and chocolate pudding (Oh, the joys of hotplate cooking!), washed dishes, done laundry, and taken a glorious shower standing in the roofless stall in the middle of the dirt courtyard. It's peaceful here for the moment, almost quiet, except for the occasional *plop* of a mango falling from the tree beside the shower stall.
   At 5:30 tomorrow morning, Doug I., Mary C. and I catch the bus for Ocotal. We'll try to speak with the Maryknoll Sisters, one of whom worked for many years in Condega, before Doug and I go on there ourselves.
   We had lunch today with Chilo Herrera, a friend of Mary's, who's a health worker. She was in Ocotal the day of the attack, and the Ministry of Health jeep in which she was riding got caught in mortar fire. Fortunately, no one was hurt and she seemed quite calm about the whole thing. Like the girls laughing at Nelson's funeral, people here really live on the sharp edge between war and peace. Can I learn to do the same?
   Chilo is an extraordinary person. At twenty she's responsible for daily health care on two *asentamientos*, with training equivalent to a nurse's aide's in the United States. She's short, plump and what the Nicaraguans call *chele* (light skinned). She wears her long hair pulled back in a pony tail. She lives with her parents, younger brother and sisters, and an aunt who suffers breakdowns because of the war. The aunt saw her husband killed horribly by the contra. She's twice been hospitalized in Managua, but nothing seems to touch her terrible depressions.
   I really like Chilo, and I'm hoping I'll be able to spend some time assisting her on the *asentamientos*.
◼ *Much love*

Monday, June 4
Dear Jan,

Oh, am I exhausted. Up this morning at 4:00 to catch the bus for Ocotal. Doug and I intended to go on to Condega, to begin collecting information about the attack there. But I'm beginning to understand how hard it is to make plans in the middle of a war. We stopped in at the Maryknolls Sisters' house in Ocotal, where Peter has been staying since the attack three days ago. Peter told us we were desperately needed to help sack up what's left of the grain at the silos the contra nearly destroyed. So here we are still in Ocotal. I begin to doubt we'll get to Condega at all.

I should probably back up and tell you about the attack on Ocotal on June 1st. It appears that five separate groups of about twenty attacked some very specific economic and po- litical targets. They got the sawmill; the offices of Radio Segovia (but not the transmitter); the offices of INE, the Department of Energy (but not the transformers); a coffee processing plant; and, most importantly, six grain silos in which were stored the corn, rice, beans and sorghum which Ocotal intends to eat in the coming months. Several people died in the attack, including two who were burned alive in the Radio Segovia offices. Witnesses say the contra carved a cross on the back of one of these. The contra often accuse the FSLN of atheism. I guess this is an example of contra Christianity.

The morning after the attack, several of us were sitting in the little *comedor* where we eat in Jalapa when the radio suddenly crackled back to life. "This is Radio Segovia," shouted the announcer. "They could not destroy us! They could not shut us down!" And then everyone in the place was cheering.

A sixth group of contra commandos was caught in a truck loaded with explosives. They were carrying a list of other targets—including the Centro de Desarrollo Infantil, the brand new Child Development Center.

So today Doug and I hiked out to the edge of town where the silos are. I think both of us were glad to have some actual piece of work to do after so many days of meetings and orientations. And there was plenty to do. The silos were hit with grenades, the tops blown completely off, and the sides split and twisted. They've covered them with tarps, to keep the rain off. We only have a few days to get the grain in sacks before the rain really sets in.

About fifty students were working when we got there, along with a number of adults. For hours I stood inside a silo, pushing beans out through a hole blown in the wall using a big wooden shovel to move the beans around. Two women stood outside, holding the sack. As each sack neared full, they'd shout out, *"¡Ya! ¡Ya! ¡Está lleno!"* They'd pull that one away and shove another sack up under the stream of red beans.

The beans that were burned by the explosion are black and sticky as pine tar. Three days later, they still smolder. Meanwhile, the beans that have gotten wet begin to ferment, growing clouds of spidery white mold, creating their own heat. Combine that with the heat of the sun, and you can imagine how hot this work is. I'm glad I'm in some kind of shape, though I have nothing like Nicaraguan stamina!

When Doug and I first got to the silos, the job of the moment was moving the full *quintal* (100 lb.) sacks from the silos to the trucks waiting to take them to warehouses in town. This, apparently, was a man's job, and a number of shirtless men stood in line, as two others hoisted each sack onto one man's back. Since I can't carry a hundred pounds but I can carry fifty, I worked with some of the school girls carrying one sack between two of us. I found myself envying Doug's strong back.

What a day. And there's so much work left to do. Doug and I plan to go back tomorrow, along with Peter. Then Mary C. and I will probably return to Jalapa, if the road is open, because Mary D. and Miranda are alone up there and things are pretty tense in the whole area. Mary doesn't want them to be alone, especially if Jalapa is going to be attacked. All day while we were working, I could hear the sounds of mortars— apparently there's fighting going on outside of Mozonte and San Fernando, between here and Jalapa. Doug will stay in Ocotal, to help set up for the Rocky Mountains Delegation, which Mary, Doug and I will be accompanying. Because of the attack, the delegation will come here, instead of going to Somotillo.

Just one more detail from Ocotal—a piece of grafitti on the wall of a house. It's a heart, pierced by an arrow. Underneath, the legend reads, "I'm in love with a four-year-old girl." The four-year-old girl is the Revolution, a child to be loved and protected. Nicaraguans would be horrified to know that in the United States such a statement might appear pornographic. On a wall in Ocotal, it expresses the Nicaraguan love of children, and a tenderness toward the future. ◼ *All love*

◼   ◻   ◼

Miranda and Mary D. were glad to see Mary C. and me when we got back to Jalapa. After our bus arrived, the road to Ocotal was closed, for fear of contra ambushes. The whole town had a strange, tense feel.

Mary and Miranda had collected a couple of guests in our absence, both North American—a priest named Tom, and Adele, who had taken a break from Spanish school in Managua and got stuck in Jalapa when the road closed.

About four that afternoon, I heard a terrifying squawking outside the house. "Oh damn," said Mary C. "they've got that thing working again!" "That thing" turned out to be the *altavoz*, a loudspeaker mounted on a small tower outside the Casa del Gobierno (City Hall) a block away from us. There followed a period of crackling music. Then a voice began to address the "heroic people of Jalapa," explaining the meanings of various siren signals we might be hearing shortly. Jalapa was on full-alert.

Arnoldo Vallejo, the head of Jalapa's government, came by our house a few minutes later to explain the situation to us: Jalapa was surrounded by contra, and an attack was expected sometime that night or early the next morning. When it happened, he said, someone would come to show us the way to the *refugio*, Jalapa's shelter for children and old people who cannot fight. We told him we didn't want special treatment, that we were already signed up to *work* at that shelter. Arnoldo nodded and said he'd be back to see us later on. It was typical of the genuinely heroic and courteous people of Jalapa that they should be concerned at a time like this with the safety of a few foreigners, when there was so much work to be done. We also knew that the *refugio* in question was only half finished, and wondered what shelter it would offer anyone.

We began pulling together a knapsack of first aid materials, and collecting our own "crash packs"—the few things we thought we'd need with us in case we had to leave suddenly. Marta, the *responsable* for the children's *refugio* came by to check on our preparations. She had with her a booklet, run off on a copy machine, describing how to organize a children's shelter and what steps to take in the event of an attack.

Around 8:00 that night, two men in green fatigues came by. Miguel and Salvador had been assigned to our household, in spite of their major responsibilities elsewhere. Jalapa was taking no chances on the safety of its North American guests.

In the midst of all our getting ready, I was also getting ready to die. At midnight I sat down to write to Jan.

◻ ◻ ◻

Thursday, June 7, 12:15 a.m.
Dear heart,

I am writing to you sitting on the steps of our house in Jalapa. Two *compas* (soldiers) are sitting with us, two of the coordinators of defense for this whole zone. All of Jalapa is on alert tonight, as we await attack. Depending on who is telling the story, we are surrounded on two—or three—sides by 1500 contra.

If this ever finds you, I want you to know that you are always the star of my heart, and that She will not desert any one of us. For the women I have met here, and even for the men, it has been worth it, Jan. For the hope that's here.

Arnoldo, Jalapa's mayor, calls the contra demonic. In true Nicaraguan style, he has spent two hours here tonight. Surely he has more important places to be. His assistant has been here, too. How strange to sit with the *compas*, their weapons laid aside for the moment as Miguel plays the guitar and we sing in Spanish and English—love songs, religious songs, songs of the Revolution.

Every two hours, the *compas* on *vigilancia* come by for coffee and conversation about life. About how the people keep their hope and their joy in the midst of war. And how necessary that is for life. Arnoldo says, "Sometimes one is tired, and then one rests for half an hour or so, sleeping like this." He bows his head over his AKa rifle. "Carlos Fonseca said, 'A person who is tired has the right to rest. But a person who rests does not have the right to be in the Vanguard.' "

Ah, heart, to touch your skin at this moment, to remember the joy I have taken from your body. God has been so generous with us: the mountains, the friendship, the marriage we've made. I'm trying hard tonight to love God as dearly and as fiercely as I love you.

Had to stop here for a while to give out coffee, lend my running shoes to a woman wearing plastic sandals. She whispered to me that she also has her period, with terrible cramps, so I gave her some Motrin. Hope she has the right kind of cramps for Motrin.

I'm going to stop now. It's 1:30 a.m. The attack, if it comes, will happen around 4:00 a.m. At least the others have. Always you are in my heart.   ◼ *In God and in love*

Sunday, June 10
Dear friends,

Jalapa is breathing again after four days of terror. Ocotal was attacked last week, the granaries and sawmill destroyed. Jalapa, with its even greater strategic value, looked like the likeliest of next targets. The contra wanted very much to take Jalapa, as a seat for a government-in-exile, and because it sits in the middle of some of the most fertile land of Nicaragua.

No one has slept here very much for the last week. As the maneuvers of Granadero I (Big Pine I) ended last night, people began thinking once again of a normal life of work and sleep. But for the last few days, we've lived on the edge of attack—never knowing when it might come, but prepared with fierce determination to deter it.

Thursday night, our household was awake all night, showing the light of our house, sitting out on the sidewalk with the militia members and soldiers who were doing *rotativa*—walking *vigilancia*. We served coffee, talked and sang, disputed feminism until dawn, kept company most of these hours by the loudspeaker half a block away, which put forth a mixture of propaganda, music and advice on defense. It quit about 1:00 a.m. then started up again at 4:30 a.m., calliope music announcing we'd made it through one more night. The half hour between 4:30 a.m. and 5:00 a.m. is the one when an attack is most likely. The moon is down and it's as dark as it's going to get.

I slept a couple of hours in the morning on Friday, while Miranda went to teach and the rest of us organized our "crash packs," a little money, canteens, whatever medications we might need. As a household, our assignment in case of attack is the care of children in their unfinished air raid shelter. We waited to hear more from Marta, the *responsable*, about our particular assignments.

At noon, Miranda came home saying, "We have to meet right now. It won't wait." She'd just spent the last couple of hours getting the children into trenches and shelters at the school. There were 15,000 troops massed on the Honduran border—not the 1500 we'd heard were surrounding Jalapa the night before. The attack might come at any minute.

Jalapa is usually a noisy place. We live across the street from a clinic, and all day long children express their outrage at being hauled in there. Most vehicles have only vestigial mufflers. People yell and call to each other on the streets. Even the birds and insects are loud. Friday, Jalapa was silent, the clinic shut, most people mobilized for defense, or sitting with their children. We attended a funeral for a soldier who'd died in Zelaya. The shouts and songs in the graveyard were swallowed up, absorbed by the terrible silence.

I'd been terrified all the night before, all the hairs on my spine raised, the back of my neck burning with fear. When Miranda came home with her news, her descriptions of twelve-year-old girls receiving last-minute rifle training, I knew I was likely to die that day, and I was ashamed of my fear. Ashamed that at such a time my thoughts were as much with the people I love and have left in the United States as they were with the people in Jalapa, facing with determination one more assault.

It takes a dual set of emotions to live in Jalapa, I think: one for everyday life and one for the realities of the struggle these people have taken on. Estela, the *responsable* of our CDS, came by to visit us the other day. She looked around our house, peered at the courtyard and said, "You should have a *refugio* (a shelter for mortars and grenades)." I told her I thought that *refugios* were for children and disabled people, that able-bodied adults had other work to do during an attack. "No," she insisted, "they're for adults, too."

"Do you have one yourself?" I asked her.

Estela smiled. "Yes, of course I have one," she said. "For my children. I must die fighting."

This same woman a few minutes later was discussing her high blood pressure and her plans to see a doctor in Managua, maybe as soon as Tuesday. That's what living in the war zone is like: Maybe the attack will come tonight—and there's plenty of reason to think it will—and maybe I'll go to the doctor next Tuesday.

The torture of these alerts is that no one sleeps, and all the important work of planting is slowed down. The captain of one barrio told us he hadn't slept for eight nights. A local doctor says a human being can do this, that he himself hasn't slept for four nights. A human being can do this, but for how long?

When people here say, *"Patria Libre o Morir,"* (A free country or death), it's clear how much they would rather have the former. I do believe there is a freedom in Nicaragua that I have never had in the United States. There is something here worth defending, and I believe that, at least in Jalapa, people will die in thousands to defend it.

Having lived through the last few days, having found myself alive and a little astonished on the other side of the most recent alert, I want to tell you, my friends, that the situation here is real, is serious, is desperate. But there is no desperation in the hearts of the people; they have a faith in an ultimate victory, even if none of them now living see it.

The thing everyone fears most, and which seems most likely, is bombardment by air. I don't know what you can do, but I'm asking you: sit in your congressperson's office, clog the streets of your city, send a hundred telegrams, talk to a hundred new people. The people here don't want to be burned in their homes and workplaces by the contra. They don't want to be raped, dismembered, decapitated. They don't want to be bombed. And neither, for that matter, do I.

This is not business as usual. This is a plea.   ◼ *All love*

Sunday, June 10
Dear Jan,
   I'm so glad I had a chance to talk to you last night. Your voice was clear, so recognizably your own. It was good, too, to have chance to share the obsession I'm beginning to feel about this place. Not too surprising, I guess, since I'm living here. And to find you able—of course, always, so dependably—to answer that obsession, to feel the urgency. How strange to be able to call you up from a war.

   Naturally, though, we both feel a little urgent about the possibility of attack or bombardment of a place where either of us is living. But what I could feel from you was the joy when I told you that, yes, there is something here worth the *lucha*. Robin Morgan says that freedom has yet to be coaxed into existence, but I feel here sometimes as if I'm actually finding out what freedom is for the first time—the kind that people are willing to die for, the kind that *we* were brought up to be willing to die for.

   It's hard for me to tell, because I haven't lived here long enough, how many of the folks of Jalapa are actively involved in political life and in defense, but I know it's a much larger proportion that what we've seen in U.S. cities. I bet it's more like being part of a really popular strike. On the other hand, we took coffee to the CDS headquarters in Sector 4 the other night with a woman named Panchita, who is the sector's *responsable*. The *compa* on duty there handed her a list of folks signed up for *vigilancia*. It was obvious that about half had not signed in. Miranda asked Panchita what she would do with this list, and Panchita replied that she'd visit them and tell them that, *"¡Deben ponerse las pilas!"* (They'd better put their batteries in!)

As I told you on the phone, we've had this Jesuit priest from the U.S. with us for the last few days, and he's driving me absolutely nuts. He's the kind of unreconstructed sexist who wonders why young Nicaraguan women go to bed with men when they "know" they are just going to be abandoned. He thinks prostitutes are some kind of specially awful sinners. He's not even minimally informed on women's rights.

On top of all that, he's terrified, and his way of dealing with his terror is (1) to build ineffectual bomb shelters out of cots and mattresses—we let him work off some steam—and (2) to talk incessantly about all the possible implications and ramifications of each little piece of non-information we get about the situation in Jalapa. It doesn't help me to have a terrified person running around here like an idiot and talking about how his special "priest thing" is healing. He can't talk for more than a couple of minutes without reminding you he's a priest.

Adele, a lovely woman, another stray who landed at our house during the recent alerts, shared my feelings and helped me keep my humility, but when she left I felt a little outnumbered. She's a theology student, mother of two teen-agers, a feminist and a calm, intelligent presence. The first thing that I noticed about her, however, was that she had a swastika tattooed on her right ring finger. Naturally I had to ask about it, wondering if she'd been with some Nazi group in her youth or had lived with the Hopi, since the swastika is also a Hopi symbol. The latter turned out to be the case. She said that she received the tattoo in a ceremony marking the time in her life when she was called to work with poor people. All honestly humble. She'd been to language school in Managua, then hooked up with another student to travel a bit. They both got stuck here when the road was closed for a few days. I was glad for her soft Arkansas accent and her genuine feminism.

I'm finding it hard to be a lesbian here. Over and over I lie to Nicaraguans, saying I'm not married, and each time it feels like a little betrayal. Miranda and Mary D. try to get me to join them in their pronouncement of joy in having a man (Tom, the Jesuit) around the house. I parry by saying to them and Tom that I'm glad to have his person, but I couldn't care less about his manhood. (And, really, when he started a conversation about gang rape today, I thought I was going to break my commitment to nonviolence!)

Mary D. and Miranda have taken on a number of men in Jalapa in a half-joking way over the issue of language and women's oppression. They have a plan to rewrite the Spanish language to make all positive nouns feminine. In the last few years I seem to have come to think that language is less central—or at least shares the center with more means of oppression—than I once thought. (Odd conclusion for a poet to reach!) The night we sat up all night with the *compas*, Mary D. and Miranda were talking about how masculine generics—in English or Spanish—make women invisible, about which of course I agree. The serious young man they were speaking with kept saying, "But you have to understand; our customs are different from yours." I was able to talk a little about the idea that a custom might be a genuine custom and still a bad thing, using the example of clitoridectomy. It was a strange, intense conversation, and a strange night. Still, I think he got my point.

So with M. and M. on the offensive, they've pretty much staked out their territory as the feminists of the group, which gives them leave to criticize me for saying I find a particular woman beautiful (objectification!), while they're full of their opinion of particular men. They also seem to feel free to tease me about the possibility of my acquiring a Nicaraguan boyfriend, which I find insulting. It's hard being around that astonishing sort of heterosexual woman who has no trouble at all "handling" men. I know I will never achieve that attractive combination of bluster and flirtation I've admired in so many tough straight women.

Enough bitching. With the end of the Granadero I exercises in Honduras, there seems to be a general releasing of breath and relaxing, although everyone knows the contra are out there.

Re: women in Nicaragua—everyone here seems to believe that abandonment is a number one problem. It's exacerbated by the war, because soldiers have a tendency to beget children and move on. The law concerning family responsibility is strict but hard to enforce, especially in war time.

On the other hand, Chilo's eyes lit up when she saw birth control pills in a box of medicines brought by one delegation. I asked her if the Church's position affected women's desire to get birth control and she just laughed and waved her hand. The only problem, she says, is getting hold of the stuff!

Here's a poem. Afraid I'm a little rusty, but it's coming.

Soldier's Funeral in Jalapa

The women of the Sandinista Youth
lead chants. *¡Presente!* falls away in heat
and dust. The silence, unfamiliar, eats
at sound. *¡Still here!* I pick for truth,
bright string of mango lodged between one tooth
and another, contemplate the beat
of hands on hands. A woman's voice repeats,
¡No pasarán! Perhaps. But I want proof.

There's no proof in Jalapa on alert
the fifteen thousand, seven miles away
and panting, won't flow down like dirt
undammed and over us, like ruddy clay—
except the giggles, and the flowered shirts
of soldiers hand-in-hand this bloody day.

Thursday, June 14
Dear Jan,

Last night I dreamed that I'd gone home to the U.S. for a couple of days' visit, mostly to reassure friends that I was all right. Peter was furious with me, for having wasted WFP money (I explained that I'd used my own) and then for having had the privilege of being home for a few days. I felt horribly guilty, as if I'd let down the whole project.

The dream reflects reality, in a way. I feel guilty for my attempts to remain connected with you, and with my life in the U.S. At the same time, I know that connection is central to my work here and to my own life. There are times when I ache for just a little bit of privacy. Our house here is a lot like a Catholic Worker house—folks drop in all day and until late at night. As far as I can tell, Nicaraguans never sleep. I never know whether it's polite for me to go away—not that there's much "away" to go to—so I spend a lot of time entertaining people I think of as other people's guests.

Yesterday and the day before I visited *asentamientos* with Chilo. She was weighing children who'd never been weighed before, in order to establish a baseline for their participation in the nutritional aid program. "What do the undernourished children get," I asked, "vitamins?"

"*Sí,*" said Chilo, "*cuando hay.*" When there are any. Mostly the program gives her a chance to talk with the mothers regularly about childcare and nutrition. Yesterday for the first time, something like culture shock took me. The *asentamiento* of Santa Cruz is so poor. Everyone is filthy; everyone's almost in rags; everyone's nose is running. Everywhere mud and dirt. They've built six or seven two-family houses in one part of the cooperative, but none of them are finished—*falta concreta* (there's no concrete). Meantime, folks are living in stick shacks. Two huge tobacco-drying sheds dominate the land and more than one family has tacked up cardboard posts inside these to make houses, complete with kitchens.

The day before yesterday, we were at La Estancia, an older *asentamiento* with a population of almost 500. These folks all live in the same kind of two-family houses (front doors facing away from each other and a common back wall). Each house has its own latrine and between each two is a sink with running water. Santa Cruz has electricity, which I doubt is much use to anyone, since no one has anything to plug in. La Estancia has no electricity, but running water makes the women's lives so much easier. La Estancia also has a *comedor infantil,* and they're building a new one at Santa Cruz. The ground around people's houses is bare, although a few people have planted flowers in pots next to their identical houses. Both *asentamientos* have big, fully completed *refugios.*

Isaac, one of WFP's constant visitors, just walked in on me as I was writing the last paragraph. He's 14, bright, *listo*, as they say here (literally "ready") and has the run of the house. He often gives talks about Jalapa to WFP delegations. He's nice, but he's also officious as hell. It's cute now, but in a few years he's going to make some woman miserable. His mother, to start with. Reyna, who runs the *comedor* where we eat, was enumerating her sorrows the other day: the loss of two children in a horrible bus accident, losses of other family members. "And your husband?" we asked. "Oh, him," came the answer. "I'm glad he left. I'm better off on my own." Some days I wonder whether women shouldn't be working to create more homosocial societies, rather than more integrated ones. Not something I really believe, just something my frustration says every once in a while.
◩ *Much love*

◩　◩　◩

The dream I described did mirror a reality about working in Nicaragua, and with WFP. Jan responded, "I have thought a lot about your feeling guilty trying to stay in contact with me and with those you love here while you are there. I am familiar with the pressure in do-gooding circles to have such feelings—and I think it spiritual and emotional crap. And I bet some of the Nicaraguan people would understand that. In a way, you are there, with them, taking their risks, *because* you love me and others here, even because you love a possible future for here. It is all of a piece, though everything about the status quo conspires to convince us there aren't any real connections."

◩　◩　◩

Friday, June 10
Dear Jan,
Last night, Miguel and Salvador came by, two of the *compas* who sat up with us on the night of the first alert. Another night, Miguel told us the story of his becoming involved with the Frente—twenty years ago, now. Last night

he talked about torture, a subject he'd brushed off in the past as "secondary" to the story of his political development. He seems not to be filled with hatred, although he has a personal investment in making sure the Guardia never triumph again. He told us that the members of the Frente have an agreement that they will never be captured alive, so that they can never be tortured again. Salvador was also tortured by the Guard—in this very house. There is one room here that he will never enter.

Miguel talked about the discipline required of a Frente militant—eleven rules of personal behavior, including one about respecting women as equals and *compañeras*. He said a lot of men bounced out of the Frente because of that one. Miranda asked him which time was harder, before or after the Triumph. No hesitation. Now is harder, Miguel says. The clandestine life *era una cosa linda* (was a beautiful thing).

We had lunch with Marta Osorio, a friend of Mary C.'s from La Estancia. Marta, 16, is a *reservista*, and today, like all the militia members in the area and all the men at La Estancia, she's being mobilized. She will spend six months in the mountains, cooking for 376 people. They get one uniform apiece which they wash in the river without soap and put back on still wet. She says she's worried, not about her own safety but about how her mother will do without her.

Tonight the WFP people are going to do a singing *rotativa*—Camilo's idea, one of the *responsables* for the CDS. He comes by the house and tells us about his son, who is suffering war psychosis. "He used to love to go out with his friends, to go the movies or to play pool. Now he just sits in the front room and stares at the wall. I offered him some money. 'Go to the movies,' I said. He just looks at me and shakes his head. 'No, thank you, Papa.' He watched his best friend die in a terrible battle in the mountains. We've tried everything, but all he does is sit and look at the wall."

Sometimes there's a barrier between us the people who live here that's more than linguistic. There are times when even though I understand the words, I can't judge the significance of what is happening. Is the mobilization of an entire

asentamiento an ordinary event or harbinger of ii combat? Sometimes I just don't know. ◻ *All love*

◻   ◻   ◻

WFP often had two short-term delegations in the cou at the same time. While we were preparing for the R Mountains group, a delegation of civil rights activists other people of color arrived in Jalapa. This Third W delegation included Black historian Vincent Harding wife Rosemary and their two teenage children. Althougl delegation had very few Spanish speakers, these people ι determined to communicate as deeply as they could with Nicaraguans during their short time there. As t explained to us, they couldn't afford to be shy; there wa time for that.

The Nicaraguans who met this delegation responded kind. Often they would speak about the connectic between their own struggles and those of people of color the United States. When the delegation met later with Fel Barreda, the head of city government in Ocotal, he told the the story of his own political development. His parents we activists in Nicaragua, but as a teenager he was uninterest in politics, preferring to travel the United States as a touris He landed in Los Angeles in the middle of the 1968 riots Watts, after the assassination of Martin Luther King, Jr. " wasn't until I saw Black people in the United States fightin for their rights, for justice, that I understood what my ow parents were trying to do at home. I came home to work fo revolution here. It makes me very happy to be able to say thi to Black people from the United States."

We met one afternoon with the local members of Mother of Heroes and Martyrs, a national group of women who have lost children, fighting in the struggle to depose Somoza or in the contra war. The Mothers have a little museum in Jalapa where photographs and personal effects of their children are displayed. "Come here," Rosemary Harding said to me. "I want to speak to this woman." As I translated, Rosemary asked one of the Mothers about her daughter and how she

died. "Tell her that I'm a mother, too. These are my children. Tell her that we do not want to see our children die fighting their children."

Rosemary's daughter and son were also outspoken, especially about the role in Nicaragua of people their own age. At home, these people would just be high school kids, they said, but here they are adults, full participants in their own society. They wanted to communicate their excitement to friends at home. "The TV and everything tells us that we should only be interested in sports or parties at our age but we can do so much more."

■　■　■

Wednesday, June 20
Dear Jan,

I'm sitting in the *sala* of the Maryknoll Sisters' home in Ocotal, waiting for some little boys to come with a cart for the water jugs. Ocotal's water is unsafe, so people who can afford it drink bottled water from a town a little east of here called Mozonte. Other people drink what they can get. The government encourages them to boil it, but since it takes 20 minutes of boiling to do any good, hardly anyone does it. There's been quite a bit of fighting around Mozonte recently and I'll bet people are a little worried about their water supply. Meanwhile, people are *really* worried about Ocotal's water, because it's drawn from the river—where corpses of contra killed in the fighting on June 1st are still turning up.

Jean and I are in Ocotal, working on firming up arrangements for the Rocky Mountains group, who arrive tomorrow. Eventually, Mary, Doug and I will be working with this group, and we've have the usual hassles people working together for the first time can expect.

It seems that I may be getting a little grace, though, in the matter of insecurity and ego on this piece of work. Somehow I seem to be able to trust that my call to be here is genuine, that there's work here I have to do, and that its nature will become clear to me in time. So when I feel inadequate, I remind myself that there must be some reason I felt the need

to come here. You know me well enough to know that this certainty is grace, not merit!

I think it's possible I may be deepening in faith a little, too. Being with the Third World WFP delegation had something to do with it. For most of those folks, the presence of God was constant. Rosemary Vincent said that for her mother, that presence was as real and as much a part of everyday life as the vegetables in her garden. There was a moment—just a moment—on the way back from Teotecacinte when I got a flash of what that kind of certainty feels like.

We'd spent the morning in town talking to the mother and grandmother of four-year-old Sullapa Gutierrez, who was killed last year in a mortar attack. I'd also talked with Lucila Gutierrez, who's lost two sons and whose last son has now been mobilized. There was singing and praying, and a lot of crying. On the way back, I was looking out the window at the hills that hold the valley of Jalapa and thinking, as I often do, of how beautiful and serene this land is and what a crime it is that people cannot live here without fear and grief. I was thinking about God, I guess, and for a moment I had a different feeling about Providence.

You know that for me the fact of Creation lies at the center of my theology—and that the continued existence of the world from moment to moment is a mystery and a miracle. Often I *think* about the active love that sustains it all. But for a few moments that afternoon, I had a different sort of perception. How to explain this? It's as if somehow the existence of God had slipped over into the category of things I know without doubt about the world. I could look at those hills and say to myself, of course She's here. It was as if I were receiving from those people the opportunity to feel what it's like to rest in God—what it's like to treat that presence as part of the ordinary data of daily life. I'm not explaining this very well. In other words, for a moment I had a sense of what a faith that is not three-quarters doubt might feel like.

I've heard enough stories of torture in the last week to last a lifetime—as if one needed any such stories at all. People I know, people who are acquaintances if not yet friends, have been tortured both before and since the Triumph. Felipe

Barreda, the Junta representative (essentially, the mayor) of Ocotal, told our group his own and his parents' story. His parents, longtime political and church workers, were kidnapped in December 1982, while cutting coffee a little north of here. They were taken to Honduras, tortured for ten days and then assassinated—retribution for a lifetime of work. One of the killers was a 13-year-old girl. She was later captured by the Nicaraguan army and Felipe believes she may be rehabilitated; she's in a half-way house in Managua. They'd like to do that for everyone, especially the young collaborators with the contra, but now with the war, they don't have the resources for it.

Felipe told us how the Guardia used to recruit little boys, eight or nine years old, and train them in torture. They were better at it than adults, it seems, because they hadn't developed so many inhibitions. And it seems there was always a U.S. advisor helping with the training.

Over and over people have told me that this struggle is one of great length—of generations. Look how long it took for Sandino's dream to flower, they say. And they're willing to live it and die for it, knowing they'll never see the end of the *lucha* themselves. This is more than patience. It's a deep perception of their own history and their place in history. In the U.S. we're taught not to think historically, and the resulting inability to connect ourselves to a heritage of struggle weakens us, I think. Even if we're living at the end of history—you and I have said this to each other before—we have to live as if we are not.   ◼ *All love*

◼ ◼ ◼

Felipe Barreda's attitude of forgiveness toward the people who murdered his parents reflects both government policy and public opinion. The most famous example of Nicaragua's commitment to a rehabilitative penal system is the "Open Farm" prison on the outskirts of Managua, whose inmates are ex-members of the National Guard. In recognition of the fact that many poor men originally joined the Guard for economic reasons, prisoners receive real agricultural training and the chance to obtain land when they leave.

The farm is "open" in the sense that inmates work during the week and are free to visit friends and family on the weekends.

Although I visited the Open Farm and talked to its enthusiastic prisoners, I was skeptical, until much later when by accident a WFP long-termer friend met a woman in Corinto whose uncle was a prisoner there. The man was serving a seven-year sentence and his absence placed a tremendous financial burden on the woman's aunt. "You must all be very angry at the government," my friend said.

"Oh, no," the woman answered, "it's the best thing that ever happened to him. He loves it there, and when he leaves he's going to know how to farm. He was a terrible person when he was in the Guard. He drank and spent all his family's money. Now he's very different."

I encountered more generosity toward the enemy among poor people in an Ocotal barrio, a few days after the June 1st attack. I asked how people felt about *campesinos* who are fighting with the contra, expecting an angry and indignant reply. Instead, a woman said, "I don't really blame *them*. It's not their fault. Sometimes they don't have any chance to know better, and they really believe what the contra tell them—that they're fighting communism or that God wants them to go with the contra. The Revolution's benefits haven't reached every corner of the country yet." These remarks elicited a general agreement.

National policy reflects this spirit in the General Amnesty, which permits any member of the contra to lay down his weapon and resume ordinary civilian life, without penalty. Originally offered only to rank-and-file contra, the amnesty has been extended to include even top leaders.

People and government appear to share a faith in the capacity of human beings—even murderous members of Somoza's National Guard—to change. Often Nicaraguans, including government officials, expressed this faith to me in Christian language about human imperfection and the hope of forgiveness. The great dream is that no one who might be part of it is to be left out of building the new Nicaragua.

The Rocky Mountains Delegation arrived in Ocotal on the 21st of June, and spent its first night sleeping on the floor of the Seventh-Day Adventist church. The next morning I ran into the first and only example of genuine European-style anti-Semitism I encountered in Nicaragua.

At breakfast, Francisco, the church's pastor, gave me a curious look. "Are you *indigena?*" he asked, meaning, was I an Indian?

"No, I said, "I'm a Jew."

"Not one of the Jews who killed Christ?"

My Spanish was nothing like suitable enough to approach the ideological—not to mention theological—tangle presented by that one. My buddy Peter helped me out. "We *all* killed Christ," he said.

"Well, of course," said Francisco, and the conversation went on to other subjects.

The delegation spent five days in Ocotal, visiting the sites of damage in the June 1st attack and digging out a *refugio* behind the Child Development Center. After two separate *despedidas*—good-by parties—we went on to San Juan de Limay, where we spent another several days meeting with students, cooperative members, women of AMNLAE and the town government. We left Peter and Jean in Ocotal, to keep the Maryknollers there company. The June 1st attack had come very close to the Maryknoll house, which is somewhat isolated from other houses. Rachel and Pastora were grateful for the companionship, especially because the two other women who usually live in the house were out of town.

Nancy Donovan, a Maryknoller who lives in Limay, had planned so many activities for the delegation that I didn't have time to write again until I got back to Managua a week later.

◨ ◨ ◨

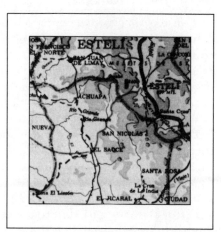

San Juan de Limay
and Managua

Thursday, June 22
Dear Friends,

This letter comes to you from Managua, where it looks as if I'm going to be for a while. Witness for Peace has discovered my office and editorial skills, so I'm stuck here running, of all things, a word processor. Our coordinator promises that it won't be forever, but I have my doubts.

Managua is harder for me than the *campo*. It's big; it sprawls; it has no center. (Except for the big phallus of the Bank of America building, downtown Managua was completely destroyed in the earthquake of 1972.)

In Jalapa, almost everyone takes *vigilancia* and works with the CDS. In my barrio here, they can't find anyone to replace the woman who is the current *responsable* for the CDS. A restructuring meeting last week was cut short when it became clear that no one was going to volunteer for the job. A new meeting date was set, contingent on everyone's promise to bring one other person to the next meeting. A *responsable* is vital: she or he will be the person to hand out ration tickets. Without a *responsable*, the barrio won't get its coupons. This is pretty ironic, in view of the U.S. government's attempts to describe the CDS's as neighborhood spy organizations. Here's the most powerful position in the barrio going begging, because no one even wants the job!

We took the Rocky Mountains Delegation to Ocotal for five days of digging on a bomb shelter for a daycare center there. The whole time we were digging we could hear the mortars falling ten miles away in San Fernando, and the *Cuarenta Bocas* ("Forty Mouths") rocket launchers that sound like a gigantic gas oven lighting.

Before returning to Managua, we spent several days in San Juan de Limay—getting there involved two hours on a mountain dirt road, fording seven rivers or the same river seven times; I never did quite figure it out. We visited several cooperatives and a *centro de capacitación*, a training school and experimental farm (grapes positive, zucchini a bust— "Tastes like water," said the *responsable*.) I also watched a woman teaching an avid class how to test a cow for pregnancy, of which procedure perhaps the less said the better. I only add that it requires the use of a shoulder-length plastic glove.

Later we attended a Celebration of the Word at Barrio Hermano Guadalupe, named for J. Guadalupe Carney, a priest from the United States. Carney spent many years in Honduras before he was deported and came to live three years in Limay. Last year he returned to Honduras where he died accompanying a band of guerillas fighting the Honduran government.

The barrio is still being built, house by house: dirt floors, rough-milled wooden walls. The destruction of the sawmill in the June 1st attack on Ocotal has slowed construction. Electricity has not yet come to Barrio Hermano Guadalupe, so we found everyone waiting for us in the gathering dark under the thatch roof of an unfinished community building. By collecting donations of coffee from every household, they'd managed to produce a huge kettle of it, dark and sweet.

They met us with songs—*"Vos sos el Dios de los pobres"*—and embraces. The Delegates of the Word read the day's lesson and invited everyone to comment on them. The second reading had to do with Jesus' response when John the Baptist sends his disciples off to see whether Jesus is really the Messiah. Jesus says to them, just tell John what you've seen: the blind see, the dead live, and good news is preached to the poor. Community members interpreted the passage for us, saying in part that all they wanted of us is that we go home and tell what we have seen—that the poor of Nicaragua now have food and shelter, health care and education.

They asked us to comment on the readings also. I said that it seems to me that the dead really do live in Nicaragua. When someone's name is shouted aloud and people answer for that person, *"¡Presente!"*, I really can feel the intensity of their remembrance of that person recreating that presence. The dead live, too, in the names of schools, hospitals, barrios.

I was a little shy about putting this idea forward, and more than a little surprised when suddenly everyone was nodding and beaming. I'd hit on one of the truths of the Nicaraguan revolution, I think: there's a way in which people feel enough a part of what they're building that death becomes a less individual event. Maybe some of the extraordinary courage I've seen in some people here comes from that feeling of participation in a struggle that began before they were born, and whose end they may not live to see. More than one young woman has said to me, "It doesn't matter if I die, because someone will come after me. We have patience. Look how long was the time between Sandino's death and the Triumph. If we have to fight that long again, we're ready."

So what is going to happen here? No one knows and everybody speculates: The U.S. and the contra are going to disrupt the July 19th celebration of the Fifth Anniversary of the Triumph. They're going to disrupt the elections in November. They're going to start bombing Managua. No one knows. Be vigilant, folks. You'll probably see it coming before I do.

Thank you for your letters, your support. I know you're doing the work—and that you have the hard part, while I have the joy of touching something awfully close to freedom. I may be scared sometimes, but my work here is easy compared to the constant effort of staving off despair that immersion in U.S. politics can be. I'm beginning to have a little faith in Nicaraguan patience. *"Eso es la guerra prolongada,"*—(this is the long war.) We may not live long enough to see the end of it. But someone will. ◻ *All love*

Friday, June 29
Dear One,

I'm sitting in the long-term team house in Managua, waiting to go to CEPAD to start work on my visa extension. Its very hard for me to be here right now, because Ocotal and Jalapa are again being threatened. The night before last, Ocotal was on the alert again, and Jean and Peter were up all night.

It's been pretty busy here. Yesterday the Rocky Mountains group had an interview with Ernesto Cardenal in the morning, a visit to Centro Antonio Valdevieso in the afternoon, followed by a trip to the market and a combination farewell and birthday party (mine) last night. In addition, two of our folks decided to get married here in Nicaragua before one had to leave this morning. They had a frustrating time trying to find the house of the woman judge who had promised to accompany them to the airport and marry them there. Well, they couldn't find the judge, so a burly protestant minister on the delegation did the job quickly before Abrán disappeared into the standby line.

Ernesto Cardenal was not expecting us; his secretary had forgotten to record the appointment. He graciously spoke with us for about 45 minutes, read a poem and answered some pretty personal questions. One guy wanted to know about Cardenal's vision of God as love—a mystical experience of which he has written. I wouldn't have had the temerity to ask, but the answer was interesting. At first he said that he'd already described the experience as concretely as he could, that words weren't much good for this. When pushed, he said that it was like falling in love. He smiled then. "And you know that when you are in love, you can't think about anything else."

I asked him about poetry, describing what passes for the stuff in artsy circles in the U.S.—how it all sometimes seems to be about, "Look how clever I can be with language and syntax!" He responded in part by naming North American poets whose work has influenced revolutionary Nicaraguan poets: Whitman, William Carlos Williams and one woman, Denise Levertov.

I think, I hope, that being in love with a human being does not mean being unable to think about anything else. I suppose it would be a very good way to be in love with God. Not so much being unable to think of anything else as being unable to stop thinking about God—no matter what else is also in one's mind. I'm not so good at that. Like you, I hope She counts some of our love for each other as love for Her.

So much has happened in the last few days that I haven't recorded anywhere, and now I don't know where to begin. We left Ocotal on Tuesday the 26th for the town of San Juan de Limay where two Maryknoll Sisters live and work. They'd set up quite a full schedule for our two days there. In fact, it was a little too full to be realistic, with something scheduled just about every hour.

One day we met with the women of AMNLAE. They served coffee and *pan dulce* (cookies), and we heard a speech by Susana, the *responsable*. I also got a chance to see my first copy of *Somos*, AMNLAE's monthly magazine. I almost cried reading in Spanish about the existence of the clitoris and where it can be found. If this is a revolution that gives women access to their sexuality, that's a new thing under the sun.

Nancy Donovan had prepared a fascinating discussion for the AMNLAE women and us. She'd come across a graphic in a magazine: a stylized drawing of a woman giving birth. The woman's face was fiercely contorted, though by what emotion was not clear. The child between her legs already stood on his own legs, holding aloft a rifle, easily identifiable by its curved magazine as the ever-present AK-47, or AKa.

Along with this picture, she gave us a biblical text to consider, one which compares the creation of the world to childbirth. She asked us to look at the picture and words, and to make comments.

At first the discussion focused on the question of whether the picture was ugly. A woman said, "When I first saw it, I thought it was horrible, but as I look at it more and more, I realize that it is also beautiful. She is obviously in pain, but it hurts to give birth."

Another woman said, "I don't think it's pain. I think it's grief, because as soon as he's born, her son has to pick up a gun. Our children don't get to be children, because of the war."

"Maybe the child is the Revolution," said Susana, "and the woman is giving birth to it. Look how strong she is, how thick her thighs are. Maybe the woman is Nicaragua giving birth to the new society."

The discussion went on in this vein, women commenting on the combination of pain and joy involved in bringing forth a new society. It was interesting that, as is often the case, they freely mixed theological and political language, sometimes talking of creating the Reign of God and sometimes of the new society, as if the two were one and the same for these women.

Who are the women of AMNLAE in San Juan de Limay? I've heard criticisms of AMNLAE leadership, that the women are too middle class to represent poor women's interests. Certainly the national leadership are women from the middle class, but the women we talked to that day wore the same cheap nylon dresses and tattered plastic shoes I see in the streets of Jalapa or Ocotal. In general, I've found that in a given neighborhood, the poorer people tend to be the most involved in mass organizations like the CDS or AMNLAE. The other day when I was searching for my Managua barrio's CDS *responsable*—whose signature I needed to obtain my residency—I picked out her house easily: it was the smallest and poorest at the very end of a dirt road lined with poor houses.

We finished the AMNLAE meeting with the Frente anthem and a few rousing *consignas*, including my favorite: *¡Sin la participación de la mujer, no hay revolución!* (Without women's participation, there's no revolution!)

Earlier that day, we'd attended an *acto* (sort of like a demonstration) at Limay's high school. The student body, mostly female now, had arranged themselves in chairs outside in the full sun. We stood on the porch in the shade, embarrassed, and listened to one more horror story, this one about the death of two People's Teachers, a married couple who used to travel to little settlements teaching adults to read. The contra were laying for them and got them both one day. The woman was pregnant. She was raped. Her breasts were sliced off, and the fetus was carved out of her belly. All of this happened in front of her seven-year-old daughter. (Later that day, our delegation met this little girl. She looked so tiny surrounded by us *gringos*. What is there to say to a seven-year-old girl whose parents were killed and mutilated in front of her?)

The *acto* finished with more *consignas*. Some popular ones: *¡Cultura es—fusil artístico de la revolución!* (Culture is the art-weapon of the revolution!) *¡Sandino vive—la lucha sigue!* (Sandino lives—the struggle goes on!)

At every gathering, there's someone, very often a woman, who likes to start the *consignas*. I can imagine that a videotape of these high school students shouting in unison might convey the image of a brainwashed and dangerous body. I think of some of the film clips I've seen of Nazi rallies. But it doesn't feel like that from more or less the inside. Why not, I wonder? Partly because the hatred is missing. There's anger sometimes, but I do believe the content matters and that the content *is* different. What do you think?

I'm going to have a go at Carlos Fonseca's *Sandino Vive*, a collection of booklets put out by the FSLN which comprise Fonseca's basic formulation of *Sandinismo*—the FSLN's political philosophy. One of the things I love about the Nicaraguan press is that they refer to beloved personages by their first names. Daniel Ortega is "Daniel," and Fonseca is just "Carlos" to everyone.

I miss you unutterably. I just got through telling my father on the telephone that the Marines have been here before; he had no idea the U.S. had been here at any time since Teddy Roosevelt. How I miss your mind and your responsibility to that mind. And how I miss the smell of you. ◼ *All love*

Saturday, July 7
Dear heart

Escape from Managua! I am in—of all places—Ocotal. I got sprung from the office because Buddy, the *jefe* of all WFP, needed to travel to Ocotal to see Jean and to Jalapa to see Miranda and Mary D. Since he speaks almost no Spanish, I'm going along with him. We took the bus to Ocotal today, where we'll spend the night at the Maryknoll house. Pastora, who lives there, says that it's been quiet for the last two days, but that they always know there could be an attack at any moment.

Sunday, July 8
Sitting in a bus in Jícaro, mulling over the driver's promise that soon, or at least today, we're going on to Jalapa. I was thrilled at 6:30 this morning when Buddy and I actually managed to get *seats* on this microbus—the last two available. We'd be in Jalapa, I thought, in three hours, tops. Well, the bus turns out to also be a plastic-ware distributorship, which means that every stop involves an hour's worth of business transactions!

For hours now, we've gone nowhere, except in circles delivering plastic bowls, plates and shoes. We have to turn right around tomorrow and return to Managua, so it doesn't look as if I'll get much time in Jalapa. Oh well. ◼ *All love*

Wednesday, July 11
Dear one,

I'm sitting in the air-conditioned office of Aeronica, number ten in line, to work on reservations for one of the coordinators of the delegation of 200 currently in Nicaragua. (This particular piece of lunacy the WFP-ers have taken to calling "B&B—short for Barnum & Bailey"—which should give you an idea of what kind of circus it is, shepherding around 200 dazed North Americans.)

In Jalapa—yes, the Tupperware Truck did finally arrive, seven hours after leaving Ocotal—I had a couple of hours with Chilo, who gave me a book of poems for my birthday, inscribed with her favorite of her own poems: *"Ser poeta"* (*"To Be a Poet"*). She writes, "to be a poet/is to be reborn in this new liberty. . . To be a poet is to give birth with every poem."

On the street which I walk to get to Chilo's house, there are three new houses being built. I've watched them go up, fascinated because they are not the usual adobe wall and dirt floor, but cinderblock with concrete slab, and real louvered glass windows. Each one sports a TV antenna on its new tile roof. I asked Chilo whose they are.

"This is hard to explain," she said. "You know that we need technical people in Jalapa, if we are going to develop at all. So many left Nicaragua altogether after the Triumph; they went to the United States where their skills can make them lots of money. The ones who remained don't want to live in Jalapa, because it's so far away from the city and so near the war. The only way we can get them to come here is by offering them nice houses. It's a contradiction, I know, when there are so many poor people who need housing, too."

She talked about her hopes for going to medical school, and her concern about stepping into the professional class herself. "I don't ever want to stop identifying with my own people and my own class," she told me, adding that she probably won't be able to afford med school anyway. Although the classes would be free, there is no money to pay for her living in Managua. Her family cannot even afford the *tejas* (clay tiles) to finish roofing their kitchen. A tattered piece of plastic covers the rafters now.

And we talked about poetry. I made a stab at translating my sonnet about Nelson's funeral. She called it my "mango" poem, because of the line about trying to pick the truth free, as if it were one of those strings that get stuck between your teeth when you eat a mango. She says she likes poetry best that isn't just one person's memories, but that makes a promise. She also says a poet has to back up every word she uses with actions, "and that is where you have to be careful." I agreed with her.

Well, I just found out that of the many things I was trying to accomplish today at Aeronica (or *"Aeronunca"*, as it's fondly known because *"nunca"* means "never"), the simplest one—confirming an existing reservation—is impossible. The poor woman, who had a perfectly good reservation, is now on the waiting list, two steps behind another of our people, who was only on the waiting list to begin with! They both now have to call back tomorrow at 3:00 p.m.

Last night I attended my neighborhood's CDS meeting. Some things, like finding people willing to do the work, are the same the whole world over! Also saw Nicaraguan TV for the first time: strange combination of Mexican soap operas, dubbed-in old U.S. movies and serials, and locally-produced news and entertainment. In our neighborhood in Jalapa, everyone gathers at 9:00 p.m. to watch the *novela*, the soap opera, in the living room of a family who has a TV. Last night I watched *Who's Afraid of Virginia Woolf?*, with Richard Burton and Elizabeth Taylor speaking dubbed-in Spanish. Very odd. ◼ *All deep love*

Sunday, July 15
Dear one,

I'm feeling pretty discouraged today, as if I'm never going to get out of Managua, because I'm doing "such a good job" here. I did take an overnight trip to Estelí this weekend with some friends from the Guatemalan Church in Exile, in order to attend a convention of Christian base communities there. There were lots of greeting and singing, a wonderful parade with floats, but it wasn't a conference in the sense U.S. feminists would understand. (No caucuses, no workshops, no plenary session for airing the inevitable criticisms any group of women can generate in three or four days!)

Interesting piece of international politics: These folks say that although Nicaragua is very vocal about its support for the FMLN in El Salvador, there's almost no mention of Guatemala in the Nicaraguan press. Apparently, Nicaragua has some important economic ties with Guatemala. The Guatemalan Church in Exile people don't seem to feel any rancor towards the Nicaraguan government which does at least allow them to stay and work here. Still, I seem, as is often the case here, to be missing a piece of the story. What do you know about it from your end?

I need to quit now and work on a letter for new long-termers, and on my article for *LesCon* (long-neglected, I'm afraid). I know this has been a pissy letter, but know that you're there in my heart. ◼ *All love*

Friday, July 20
Dear one,

Yesterday Nicaragua celebrated the Fifth Anniversary of its revolution. In Managua, more than 200,000 people gathered in the new Plaza Carlos Fonseca. Demonstrations here don't produce nearly as much paper as ones in the U.S. I sort of missed little leftist groupings like the Spartacists. The enclosed leaflet from the Frente Obrero (Workers Front) was the only offering from a leftist splinter group; showers of them were tossed on our contingent as we approached the Plaza. I couldn't see how many folks were doing the tossing, but their number was not legion, I imagine. I find the Cyrillic script on the back fascinating. Couldn't they find any other paper? Or what were they trying to communicate? Presumably they don't expect *"trabajadores y campesinos"* to read Russian!

We have a short-term delegation staying with us, so they marched in their yellow WFP T-shirts with the rest of our barrio the six kilometers to the Plaza. As we were assembling at the end of our street, our *responsable* handed each of us a mimeographed list of fifteen *consignas*. Number 7 was particularly familiar to me: *"¡Aquí, allá, el yanqui morirá!"* (Over here, over there, the Yankee will die!") When she got down the list to Number 7, our *responsable* looked over at us and skipped on to Number 8! Typical Nicaraguan courtesy.

The *acto* itself was an improvement on the U.S. version of the same thing. It began only half-an-hour late and lasted an hour-and-a-half with very little filler. One thing they don't do here is introduce the introducer of the person who is going to introduce the speaker. A nice change.

Daniel Ortega gave a good speech, comparing the efforts of the Nicaraguan people in the last five years to the composition of a great poem. He went on to announce some lifting of restrictions on travel inside Nicaragua. He added that Nicaragua's State of Emergency would end in October, but

87 ◼

that even before then the ban on anti-FSLN demonstrations would not apply to meetings and rallies of opposition parties preparing for the elections.

Ortega then introduced Fernando Cardenal, asking the crowd to raise our hands if we wanted to see Cardenal become the new Minister of Education, clearly a reference to the Jesuits' insistence that he choose between his order and the government post. The crowd's response was enthusiastic.

The *acto* finished with music: a song to Carlos Fonseca, followed by the FSLN anthem. (All Nicaraguan ceremonies seem to open with the national Anthem and close with the Frente's.) The song to Carlos incorporates Tomás Borge's words with a chorus that speaks of Carlos as *"tayacan"* ("leader" in one of the indigenous languages) and calls him Nicaragua's lover and vanquisher of death. The final line goes, *"Nicaragua entera te grita, ¡Presente!"* —"All of Nicaragua cries out to you, *¡Presente!"* It was quite something to hear 200,000 people crying out the final word.

The tendency to speak of the dead, particularly heroes like Sandino and Carlos Fonseca, as *"presente"* does have its detractors. In Managua you see billboards proclaiming, *"¡Solo Cristo vive!"* ("Only Jesus lives!")

We have to stop talking so long on the phone, but it's very hard to resist the chance to run my experience through the mill of your mind. I'm pretty lonely here for someone who sees things even vaguely the way I do. The other night I scandalized three long-termers by saying I had criticisms of Jesse Jackson. Hard to explain to those folks what words like "hymie" do to my stomach. And equally hard to explain how I can criticize some of Jackson's actions, and express doubt about his commitment to feminism, and still support the Rainbow Coalition and voter registration drives with a full heart.

Speaking of Democrats, apparently Mario Cuomo gave a keynote address at the Democratic National Convention that's being touted as the greatest speech of the century. What on earth did he say? Is a text available?

Time to stop. ◼ *All love*

It turned out that Jan was also thinking about the Jesse Jackson campaign. A few days before, I'd called her from Managua, in part to talk about how hard it was going to be to leave Nicaragua. I had a proposition—that I renew my contract with WFP and that she join me for a second six months. She wrote:

"So you want me to come down there with you for six months. My first reaction is that if right now I were to believe I should commit myself to working in an essentially hostile environment, it would be on whatever efforts are made to continue and expand the Rainbow Coalition—not in Nicaragua, and certainly not in any way with white U.S. Christians, however much I may yearn for a spiritual context. I know—all my years of training myself to be a political observer tell me—that I have seen genuine energy for change, and more Truth than I hardly ever see—in the last few days of the Jackson effort. Now whether this energy is centered on this particular individual, or whether he is serving as a catalyst (one who can change and grow) for something real, I don't know. But I know I am in the presence of real revolutionary energy insofar as one gets to be here—and it is starkly clear that it has nothing to do with white middle class. (I still don't know whether it really has room for me.) But I know I am seeing the quality of energy which makes a difference.

"Damn good feeling—and an unlooked-for gift here in the belly of the beast. So that is where I am at the moment—extraordinarily enthusiastic. And not very inclined to commit myself to being in Nicaragua, because I have even more than my usual sense that the work is here—and that I have actually been in the presence of some of what it would look like."

I knew Jan was right about where our work has to be, although it was hard to acknowledge that I couldn't live inside someone else's revolution forever. From that time on, I began to think more frequently about applying what I was learning from Nicaragua to my own country. A number of Nicaraguans had told me the same thing. In Limay, a woman said to me, "You can stop the aid to the contra this year, and you can stop aid to the contra next year, but until you change your own country, we will always be confronting some form of aggression from the United States."

◼ ◼ ◼

Tuesday, July 24
Dear Jan,

I got up to Jalapa this weekend, because a reporter and photographer from *Time* are doing a story on religious *internacionalistas* in Nicaragua and wanted to augment their coverage of WFP with interviews of the folks up in Jalapa. They needed a guide, I guess, although they'd hired a jeep and driver, so I went along. Both were women, about my age. Jan, the reporter, is Black; she's worked five years for *Time* and five before that for the *Wall Street Journal*. This is her first visit to Nicaragua. Some time ago she spent a few weeks in a language program at Cuernavaca, Mexico. Cindy, the photographer, is a white woman based in Mexico. She has been working in Central America for the last three years, including El Salvador and Guatemala.

They were hard to figure out. First of all, they were very clubby. They hadn't worked together before but they were part of the same *Time* staff and they hung together. They talked together in code around outsiders (e.g., discussing Jan's possible future articles in veiled terms, leaving out all concrete nouns). Both were clearly sympathetic to popular struggles in Central America, but neither had any illusions about what would get past their editor in New York. I guess they had a cynicism I didn't like—a sort of "mature realism" about the world I found absurd in people my own age, no matter what their professional status. Jan, for example, was quick to tell me how cheap the meals she bought me were, because she'd changed her money at illegal rates. She is sympathetic to Nicaragua, but the "reality" is that you change your money at advantageous rates, regardless of its effect on the economy. That's the grown-up way. In any event, we were heartily sick of each other by the end of the trip.

In Jalapa I saw Chilo very briefly. Yesterday she was to enter the hospital at La Trinidad, near Estelí, for surgery on an ulcer. I knew she'd been having stomach problems but this was a surprise to me. At least I managed to bring her a birthday present, a poetry anthology, and some vitamins I rescued from donations destined for a military hospital.

I may get to go to Matagalpa and Jinotega next week, to gather information about massacres that have taken place there recently. I'd be traveling with Joaquín, who did six years with the Peace Corps in Guatemala. I think we'd get along all right, because I can feel his pain so well, and because we seem to respect each other.

In Guatemala Joaquín organized beekeeping cooperatives, traveling from village to tiny village to meet with local organizers. The military government couldn't abide anything that looked like genuine community organizing, and eventually Joaquín got the word that if he wanted to live, he'd better leave Guatemala. Not one of the towns he worked in exists today. Not one of the people he worked with is alive today. The Guatemalan army killed them all.

I feel a little bit that Joaquín has a right to his sense that no one else in WFP is quite as dedicated as he—which feeling emerges not so much in comparisons he makes, as in the obvious fact that he works longer and harder than anyone else.

There's some pretty disturbing stuff going on in Nicaragua right now, but I don't have enough first-hand knowledge to talk too much about it. Dependable folks are telling me about abuses occurring in connection with military conscription. Apparently, in some parts of the country, the police are showing up at gatherings of people, rounding up the young men and holding them long enough to check their registration status.

Meanwhile, CEPAD is trying to facilitate dialogue between some of the Protestant churches and the government about conscientious objection. A WFP representative attended a meeting yesterday between 150 evangelical pastors and government officials, at which many of the pastors offered the performance of war-zone service, e.g., as medics, as long as their people don't have to bear arms. The government appears ready to make accommodations, but only on a case-by-case basis and they're pretty resistant to putting any reference to conscientious objection into law. All of this belongs in the context of the actions of the Catholic hierarchy here and a number of Protestant churches who received their right-wing politics along with their fundamentalist theology directly from U.S. missionaries. The Catholic church, which never had a pacifist position under Somoza, is now maintaining that good Catholic youths have a duty to resist draft registration. To make matters more complicated, there are a number of churches in Nicaragua which have had a *traditional* commitment to nonviolence.

This is all pretty discouraging. I know Nicaragua needs an army, and Goddess knows I'm no military strategist, but I wonder whether the possibilities of an all-volunteer force have been exhausted. Peggy and I were talking about it this evening and acknowledging to each other that we have good reasons for being anarchists. None of which means I've lost my ardor for the revolution here—just that nothing is simple in Nicaragua, as you well know.   ◼ *All love*

Saturday, July 28
Dear heart,
It looks as if Arnold and I have made a little peace about my job in the office here: I'll give a few days at the end of each month to finish up the books and edit whatever work has accumulated while I've been gone. The rest of the time I'll be free to be just like any other long-termer. This is the proposal I made myself the first week I was here, so I was surprised to hear it come back to me as something new and different—surprised, but delighted.

The immediate upshot of all this negotiation is that I'm going to get to go with Joaquín to Jinotega next week. Needless to say, I'm relieved to think I'll finally get back to the *campo*. We'll visit some little towns that were attacked in May and June and collect people's stories there. It's amazing how much less daunting that process seems to me now than it did two months ago. When Doug I. and I planned to go to Condega, I was terrified: I had no idea where to begin gathering information or talking to people. In fact the prospect was *so* daunting that somehow we never got to Condega— partly because we were working at the granary in Ocotal and then got caught in the alert in Jalapa, but partly because I was afraid to go. Now my Spanish, though not perfect, is better, and I can easily imagine going into a new town and finding out what's been happening there. What a change.

I'm curious to know what the U.S. press has made of Arturo Cruz. I see that even *In These Times*—or at least John Judis in *In These Times*—seems to be willing to give Eden Pastora (the ARDE contra leader) the benefit of the doubt. I don't. Especially when he hooks up with someone like Arturo Cruz, who really is pretty slimy, the quintessential representative of business interests.

Did it make the U.S. papers that Cruz and other members of the *Coordinadora Democrática* (Democratic Coordinating Council) are doing their best to torpedo the elections here? Cruz arrived in Nicaragua on Monday, July 23, ostensibly to register as a candidate for the presidency, representing a coalition of four conservative parties. Three days later, he's off to Europe with Pastora and Robelo (contra leaders) to raise money for the contra. In most countries, raising money for the enemy would be called treason. In Nicaragua, Cruz can get away with announcing it publicly! He'd just come from talking with Reagan. In three days, he "decided" that the Sandinistas weren't going to grant the "nine points" on which *La Prensa* and the *Coordinadora* are so keen. Of course, he'd never intended to run at all. The whole thing was a ploy to discredit the elections here and in the U.S., where they can now say that the Sandinistas wouldn't "allow" the opposition to run. Is that your perception from the U.S.?

Other question: It looks to me as if Reagan is now planning to invade (or provide air support for an invasion) before the elections. What do you think? The latest polls I've heard about put Mondale at 48 per cent and Reagan at 50 per cent. That's close enough to push Reagan over the edge, I think. I notice that the propaganda level is rising again, after a period of relative silence concerning Nicaragua. I assume you heard his cracks about how the U.S. already took out one Soviet base (Grenada), and we're not going to let the other one (Nicaragua) continue to exist. You can't get much clearer than that. All of this is pretty scary to me, not so much because I'm concerned about my personal safety, but for the thousands of people who will die here if they start carpet bombing Nicaragua.

Did the news reach the U.S. that two days ago the Salvadoran Air Force began saturation bombing of an area 35 kilometers north of San Salvador? They had bombed the civilian population before, but this is a definite escalation. Apparently, the whole thing can be heard on the outskirts of San Salvador itself.

It has to stop, Jan. I don't know how, but it has to stop.

We're going to have a lot to put back together—not love, but dailyness of our lives. How I miss that. All for now. ◼ *All love*

P.S. My hair is driving me nuts. Would you grieve if I cut it?

◼ ◻ ◼

Arturo Cruz's three day candidacy was the closest the *Coordinadora Democrática* came to entering the elections. Cruz, a career-man with the Inter-American Development Bank, served briefly after the Triumph as Nicaragua's ambassador to the United States and was a member of the first Junta. He was also one of Los Doce (The Twelve), a coalition of conservative businessmen, moderate professionals and liberals who opposed Somoza. Although a Nicaraguan citizen, Cruz has lived half his life in the United States and is no stranger to the U.S. State Department and its machinations for Nicaragua.

The *Coordinadora*, which the Reagan administration insisted on identifying as the only opposition to the FSLN in Nicaragua, represents upper-class and business interests. It is an amalgamation of three small parties (Liberal Constitutional, Social Christian, and Social Democratic), along with a fraction of the divided Conservative Party. It's membership also includes two small labor organizations, the Conference of Professional Associations of Nicaragua, and perhaps most importantly, COSEP, an organization representing private industry.

Backed by such a coalition, and arriving in Nicaragua with the blessings of the Reagan administration, it's not surprising that Cruz's favorite election slogan was *"¡Con Arturo el Presidente, habrá pasta de dientes!"* (With Arturo as President, there'll be plenty of toothpaste!)

Since the November 1984 elections, Cruz has worked very closely with the U.S. government and contra. When the Reagan administration in 1985 attempted to create a new, unified and sanitized contra force, known as UNO (United Nicaraguan Opposition), Cruz was there. When in January 1986 UNO announced its program for a provisional government, Cruz was present, along with Secretary of State George Shultz, for the ceremony. Arturo Cruz is certainly the man the United States would like to install as head of a provisional government in Nicaragua, should it succeed in overthrowing the present government.

◼ ◼ ◼

Sunday, August 5
Dear heart,

A day with slightly less to do than usual. One short-term team left Managua yesterday for Somotillo, and another arrives here tonight. This house where they stay, along with whatever long-termers are currently in Managua has been full to overflowing. I'm reminded a little bit of how rich Dorothy Day used to feel when she had a little room to herself. Everyone has been feeling the crowding, but we have different ideas of what to do about it.

My idea is to get the hell out of Managua, which it now appears I will be doing tomorrow. Joaquín's idea is that WFP should rent a palacial place up the hill from here, so that each of us will have a little work cubicle and some peace and quiet. Fortunately the place is not really available, so he contents himself with fantasies. I say "fortunately" because I don't want to contend once again over the issue of what sorts of accommodations are appropriate to WFP.

Last time we got into this I'd just come back from Jalapa. The next morning everyone decided to go to breakfast at Managua's fancy hotel, the Intercontinental. They offer a brunch involving, for Nicaragua, an extraordinary array of food. When I walked in and saw the meats, breads, cakes, eggs, sausages, fruits and vegetables, my knees went watery. All I could see was Chilo's kitchen, with the torn plastic covering the rafters and her mother making beans and tortillas. I tried to describe my reaction to the other WFP-ers, but made no contact, so I gave up.

I hope you'll help me think through all this lifestyle/comfort stuff when I get home. I do believe that these WFP folks are wrong when they assume that "we" *gringos* all live a certain way, but I'm not sure how wrong. The upshot of my queasiness with the Intercontinental is that everyone teases me now about my "favorite" place—which actually feels fine to me. We haven't been there since.

Women in Nicaragua still have a long way to go. Last night, Sharon was watching her new toy—a TV—and on comes this variety show with a highly made-up woman crooning about how macho some guy is. Full face filling the screen, rocking out *"¡Ma-acho!"* Over and over I'm reminded that liberation doesn't happen all at once.

It looks as if tomorrow we'll be heading north to Matagalpa and Jinotega. We have letters of introduction to the Frente there from the Frente here, and from CEPAD. I'm hoping we'll get a chance to get out to some of the smaller places, like San José del Bocay and Pantasma. I'm also harboring a secret plan to go overland as far East as Siuna, although that rightly belongs to another trip, I guess, as it's getting into Miskito territory. ■ *Adelante, compañera*

■   ■   ■

Matagalpa

Dear Janny,

It's a few minutes after 6:00 in the morning and I'm lying in my little cubicle in the Hotel Don Diego in Matagalpa. We have an 8:00 a.m. appointment at the zonal Frente office to be taken to two different cooperatives to speak with folks who've been present at recent contra attacks. Lucila Lurio, the *responsable* for this zone was very friendly and helpful when we went by the office yesterday, probably due in part to the letter of introduction we carried from the Secretariat of the Frente in Managua.

The bus took three hours from Managua to Matagalpa. I don't know what the land looks like between those two cities because we stood up the whole way, along with many other folks, and the windows were well below eye level. The wind blew my hat off, pulled my braids apart so my hair nearly strangled fellow passengers, and left me looking a bedraggled mess. So I gave up and took myself off to a *sala de belleza* (beauty salon) where a very nice woman removed the braids—and most of the rest of my hair. "Ah," she said, "you're going to the mountains." Meaning I was joining the militia and going to fight in the hills. I allowed that I was going up in the mountains, but not to fight. "Never mind," she said. "I'll give you the cut I give all the *muchachas* when they go to the mountains." So she did. It's the dykiest cut I've had in years!

Matagalpa is built in a valley, sort of spread for a mile-and-a-half along a dip between the mountains. There's a new hospital (Swedish) and several other big installations whose purposes I haven't discerned. There's a lot of military around; things are tense in the region. Last night an *acto* of more than 500 FSLN supporters passed by in the dark street. The electricity was out, more or less as usual, so a few folks carried candles or flashlights.

This *acto* was a response to an incident that occurred here Saturday in which a group of Arturo Cruz's supporters apparently threw rocks at the Mothers of Heroes and Martyrs who were protesting Cruz's presence in Matagalpa.

We went this morning to the Frente office, where Lucila Lurio met us. She'd had a letter prepared for us, but she suggested we wait until she gets through with a meeting today, because she'd like to take us around herself in her jeep. We called at 3:00 p.m. but the meeting was still going strong, so we're going to wait. She said that if she doesn't leave today, she'll certainly go tomorrow at 7:00 a.m.

Meantime we walked up a road into the hills outside Matagalpa. These hills are volcanic I think, but worn down by time. Some are almost mesas, others look from a distance a lot like Vermont's Green Mountains. From above it's easy to see why Matagalpa grew up where it did. It's in the middle of coffee country in a mountain pass beside a river. We spoke with a *campesina* who lives on a *finca* (farm) of about 15 acres. A windmill pumps the water for her house. "We're *mozos*," she said. Joaquín says he hasn't heard that word since leaving Guatemala; it means people who live on and look after someone else's land. It indicates a tenant's relationship to the landlord except that these people probably don't pay rent, but must give up a share of the crop in return for a place to live.

Matagalpa is the regional capital and there seems to be lots of commerce here. Plenty of vegetables in the market, lots of clothes and plastic goods in the stores. I've seen two hardware stores, four bookstores and a yoga center! Our hotel is right near the highway and there's a lot of traffic north to Jinotega and south to Managua.

Up in the hills we ran into Claudia, a woman I'd met earlier at the WFP house in Jalapa. She and I took the bus together from Ocotal to Managua a few weeks ago. Her father is from the Virgin Islands and her mother is Puerto Rican. He's worked for the Department of Defense for 40 years, and Claudia's pretty rich herself (owns a condo in D.C.). But after nine years of well-paying government work, she's been traveling in Central America for a year and it's changed her life. Never can she go back to her old job and friends. But, Jan, she's taking in all this new information and she has nowhere to put it, so she's horribly confused. I suggested a few basic books (she's a reader). Everyday she makes some new discovery about the perfidy of the U.S. and it's still one surprise after another.

I'm reading a book by the Guatemalan Church in Exile called *Cristianos: ¿Por qué Temer a la Revolución?* (Christians, Why Be Afraid of Revolution?) Very interesting to read liberation theology's interpretation of Exodus and to lay it alongside that of someone like Merlin Stone. I remember that for Stone in *When God Was a Woman*, the story of the first five books of the Old Testament is the story of the triumph of a monolithic male God and patriarchy over the Goddess in her various manifestations, and over matriarchal society. I don't know how much credence I put in the primeval matriarchy, but I do think that both ways of looking at Exodus are true in part.

Exodus is certainly the quintessential story of God as the liberator of slaves. I remember ten years ago, celebrating the Passover seder with a group of other Jewish students in Oregon. As we went through the familiar service, answering the questions for each of the four sons, I realized for the first time what the point was: the seder is for the children of the family, a ritual performed so that each new generation will remember that we were slaves in Egypt, and that we were freed.

And feminist theology is also right: the golden calf the Jews built in the desert while Moses was off on Mt. Sinai was a symbol of the Goddess. Jahweh's triumph was also the triumph of men over women.

How to reconcile these different understandings of the same history? I think they're symptomatic of the reconciliation women still must work out today, in Nicaragua as elsewhere, between justice for their people and justice for themselves as women. Not an easy peace to make.

Joaquín and I were talking yesterday about possible plans after WFP holds its end-of-August retreat. I might go to Siuna with him. It would probably involve more risk than anything I've done up to now, as things are pretty woolly out there, but that's just why WFP needs to go there. This war is no longer a border affair and we need to be in the middle of the country as well.

Keep writing to me about the *lucha* in the U.S. I need to remember where my struggles are. I never manage to forget I'm a woman for very long, though. Claudia and Joaquín were saying today how they feel freer here than anywhere else they've ever been. For me it's a little more complicated. I still lower my voice when I tell some North American the name of the paper you and I publish. And I've never come out to a Nicaraguan. Will there ever be a world where I don't have to be afraid, as a woman, as a lesbian? Yes, there will be. But you and I won't live to see it.

I'm going to have to come back to Central America someday, Jan. Is this seduction? Is it just that it's easier to identify with the poor of another culture? Maybe. Will you help me to remember the poor women of my own country? The longer I am here, the more I understand why what we have to work for in the U.S. is a genuine revolution. Nothing less will shift the power in the world. But a feminist revolution. And do I even know what that means anymore?

Heart's desire, I never forget you, although sometimes San Francisco seems decades away. A short-termer I met recently is the best friend of one of the Ploughshares folks in the U.S., who've just been sentenced to three years in federal prison. His friend's been married just a year. One of the possible futures I see for either of us is prison. I heard this man's story with tears standing in my eyes. No more separations, please the Goddess. And no prison. ◼ *All love*

◼ ◼ ◼

This conversation about prison might seem a bit melodramatic. Certainly, white activists in the United States have not suffered the kind of wholesale repression Somoza visited on his people. Even the Ploughshares people invited their own imprisonment, by beating on nuclear nosecones. It's not surprising they were arrested. After all, damaging nuclear warheads is decidedly illegal in this country.

It can be tempting to romanticize civil disobedience and *voluntary* imprisonment, which have a long and honorable history as tactics of nonviolent movements. I suspect these methods have the greatest power when those who employ them are the most at risk, as were poor Black anti-segregation demonstrators in the South of the 1960's. For these people, going to jail meant placing themselves at the mercy of a system in which they had no stake and no power. It meant hunger; it meant beatings; it meant the possibility of death.

The tactics of the Civil Rights movement have been adopted by the largely white and middle-class anti-nuclear and peace movements. The music, too, has been borrowed from liberation movements. "We don't care if we go to jail," the South African song goes, "It is for freedom that we gladly go." But "going to jail" there is not the same thing as here where all the steps of the dance have been orchestrated in negotiations between police and demonstrators, or when "jail" is a circus tent hastily erected to house hundreds of demonstrators for a week or two.

I wonder whether too many such "jail" experiences might not have a distorting effect on a movement. First, they reinforce the lessons of a middle-class upbringing which teach that the system is essentially friendly, if misguided on one or two points. Second, they leave a movement unprepared, should a friendly and apparently tractable law enforcement and legal system suddenly turn nasty.

Since my return from Nicaragua, events have taken at least one such nasty turn. The Immigration and Naturalization Service decided to prosecute several people working with the Sanctuary movement in Tucson, Arizona. Some of their co-workers who refused to testify against them were held under house arrest, as far away as Seattle, Washington.

The government did a poor job of presenting its case and it seemed likely, in spite of an extremely hostile judge, that the Tucson defendants would be acquitted. Those who followed the case were shocked when the jury returned with "guilty" verdicts. The INS has recently announced its intention to open Sanctuary investigations in the San Francisco Bay Area as well.

When I wrote to Jan about the possibility that one of us might spend time in jail, I didn't mean that I thought either of us was likely to go out and attack a nosecone. I meant that in the course of ordinary, even completely legal, political work, it is possible to provoke a nasty government response. Thinking very much about that possibility can be immobilizing (or give you an overblown idea of your own importance), but never thinking about it at all can make you unnecessarily careless.

◼ ◼ ◼

Thursday, August 9
Dear heart,

How I ached for you yesterday. Is it insulting that the times I miss you most are the hard times? Yesterday there was a big part of me that wished I'd never left San Francisco and the comfort of our life there. The emotional comfort, I mean. A little diarrhea and sleeping on a floor I can live with. But I miss the comfort of a life unbroken by events like the meaningless slaying of a child or *compañero*.

We left Matagalpa in a Frente jeep yesterday. By 10:30 a.m. we were sitting in the Frente house in La Dalia, a little town southeast of Matagalpa. We spent a couple of hours talking with Luís Vilchez, the *responsable*, and a member of the zonal committee. He arranged transportation for us in a little pickup to the homes of some of the people who were killed here a couple of weeks ago.

The first place we stopped was a state-run farm. It's big—over 900 acres. Before the Triumph, the land belonged to the president of Somoza's Senate. The folks live in a barn divided into little private areas. There we met Corina Ruiz and Andrea Picado, the wife and sister of Brígido Picado, who was bayonetted to death on the 26th of July. I'll write more about their story in a group letter. For Corina, this violence had nothing to do with the voter registration due to begin the day after her husband died. They cut the tongue out of this man's mouth, they castrated him, they cut his throat, and for what? They didn't even get across their message.

Corina and Andrea came with us in the cab of the pickup truck and we went on to Taspale, a little crossroads of a town. Taspale consists in part of the buildings of an old *finca*, La Hacienda. One of these has been converted into a little store run by Pedro Lopez Castro, father of German Lopez Zamorra who was also killed. Pedro searched from Thursday until Saturday when he found his son's body under a coffee tree, hacked into so many pieces he had to bury it right there. Pedro had no idea why they'd killed his son. Nothing like this had ever happened before in this quiet valley.

We went back up the road towards La Dalia about a quarter-mile to the little dispensary. María Dormos and her children live in a shack behind the dispensary. Her son Miguel, 18, was kidnapped, leaving her with no way to support herself and the seven other children. And now I have to tell you about one of the most shameful things I've ever done. Even as I think about writing it down, my face and back are burning with shame.

There were five or six of us there, besides María and her children: Luís and a couple of *compas*; Iliria Guttierez, the nurse; Joaquín and myself. Luís pulled me aside and said, "Look, *compañera*, you know Miguel was her only support. She has nothing now. Do you think you and your friend could help her a little?" I spoke to Joaquín in English, explaining what Luís had asked. He shrugged. "Go on and give her something, if you want to."

Oh, God, Jan. I didn't know what to do. Luís was staring at me; Joaquín wasn't going to help me (and considering how things turned out, he was probably right). I couldn't see any way to get my wallet out of my pocket without everyone watching. My Spanish wasn't good enough to manage using a ruse to get María by herself behind the little building. So, in front of everyone, I walked up to her and gave her 300 *cordobas*, saying something like, "I know that you are alone now. This isn't much, but maybe it will help."

Everyone but María looked disgusted. She smiled and tucked the money inside her dress. Later Joaquín asked, "Didn't anyone ever teach you how to palm money?" and showed me how to fold the bills up and pass them palm-to-palm in a handshake. But he was too late; I'd already stomped all over a delicate moment, and nothing could rectify it.

At the dispensary we also talked with Iliria Guttierez. Her husband was kidnapped the same day as Miguel, but her situation is a little different. She has only four children, the oldest already 14. Her sister works in the hospital in Matagalpa and wants her to come live and work with her. Iliria would like to go, "But the people here won't let me go. There's no one else here who could do my job, and I can't leave them."

Much later. This is our second night sleeping on the floor in the outer part of the Frente's dormitory. I'm writing this with a fading flashlight in one hand. Today by way of contrast, we visited the Cooperative Daniel Teller Paz, named for a young man who fell fighting the contra. There's a Swiss brigade building 40 little three-room houses. They have corn, beans, bananas, coffee, cattle and a vegetable garden. They're organized for defense, and a popular teacher newly arrived from Managua teaches reading to children and adults. She's also organizing a music and theater group.

Poor Joaquín! I seem to be determined to embarrass him wherever I go. Some of the women and children were showing us around the garden. In an effort at conversation, I asked them, I thought, whether they had any problems with rabbits. They stared at me, obviously trying to suppress giggles. I watched the red rise up Joaquín's face. Instead of saying *"conejos"* ("rabbits") I'd said *"cojones"* (slang for "balls")! Oh well. We get along. ◘ *Love*

Friday, August 10
Dear friends,

This letter comes to you from a little cubicle in the Hotel Don Diego in Matagalpa. Joaquín, my traveling companion, and I returned to the city of Matagalpa this morning after two days in the *campo*, where we visited the families of people who were killed or kidnapped at the end of July.

We slept two nights at La Dalia, a little crossroads on the way east to Waslala. From there the local FSLN folks took us out farther into the country.

Wednesday we went to Taspale where, two weeks before, a group of FDN (National Democratic Front, operating from Honduras) contra had taken over the town, terrorizing the population, kidnapping two men and leaving behind the mutilated bodies of eight others. The contra killed the men silently, one at a time, cutting their throats with bayonets, so no gunfire would alert people to what was going on. But first they castrated them. They cut the tongue out of one's mouth, the eyes from the face of another. They used a knife to scrape away all the skin on the face of Adán Flores, a 70-year-old *campesino*. No one knows whether he was alive or dead when they did this. We spoke to the families of these people. We heard them describe discovering bodies, one by one, of the missing. One man had been hacked to pieces. His father had to bury him in the coffee field where he was found.

Midday in this day of terror, the contra herded everyone they could find into a little meeting hall. "Everyone" consisted mostly of women and children, as the men were all out working in the coffee. The contra delivered a lecture on their efforts to combat communism. They warned the people of Taspale not to participate in the four days of voter registration scheduled to begin the following day. It was only later that the people discovered the bodies of the men murdered in this "crusade against communism." In spite of threats, so many people appeared to register that the elections board ran out of materials. A supplemental date will have to be set.

We spoke to Corina Ruiz and Andrea Picado, the wife and sister of Brígido Picado, whose body was found in the road. They live in a converted barn on a state-run coffee farm. Corina is tiny. She held her month-old baby in her arms and stared into the distance, telling her story in a dull monotone: how they found her husband in the road, how he'd been castrated and his throat cut. Did she think this had anything to do with voter registration? She didn't know. Were they organized for defense on the farm? No. Did she think that now they would begin to organize? No.

Her pain was untouchable. This eruption of violence into her life made no sense to her, and it didn't seem even to occur to her to try to understand it. She was bewildered, as if a hurricane or flood had carried off her husband. One more sorrow in a life full of sorrows, over which she had no control.

Andrea, her sister-in-law, was more animated. She told me that the contra had come to her house looking for her other brother, who is an officer in the militia. "I told them I have no brothers," she said. "The Frente never treated us like this," she went on, "People call the contra beasts, *Somocistas*, and that's really what they are. Dogs!"

Later we stood in the presence of María Dormos, whose 18-year-old son was kidnapped. "Go say goodbye to your mother," they told young Miguel. "We're going now." She has seven other children, all very much younger. Miguel had supported the entire family. María stands in the grey drizzle, her dress held together with safety pins and coarse white thread, her face a mask of defeat. No tears, just a terrible resignation. What could I say to this woman whose son has disappeared? That I'm very sorry? That I've come here to stand at the side of the Nicaraguan people in their suffering? That I hope Reagan will be defeated in November? Absurd. I'm going home in a few months. And Miguel is gone, gone, gone. And I'm standing there in the rain, my North American arrogance pooling at my feet.

Understand, all this killing, this mutilation, happened in the middle of lush green mountains, volcanic ridges and mesas rich with corn, coffee, bananas. This land is so rich, the green hills luminescent in the sun. People could live well here, if they weren't being murdered in the service of the rich people of our country. If they didn't have to fight a war.

The next day, we saw a little of how things might be in Nicaragua, a possible future. We visited a cooperative at Yale, way out in the hills. Once the property of three rich men, the 3200 acres of Co-op Daniel Teller Paz are now shared by 36 families. Two of the previous owners sold their land to the government. The third was the subject of expropriation; the land was lying fallow and unused. The expropriated owner was compensated for his loss.

There are still big landowners in Matagalpa. Luís Vilchez of the FSLN in La Dalia explained the problem of what he called decapitalization: as a conscious counter-revolutionary strategy, big landowners allow their land to deteriorate. They don't plant, they don't tend the land, in order to diminish its value and contribute to food shortages. Rather than invest their capital in Nicaragua, they send it to the U.S., for example to Miami banks, where they can obtain numbered accounts, like those in Swiss banks. Many times, Luís said, they will farm a little on the perimeters of their land, to give the illusion it's being worked.

At Co-op Daniel Teller Paz they're growing corn, coffee, cacao, bananas. A herd of 20 dairy cattle provides milk for the children. A Swiss brigade of men and one woman is helping to build 40 houses. The government has sent them a teacher and a health care worker.

This is the Nicaragua we're supposed to believe threatens us. This is the Nicaragua which the U.S. embassy here recently informed a Witness For Peace delegation is "finished." They imply that it is only a matter of time before the U.S. pulls the plug on Nicaragua Libre. The folks at Co-op Daniel Teller Paz don't believe they are finished. They're just barely beginning. The absurdity is that it is in our hands. Goddess give us a little courage and a little wisdom.

Saturday, August 11
After we got back from La Dalia, we spent an afternoon with the Mothers of Heroes and Martyrs, in Matagalpa.

Juana Centeno is the local *responsable*. She sat beneath a portrait of her son Roberto, who was killed in an ambush last year, and talked to us about the Revolution and her faith.

"Our children couldn't live to finish the struggle," she says, "so now we have to take up their work. You have to understand: before the Triumph of the FSLN, Nicaragua was Somoza's private *hacienda* and we were his slaves. We were terrified of the National Guard, but today we laugh together in the streets with the *Commandantes* of the Revolution. We are poor women, but we have our dignity."

To people in the U.S., Juana had a special message: "Now is the time in history to make a choice. Will you remain on the side of the rich, who kill as the whim takes them, who cut people into pieces? Or will you place yourself on the side of the poor?"

The next day we accompanied some of these women to visit a military hospital in Jinotega. We talked with wounded soldiers there and helped distribute the cigarettes and candy collected for them by school children in Matagalpa. One kid was 15; he'd lied about his age to join the service two years before. He was almost well now, and aching to rejoin his *compañeros*.

The Mothers received some recruiting posters as gifts. One woman handed hers quietly to me. "Here," she said. "You take it. Even today I couldn't bear to have it in my house. My daughter died five years ago in the liberation of León. She was twenty, studying medicine." My mind was flooded with images given me by a woman I'd met at the Plaza in Managua during the July 19th celebration. In León, she told, there were rivers of blood in the streets.

Be well, folks. I think of you often. ◼ *Much love*

Saturday, August 11
Dear one,

Back in Matagalpa. This afternoon we interviewed the Mothers of Heroes and Martyrs. In a demonstration last Saturday, a gang of Arturo Cruz's supporters threw garbage and rocks at women who'd come from all over the department (state) of Matagalpa to witness silently against Cruz's pro-contra stance. These women, many of them poor *campesinas*, had brought with them photographs of their dead sons and daughters. These irreplaceable pictures, Cruz's thugs tore out of the women's hands and pulled to pieces in front of them.

On the face of it, this seems like a pretty stupid move on Cruz's part, since no one is more respected in Nicaragua than the Mothers of Heroes and Martyrs. *Barricada* (The Frente daily) interprets it to mean that the right wing is trying to create the impression that an atmosphere of anarchy surrounds the elections. Since the same kind of thing happened the next day in Chinandega, it does seem to be part of a general plan. Seems to me like a plan destined to backfire, but the Right has never been noted for its subtlety in Nicaragua.

We visited with five of the Mothers yesterday. What fine women! One, when telling us her name, stopped to correct a friend who'd interrupted to add the first woman's ex-husband's name. "No," said Herminda Díaz, "I'm not Herminda Días 'de' anything. I'm single now. Or better—I'm married to the Revolution!" There was laughter all around the room and a general nodding of heads in agreement.

I'm still trying to assimilate my sense of my own inadequacy over the last few days. I really found myself unequal to the task of responding to the wife of someone killed and mutilated the way Brígido Picado was. What hubris to think I *could* respond, beyond telling the story to other North Americans. I wanted Corina's pain to go away—because I couldn't stand it. *I*, who am going back to San Francisco in a few months, I who don't have to live in a converted barn, waiting for the next attack. Being in Managua so long, I'd forgotten what fear felt like. It's important that I remember it. I wanted Corina to be a brave revolutionary and she wasn't. She was a terrified little woman with a month-old baby and a bad cough. ◼ *All love*

◼   ◼   ◼

Bocay

Sunday, August 12

Dear heart,

This comes to you from a truly tiny cubicle in a row of cubicles in the only *hospedaje* (guest house) in Bocay. It's a seven-hour trip from Jinotega to Bocay in the canvas-covered back of a Chevy pickup, carrying people, dogs, chickens, and *quintales* (hundred pound sacks) of corn and rice. Several times the 30-or-so of us had to get down from the truck and walk up or down a particularly muddy stretch. Several times the truck lost all traction and we slid sideways down a slope, with mud up over the hubcaps.

But, oh, it's been well worth the trip already. We got into town—about 50 houses spread along a bend in the Bocay river—at about 2:30 p.m. After finding the Pensión Jaquelina, we took a little walk down to the center of this settlement, a bare flat place flanked by the new health care center, a school, a bank, a coffee warehouse. These buildings are of brick, but the rest of the town is thrown together out of rough-hewn wood. Bocay turns out to be an R&R place for the *compas* fighting in the mountains near by. We've been befriended by a battalion from Somotillo, where Joaquín spent two weeks back in April.

Apparently, we're the first North Americans to appear in Bocay, and people have guessed we're everything from Swiss to Cuban. Folks have gone out of their way to point out to us our "valor" in undertaking this journey, because Bocay is a pretty dangerous place. It's been attacked several times, and most folks live here in the first place because they've been forced down out of the mountains by the contra.

The first *compa* we met was Fátima, the only woman in her battalion. She's been in the *lucha* since she was thirteen, when she served as a *correo*, a clandestine messenger for the FSLN. Now she's a full member, a *militante*. Four of her brothers have died in this struggle: three murdered by the National Guard before the Triumph and one killed in combat just two months ago. Still, she carries a spirit of hope. ◼ *Abrazos*

Sunday, August 13
Dear Jan,

A little more light this morning. There's no electricity in Bocay, so folks go to bed pretty early. Joaquín and I sat up last night talking with Carlos, Political Secretary of the battalion from Somotillo. All the *compas* we talked to yesterday seemed to have clear political views, and Carlos was interested in the progress of *our* political development. How had it been possible for us personally to break though the lies and conditioning of our socialization in the U.S.? Carlos has a mild Asian face, wire-rimmed glasses, and a sparse, almost blond, Fu Manchu beard and mustache. He introduced us to his mascot: a little squirrel who lives inside his shirt, named Napoleon.

Imagine the three of us in a little room, two-thirds of it occupied by a single cot. A bottle of kerosene with a rag wick gives us a little light. Here we sit, planning how someday we'll make a revolution in the U.S., too. Napoleon nibbles on a big kernel of corn. Revolution almost seems possible.

Joaquín told the story of his time in Guatemala, how every single person he knew there is dead now, the towns where he worked obliterated by the Guatemalan army. We talked about how to motivate people in the U.S. to care about aggression here in Central America. Carlos agreed with us that a full-scale invasion with U.S. troops is the Pentagon's last resort, which means we'll have a harder struggle than we did even against the Vietnam War. If U.S. citizens aren't coming home in boxes, it's hard to make other U.S. citizens notice a war. All the time we were talking, the rain fell on the tin roof and water flowed by the building into the river 50 feet below us. It rains ten months out of the year in Bocay, and nothing ever dries here.

A *campesino* family—two women, a man and a twelve-year-old girl arrived at 4:30 this morning. They'd walked all night to do their shopping here and will return home this afternoon or tomorrow. One woman said there's a lot of sickness in the mountains, but that people do come to the health center here for care.

We have an appointment this morning at the Frente office—a back room in the bank building. Doesn't look as if we'll need the letter we brought from the Frente in Matagalpa; our mere presence here seems to be recommendation enough.

Before the Triumph, there really was no Bocay, just an aggregation of seven or eight houses at a bend in the river. Travel to and from Jinotega was strictly a mule-back affair. In the last five years, the government has brought in a road, education and health and care. The bank offers low interest loans, so small farmers don't have to mortgage their crops to big landowners in order to plant, as they had to do in the past.

As violence increases in the mountains more people move into town. We ate lunch yesterday at a *comedor* run by a woman whose *finca* was burned last year by the contra. She and her family didn't want to leave, but they had to, in part because they'd been involved in community organizing and so were marked by the contra. She says, "There we had our animals, our crops. Here we are able to make a living, but it is not the life we had before." She went on to describe how beautiful the view had been from her house. "We were happy there—write this down; I want people to know how much we loved our home." Imagine living somewhere so beautiful all your life, knowing it was beautiful at the time, not only in retrospect. When they first came to Bocay, the government helped them build the house, and gave them food to eat until the *comedor* got started.

A cardboard sign on the bank building reads, (sic) *"Campecino, ci tu problema es falta de tierra, precéntete a la oficino de Reforma Agraria."* (*"Campesino*, if your problem is lack of land, go to the Agrarian Reform office,") terrible spelling, in painstaking print. These people are supposed to be our enemies? On the road to Bocay, we passed a huge barn. Someone who had clearly only recently learned to write had scrawled across the wall, again with the most creative spelling, "We won. We are free. We will never return to being slaves!"   ◼ *All love*

Tuesday, August 14
Dear Jan,

We'd hoped to get out yesterday to one of the fourteen cooperatives in the Bocay area to talk to folks there. At first it looked as though something could be arranged, but later Ernesto of the FSLN told us that it was too dangerous because of the fighting going on not too far from here. We certainly didn't want to put anyone else at risk, and because there are no vehicles in Bocay, it would have been a matter of someone's accompanying us on foot, so we didn't press.

It did happen that about 40 members of another co-op were in town to sign papers at the bank for a loan. We had a meeting with them on the porch of the little school. They told us about how they formed the co-op and the damages they've suffered in the war.

The most interesting part of that meeting was an exchange between the president of the co-op and the representative from UNAG, the union of small farmers and cattle raisers. The co-op president was frustrated at not being able to get any sugar. The man from UNAG assured him that he could get sugar the next morning—500 pounds or more—but that they needed a census of the co-op to know how much to apportion them in the future. Then he went on to explain how the war had prevented their getting sugar, citing transportation problems, etc. But what was interesting was his attitude. After all, he's a *campesino*, too, not a big shot. He said, "I'm not here to hassle you. If you tell us you have a problem, you need something, I'm here to listen and believe you and help solve the problem." Which was true, of course. But he was the best union rep I've ever met. As far as I could tell, his position had given him no sense of superiority over the people he serves.

Bocay is a pretty scary place, even for its own residents. The whole town is uneasy. Many people are newly arrived, having fled the contra, so folks don't know each other very well. You never quite know to whom you're talking, or where her or his loyalties lie. Many people are confused by enormous changes they've seen. Some are undoubtedly contra sympathizers. And some are outright collaborators.

It's true that many *campesinos* are fighting with the contra. They're kidnapped, tricked, lied, bribed and drugged into combat, where they are first to die. The contra commanders make no effort to rescue their wounded who are saved many times by the Sandinista army. Often the contra will kidnap an entire village, taking everyone to Honduras where the women and children become "refugees" and the men are forced to fight.

There are a number of posters up here, encouraging people to take advantage of the amnesty program for rank-and-file contra. One features a full-face photo of a *campesino*. The caption underneath reads, "I turned myself in, and I'm alive!" Another is a comic strip in several panels, showing a poor *campesino* wandering the hills in blue rags, the remnants of his contra uniform. He realizes that he was tricked; he's not getting rich and he misses his farm and his family. The last panel shows him home safe, having taken advantage of the amnesty.

Yesterday two FSLN members and some of the *compas* held an election rally. They'd received a lot of paper flags and posters which they stapled up all over town. It doesn't seem to be the custom here to ask someone if she wants a flag stapled to her wall. And these folks are terrorized enough that I don't think they'd dare object if they did mind. (I want to be clear here. I'm not saying that the FSLN have done anything but good in Bocay. Only that the people here are too buffeted by the war to feel safe around any authorities. I've seen other political parties be just as aggressive about spreading their propaganda. Not only the Frente is electioneering.)

After the postering there was an *acto*, a little procession up and down the muddy street, in the rain, attended by about thirty *compas* and twenty townspeople. Bocay still isn't organized for self-defense. The people aren't armed; there are no branches of the CDS or other mass organizations here. That work is just beginning. To their credit, the Sandinistas started five years ago with the provision of services and only now are looking for support. I hope the people here will recognize the FSLN by its fruits.

One problem the Frente has in a place like Bocay is that their organizers often come from outside. You plop a nice kid from Managua down in a mudhole like this and he's going to have troubles. It takes time to win people's confidence.

On the theological front (excuse the military metaphor; they seem to creep in these days), some good news. It's been so hard for me to know what to say or do when confronted with the grief of the people we're interviewing. Partly because of the language barrier but mostly because of my own self-involvement, I feel overcome with self-consciousness and have no idea how to behave. In the last few days, I've been able to give some of that to the Goddess.

How to say this without sounding sappy. . .if I can let Her move through me a little bit, I find I don't have to be so self-conscious. The point isn't what this grieving woman before me thinks of *me*, but whether I can hear her grief in a way that touches her. I know the Goddess can do that, so what I'm trying to do is let Her do it through me. Never thought I'd want something like that before, but it's such a relief.

Well, it looks as though we may spend a few more days in Bocay. We're about 140 kilometers from Jinotega—a long way. The pickup that brought us hasn't returned to town and there's no other vehicle around. We're hoping maybe to catch a ride on an IFA—a big army truck—but at the moment we seem to be stuck. It's a four to five day walk to

Jinotega, a bit grueling, even apart from the danger from the contra.

Speaking of which, that's another reason I'd sort of like to get out of here. The owner of this *hospedaje* is a not-very-bright young man who is *pura* contra. He's spent quite a bit of time whispering to us about how much better things were under Somoza. He stood this morning in the doorway of my little dirt-floored room, looking at the stuff laid out on my bed. "Very nice," he said, fingering my extra pants. "We used to get things like this, before." He's angry that he can no longer get clothes and other goodies from the U.S. because, he says, the Nicaraguan government refuses to trade with the U.S. I suggested it might be the other way around, but he says that's all lies. "The Soviet Union," he went on, "is far away from Nicaragua. The United States is very close to Nicaragua. Nicaragua belongs to the United States." He is probably the richest man in Bocay. He owns the town's only electric generator, although he's been out of diesel fuel for a few weeks now.

This guy is mostly just dumb, but he has a friend who's vicious. All last night I could hear him in another cubicle, hassling the woman he's with, trying to force her to have sex with him. Both of these men tend to drink too much rum, and I don't trust either of them. We've told them we're here just to listen to what people have to say, but the landlord keeps asking us to explain again what our "mission" really is. Frankly, I'll be damned glad when we get back to Jinotega.

Other folks are very much pro-Process, and we've heard some important stories from them. The place is full of soldiers, which makes me pretty sure that nothing will happen to us *here*. But on the road? I'm not so sure. *Así es la cosa* (that's how it is). ◼ *All deep things*

Thursday, August 16
Dear Janny,

Well, we're safe back in Matagalpa. Got in yesterday afternoon after about nine hours of travel. We'd expected to leave at about 6:00 a.m., but at 3:30 a.m. one of the four trucks that rolled into town the night before began blowing its horn. I leaped up and ran out to ask the driver to wait. (I had visions of spending another three days in Bocay with Vicious and his friend planning Goddess knows what for us, and I didn't want to miss our ticket out!) No problem getting on the truck. The proprietor of the *hospedaje* stuck his head out the window to let us know there would be a truck leaving at 6:00 a.m., too. That was all I needed to confirm our decision to risk the dark over getting a couple hours more sleep. Whatever truck he wanted us to take was not the one I wanted.

On the way out of town, we stopped at a comedor where Joaquín and I had eaten several times and gotten to know the family a little. They're the ones who were burned out of their farm by the contra. We sat in the dark kitchen drinking sweet, hot coffee. (Imagine a room, a third of it occupied by a fireplace for cooking and a clay oven. The walls are rough wood; the floor, dirt. The fire provides the only light.)

This was the morning Fátima, their 15-year-old daughter, was leaving for six years of study in Cuba. We overheard her whispering to her sister, "I'm saying goodbye to my Nicaragua, but I'll come back to serve my community." Six years is a long time. Fátima climbed into the back of the canvas-covered pickup, sitting at the very edge of the bench, one leg swung over the tailgate. As we bounced along, she stared back into the lightening mist.

Dear heart, today my skin remembers you. I know now how ready I am going to be to come home. ◪ *All love*

◪ ◪ ◪

Managua

Saturday, September 1

Dear heart,

It was good to talk to you last night. Sometimes everything here seems so unreal; other times it's the U.S. I can't quite believe exists. It's funny, though; I don't think I'm going to have terrible culture shock on re-entering the country. San Francisco, 22nd Street, the curve at the top of Golden Gate Park—it all seems more familiar to me than Managua, maybe because I've moved around so much in the last few months.

Talking to you eases the sensation of unreality. We WFP people are such babes in the woods here. What do you think about the following?

No doubt you've heard about the *Sojourners* magazine interview with David McMichael, the CIA agent whose contract wasn't renewed because he refused to supply false evidence of Nicaraguan arms shipments to El Salvador. Turns out that he has been working in the Washington WFP office for the last three months. The woman who runs that office says that he's going through a crisis of faith. She's especially impressed by his willingness to perform menial tasks like collating and stapling. (As someone who makes her living performing such tasks, I'm not so impressed.) She also says he remains deeply committed to the need for intelligence gathering; he just objects to being asked to alter facts in order to substantiate a particular White House line.

Well, he's in Nicaragua now, visiting. He was over the other night, gathering information for a speaking tour back in the U.S. He says he wants to beat Reagan at the polls and get the U.S. out of Nicaragua like he's never wanted anything in his life. Naturally, he wanted to know from us long-termers where we'd been in Nicaragua and what we'd seen. He was especially interested in contra violence, but also in the psychological effects of that violence, particularly in hearing about demoralization, resistance to government policies, etc. He also told us that in order for WFP to retain credibility, we have to be willing to criticize the FSLN, and was interested in hearing about any abuses by the Frente we might happen to come across. We were asked to say a little about where each of us had been and what we'd been doing. I just said that I'd been in Matagalpa and Jinotega, nothing more.

McMichael also talked a little about what kind of infiltration WFP might expect. He said that since we do everything publicly, without secrets, that we're vulnerable only in two ways: (1) creation of dissent and disagreement within the organization and (2) attempts at public embarrassment, e.g., through revelation of the sexual peculiarities of WFP members. This last he said while looking right at me, but that could have been entirely accidental. On the other hand, he *is* a CIA agent; he has seen all our files; he obviously kept track of our names as we were introduced, so it may have been intentional.

I suppose he's another Daniel Ellsberg, but I don't entirely trust him. Of all the places he might end up, he can probably do the least harm in WFP. He did say one thing with which I agree, however: WFP has to be very careful to do the best we can to protect our informants while retaining our credibility.

This subject came up a few days ago at our August retreat. Arnold and other members of the WFP had met with the new U.S. Ambassador to Nicaragua, the first time since his arrival that he's agreed to meet personally with anyone from WFP. They said he was smooth and ordinary, that he pretended he needed to be informed about WFP and our work here, as if he'd never heard of us. He also mentioned that he'd be *very* interested in receiving copies of all our reports. It was during our discussion of whether or not to comply with this request that I began to see just how useful we can be to the embassy and all the information gatherers who work there.

Of course, anything we publish will get into the government's hands eventually, so we might as well pass it along directly, I suppose. But what fools we've been! For months we've been marching our short-term delegations into the embassy to tell the stories of the outrages they've seen. And for months, we've been passing along information with military significance, e.g., how the war has affected the kind of equipment and supplies available at a particular hospital, or how determined (or discouraged) the people in a particular community may be feeling. We've thought we had the right to meddle in something—the machinations of intelligence gathering—that's so far outside our knowledge!

Worse, we're in a position to put a lot of Nicaraguans at serious personal risk. Some people wouldn't talk at all to Joaquín and me in Bocay, or would only talk if we didn't use their names. These folks are not paranoid. Their friends and *compañeros* have been selectively murdered. And we could easily get them killed, if we're not careful. Not that they aren't already in danger. I don't want to exaggerate our possible importance. Besides, I haven't the vaguest idea how to be "careful." As you know, deception is not my strong suit, and intelligence agents are undoubtedly more "intelligent" about this sort of thing than I am.

I brought some of this up in the discussion about sharing information with the embassy. We've agreed to use fictitious names in our reports when necessary, but to maintain a file with the real names available, in case an international legal body or human rights organization should want to use them.

So part of me is sort of shocked that it took this long to realize how easily we can be used. And part of me wonders now whether the reporting we do might not cause more harm than good. It's not as though we reach that many people—although apparently a lot of our stuff gets to Congress. Who knows? I just know that I'm not very well trained for living and working somewhere so filled with danger. And Nicaragua is so much better a place to live in that way than El Salvador or Guatemala. Someone like me would be dead in a few months there. We talk about repression in the U.S., and it does exist. But it's not on the scale of the fear that people live with in Central America. I've only seen the tiniest bit of that kind of danger—but enough to know why our friend from Brazil has such a hard time taking U.S. political activists seriously. It's a whole different kind of nightmare in Latin America. ◼ *All love*

◼ ◼ ◼

Jalapa and Limay

Wednesday, September 5

Dear Jan,

This missive comes to you in the absurdly tiny print of the typewriter that lives in the WFP house in Jalapa. I'm up here with Gray to get things ready for the next delegation which arrives this Sunday. As I told you on the phone, my mother's coming with them!

This has been a sort of frustrating morning. Gray is off at La Estancia, one of the *asentamientos*, trying to arrange for us to spend a night there. This involves transportation arrangements that would make you cringe. The way we get out there is to work that morning with IRENA, the reforestation agency, and be dropped off at La Estancia at noon. Getting back to Jalapa will be a bit more of a challenge. We have to hire a truck—not easy in itself—to pick us up; further complicating matters is the fact that the bridge entering La Estancia has a huge hole in it. It's another quarter mile up a steep hill into the *asentamiento*. I'm hoping the IRENA truck will be willing to negotiate this bridge because, otherwise, a morning of tree-planting followed by a stiff, if abbreviated, hike will be enough to do in the less fit members of this delegation.

Oh yes—frustration. Well, first off, both of our contacts at the Casa del Gobierno (the equivalent of Town Hall) are off at a *seminario* (workshop) in Ocotal, which won't be over until Friday. Since they both have wives and children in that area, they probably won't be back in Jalapa until Monday. From the Casa del Gobierno, I went to the FSLN office, to enlist the Political Secretary to speak to the group about the history and ideology of the Frente. (This is something we've never done with a group before, and I'm curious to hear what they'll say.) Damned if one of the FSLN members—one of the few men in Jalapa who seems to be able to tell Peggy and me apart—doesn't make a pass at me! It's been so long since any man has made a pass at me that I was quite surprised. Obviously I'm not visible as a lesbian in Nicaragua. Well, I got out of it with a laugh and a reference to the fact that I'm here to work and nothing more. He gave me a pretty good handshake and a smile, so I hope he emerged with ego intact, as I wouldn't want to occasion an Incident. ("Bad enough she's a lesbian, but now this?!")

Later, Gray and I went around to firm up a few more interviews. There really isn't all that much to do in Jalapa, especially as we won't have transportation. There are several places we can walk to but several people on this delegation won't be up to really strenuous exercise.

Don't tell our cat, but I've been being unfaithful. The object of my attentions is Maude, the little cat who lives here. She's constantly having kittens (four tiny ones at the moment). The last time I was here she was too shy to be touched, but Gray, who's a little shy himself, has been feeding her, and today she sat uninvited in my lap. She a tough little grey tiger—very common, but very pretty.

I'm curious to know whether the papers are making anything at all of the fact that the pilots of the helicopter shot down at Santa Clara were *gringos*. Naturally, it's a big deal here, although I don't think anyone is terribly surprised. Peter and Sharon, who were in Santa Clara the day of the attack and assisted in collecting the parts of the body of one little girl, had a meeting with the UPI people the following day. I don't know what came of it, but I have a feeling that WFP is becoming enough of a bother that the U.S. government would just as soon we didn't exist. I think we may be beginning to have some effect, in our own bumbling way.

That's on the positive side. On the negative side, I'm a little discouraged about the effects of the war in Nicaragua. I guess the worst is the draft. On our way back into Matagalpa from Jinotega, our bus was stopped by the police. They were checking all public transportation that day, looking for young men who hadn't registered for the draft. One guy who was sitting behind me didn't have his ID with him, so the police made him get off the bus. He swore up and down that he was registered and had his papers at his house. The police were very polite, almost apologetic, but firm. The young man was disgusted and angry and, I kind of suspect, not registered. I'm not sure how much liberty you end up with when its defense has to be coerced.

Food shortages, too, are depressing. There's been mismanagement, and even some corruption, although most of the shortages and poor distribution are attributable to the war.

I guess what frightens me is the possibility that as things get harder here (and it looks as if they will) the Junta will clutch—lose their trust in the people—and betray the people's trust in them. So far, that seems very far from happening, but every day it's clear to me just how true was what you and I said to each other before I left about the difficulty of maintaining an open society in the midst of war. The papers are full of phrases like, "Peace, yes, but peace with honor," which of course reminds me of Nixon's Vietnam-era pronouncements. Naturally, the circumstances are very different today in Nicaragua. Another common expression is, "Peace, yes, but not the peace of the grave." Funny, though, how Richard Nixon and FSLN—who represent two opposing ideologies—can arrive at an identical rhetoric of peace and honor. I do believe that these two poles represent completely different understandings of the world. I'd certainly vote for the FSLN if I were Nicaraguan. Hell, I'd probably *belong* to the FSLN. But in my heart I guess I'm still an anarchist, and a feminist, and therefore given to a bit of skepticism about any government.

I am certain that the FSLN is struggling to maintain liberty. They've all but ended the State of Emergency, although strikes are still prohibited. In my time here I've seen people participating in the basic public decisions affecting their lives in a way I've certainly never done myself at home.

Another depressing item: a story two days ago in *Nuevo Diario* about Israel's role in Central America. The headline and the whole first paragraph referred to *Jewish* arms and *Jewish* involvement. It wasn't until the second paragraph that I was sure I was reading a story about Israel. I think when I get back to Managua, I'll try my hand at a letter to the editor pointing out the distinction between Jews and Israelis. Although, as our Lebanese friend Tina points out, if Israelis insist on calling theirs a Jewish state and proceed to murder people in the name of that state, it won't be surprising if a new kind of anti-semitism takes hold, in Latin America as well as in the Arab world. It's painful to find that conflating of Israel and Jews here in Nicaragua, too. But the amazing thing about this place is that I can probably walk into the offices of *Nuevo Diario*, have a conversation with the man who wrote the article, and effect a change in policy. The whole feel of the thing was that it had been written by someone who was ignorant, not malicious.

No one in WFP takes the kind of interest I do in questions like these, although people are polite about being willing to discuss them. It's true that these folks do not have the automatic reaction of examining themselves for evidence of one sort of prejudice or another, which is actually rather endearing in many of us nice white feminists.

I'm currently making myself miserable by reading a little book of primary documents concerning the different behaviors of various Christian churches in Germany during the Third Reich. Fascinating, actually, in a horrifying way. My time here had convinced (or re-convinced) me of the possibility of deeply revolutionary action arising out of religious faith. But it's important to remember religion's long history of faithlessness and duplicity as well.

Well, what a cheerless letter this has been. I hope you understand that what's happening to me is that I'm learning to love this revolution enough to risk criticizing it.

◘ *All deep love*

Tuesday, September 11
Dear heart,

I find myself once again alone in the WFP Jalapa house. The reason I'm here alone is that this morning, when the delegation that includes my mother was to go to La Estancia, I found myself too ill to accompany them. So I've spent the day sleeping a little and reading a strange novel about an anthropologist in Burma, and then something else called the Santa Fe Document—a 1980 conservative think-tank document on Latin America. This charming item was prepared to guide Ronald Reagan, should he accede to the presidency, in his treatment of Central and South America. The rest, as they say, is history.

The Florida delegation seems to be a little different from some of the other WFP groups, in that it contains a number of radical pacifist anarchists. Several of these folks are deeply suspicious of government in general, and so disposed to be suspicious of the Nicaraguan government in particular.

Now I happen to think that a healthy suspicion of government is probably a good thing. Unfortunately, these folks are also deeply connected by class and color to the dominant culture of the United States. This means that however much they may oppose U.S. government policies, they still think that the experience of the white middle class in the U.S. (their experience) is the norm. So it's very hard for them to imagine that the majority of Nicaraguans might have a different relation to *their* government.

In addition, they're used to describing the faults of the United States in terms of its culture of "militarism"—as if U.S. military power existed somehow divorced from U.S. military and political objectives! If what's wrong with the United States, in their view, is that it is full of soldiers and weapons, it's not surprising that they find the presence of soldiers and weapons in Nicaragua equally distressing.

I don't think it's a good or happy thing that so much of Nicaragua's human and financial resources have been diverted to defense. Nor do I like the way that the military is sometimes romanticized here, particularly because a culture that overvalues battlefield valor tends to erase women. I don't like it that it sometimes feels as if the greatest contribution a woman can make to the Revolution is to be a Mother of a Hero or Martyr. It doesn't make me happy to see little boys playing with wooden AKa's. But the problem is not that Nicaragua is becoming "militaristic." The problem is that Nicaragua is, through no fault of its own, at war.

On the other hand, I should add that irritating as I find these folks from Florida with their transplanted North American vision, I respect them more than I do U.S. lefties who adore the idea of guerrilla war in the Third World. More than once at home, I've sat in a hall filled with North Americans who burst into applause whenever a speaker pronounced those magic words "armed struggle." I guess I think it takes a fair amount of gall to be urging people thousands of miles away to take up arms, when you have no idea at all what the reality of "armed struggle" is: the loneliness, the hunger, the illness, the dying. Fifty thousand people died in the struggle against Somoza. That is a terrific price for comfortable North Americans to wish on a tiny country.

This working with a group has driven me to near exhaustion. I'm holding the web together on this one. Jenny's worked five or six groups already and is tired. Gray has been in Jalapa since the delegation arrived in Nicaragua, and so only met them for the first time yesterday. And I feel like a piece of meat left out for the crows: every two seconds they *want* something from me—either a history of the town of Estelí (which I don't know) or photocopies of some song sheets (which I can't supply). I have tried over and over to explain to them that there is a paper shortage here, that Nicaragua doesn't produce paper, and that we can't make them 12 copies of everything, the way we would do at home, but they don't *get* it. They say, "Yes, of course," and ten minutes later ask for photocopies of a 20-page document.

When the secretary to Monseñor Obando y Bravo canceled our next day's appointment for 11:00 a.m., I offered these folks some options from among things one can do in Managua without prior arrangement. A trip to Centro Antonio Valdevieso, for example, or a photo opportunity at the ruined Cathedral, both of which they'd already shown an interest in doing. "I'd like to talk to a women's group," says one, "or a labor union."

"I think it's very important to talk to someone from the Catholic church hierarchy. Will you explain that I bring a message from a bishop in Florida? I'm sure they'll see us then," opines another. Yes. Promise to try again with the hierarchy. Try to explain why at 6:00 p.m. it's too late to set up an appointment for the following morning with a "labor union."

So by dinner the next night I'd about had it, after a day during which I grew to detest the sound of my own name. I'd invited Ani Wehby, a Sister of Notre Dame, to come speak to the group. (She's a kick in the pants, and I love her. Her family is Lebanese—Maronite—and as a child in the U.S. she spoke Arabic and French as well as English. Other kids teased her about her accent, and she blocked out the first two completely by the time she was seven. Now she's having to learn French again, with the rest of her order.)

Ani was wonderful, and this largely suspicious, anti-Sandinista group warmed up to her in spite of her partisanship. The dinner ended with her description of how, after many years of working in the nonviolent, radical Christian-base communities in Brazil, her time in Nicaragua had changed her commitment to nonviolence. She said that she'd been challenged by the *campesinos* here in a way that shook her to her foundations. A friendly discussion took place between her and two of the hardcore exponents of nonviolence. One, Harry, 71, made the eloquent, but irrelevant, point that the state, any state, must employ violence to maintain power, and that Christians must never mistake a state for the Kingdom of God. (I agree with him about that, but the issue actually under discussion at the time was the options open to individual *campesinos* when the contra threaten them in their own isolated homes.)

After Ani left, the discussion continued and I'm afraid at one point I lost it and found myself in a shouting match with Harry and Dick. Dick was going on about how all violence is evil, including the violence of shooting in self-defense. He was talking about how *campesinos* who take up guns to defend their children are just making things worse, and how they embody evil by so doing. I suggested to him and Harry that maybe North Americans should be looking to the beams in our own eyes, rather than the motes in the Nicaraguans'. This quotation from what these folks call Scripture did not go down particularly well. Dick's wife entered the room—and the discussion—briefly to suggest that maybe it wasn't their purpose to judge the Nicaraguans, but Dick stood firm.

"Violence is evil and has brought us to the brink of nuclear war. I'm in a position equivalent to that *campesino's*. I'm a tax-resister. But when the IRS comes to my door, I don't pick up a gun." I said that was hardly an equivalent situation, that the IRS would not arrive to kill him and the children in his house who could not defend themselves, that these discussions in living rooms were different from the real thing. "Oh, but we talk about these situations all the time in Tallahassee," says Harry. " 'What would you do if a man were trying to rape your wife?' And there's plenty of rape in Tallahassee."

You may well imagine that this is the point where I lost it. The issue here was not rape, I shouted, and don't give me those tired old stories about two men haggling over division of property rights to an inert woman who has nothing to say or do herself about the question of whether or not she'll be raped! What had really set Dick off in the first place was Ani's assertion that Jesus was not a practitioner of non-violence. What do I say, she had asked, to a *campesino* who asks me how he should behave when his family is under attack? "Then it's Easter time," says Dick. "Time to go to the Cross."

So now Dick is shouting how there's only one way to interpret the Gospel. I allow as how, although the non-violent interpretation of the meaning of Christ has a long and venerable history, there are other theologies, other understandings of what is after all a Mystery, written by other equally sincere and venerable authors. (And me not even a Christian!) By this time, Dick is back on the theme of the evil of violence. It was clear, too, that evil has a capital "E" in his lexicon; that not only is the action of bearing arms Evil, but the bearer of arms as well. At that point I said I hoped that if in the course of this trip a Nicaraguan had occasion to tell him a story about defending her or himself and children with a gun, that he wouldn't tell that person she or he was Evil. "Of course I wouldn't," said Dick. "I'm a sensitive, compassionate person. I'd probably be very compassionate. But I'd still think it." I nearly puked.

Jan, it's not that I'm unwilling to listen to arguments about nonviolence, even when it means "going to the Cross." It was the unbearable arrogance of this man, to assume he had the right—he, and not even his god or his Christ—to decide that *campesinos* defending themselves from the contra are Evil. And never a word about the Evil of the forces that rule the U.S., who force *campesinos* here into a choice about bearing arms and killing other human beings. Where is the authorship of the violence in this situation? It's not in the shacks of Taspale.

Later I recounted the conversation to Jenny, Arnold, Joaquín and Sharon. All agreed these guys had been just as arrogant and repulsive as I'd thought, and they didn't blame me for losing my temper. Jenny pointed out that a few conversations with Nicaraguans would make a difference, that I should have faith in them, and of course she's right. I said I hoped the Goddess would give me the humility not to think I was wiser or better or less ignorant than these delegation members. Arnold said, "But you are." I don't think that's true. But I do think that the reason Dick believes his situation is exactly equivalent to a Nicaraguan *campesino*'s is that he's a victim of the North American middle-class disease: the belief that his way of life is normal.

One member of the delegation I like a lot. Greg is a young gay, also devoted to nonviolence, whose grandmother was of the Pueblo people. He spent a lot of time with her when he was growing up and identifies deeply with indigenous peoples. During reflections after the day we'd talked with Fernando Colomer, who is a Miskito and a Moravian pastor, Greg said, "I'm going to speak from bitterness. Talking to Fernando today, I remembered what my grandmother told me: 'No matter what government wins, the native people will always lose. And our way of life will never be as it was.' " He went on to convey to the group the apparently new (except, bless her, to my mother) information that "Indians" live in the place where Ghandi came from, and that the Miskito are "indigenous" people. I added that in Spanish the word is similar: *indígena*.

Well, that's enough *kvetching* for one night. The *altavoz* has just finished it's evening address—an invitation to the North Americans who are visiting to attend an *acto* tomorrow at the school, in celebration of September 15, the anniversary of Central American independence from Spain. ◼ *Love*

Saturday, September 22
Dear Janny,

This letter comes to you from the table in the living/dining room of the long-term team house in Managua. My mother's delegation are busily writing their report, so I'm taking this opportunity to write to you. Enclosed you'll find a few little things. Play the tapes on my machine. The other thing, the black clay necklace, goes either once around your throat or twice around your wrist, as you prefer.

I think it's been good for my mother to come to Nicaragua. She's been hungry for a long time for a political involvement that makes sense to her, and this may turn out to be it. I will say that she was the best prepared member of her delegation, in terms of arriving in Nicaragua with some familiarity with its history and struggles.

Her health isn't good, though, and she's caught a terrible bronchitis here. Being in Nicaragua has allowed me to let go of the worry I carry for her all the time; there just wasn't room for it in my chest.

This package comes to you via Jerry, one of my favorite members of this delegation. He's the first humble genetic engineer I've ever met. In fact, he's the first genetic engineer

I've ever met. He never travels anywhere without his gold pan—quite a hit at the gold mine in Limay. In fact, he traded his new plastic one with the miners for an old aluminum one they had. ◼ *All love*

Saturday, September 22
Dear friends,

It's been almost a month since I've written, but I haven't forgotten you. WFP held a retreat at the end of August, and since then I've been preparing for and accompanying a short-term delegation which included, among other people, my mother! We took these folks to Jalapa and to San Juan de Limay.

Nicaraguans who found out my mother was with this delegation were delighted. Many older Nicaraguans remember how they were radicalized through the activities of their revolutionary children. They assumed that the situation was the same with my mother and me, that my political work had inspired her. I had to tell them it was the other way 'round: that my mother *raised* me to do political work.

In Jalapa I had a chance to spend some time with my friend Chilo, who works six days a week providing health care on two *asentamientos*. She's recently added a seventh day of labor, teaching first aid to women at Santa Cruz settlement on Sundays. At night she takes classes to finish high school. When I talked to her two months ago, she had hopes of becoming a doctor. Lately she has decided on technical training in agriculture instead, in part because it is cheaper but mostly because she'll be able to help her people so much sooner. Her medical skills won't leave, she says, but she doesn't want to move into the professional class; she wants her own interests to continue to lie with those of the poorest people of Nicaragua.

Chilo's decision echoes the rumblings of my own deepest thoughts these days. Chilo is poor. She doesn't want to live in a house with a dirt floor, half of whose roof is nothing more than torn plastic. But she doesn't want anyone else to live that way either. And for her, that means deciding against the steep but possible step up into a physician's status and physical comfort. I experience this kind of choice as a clear challenge to many North Americans, especially North American women, who may be savoring professional success for the first time, maybe buying a house or making a few investments. Can we really afford in the long run to have that kind of stake in the status quo?

From Jalapa, we went on to Limay, where we spent three days in seemingly constant contact with death. The day we arrived we heard that they'd just brought in the body of a soldier who'd been killed the day before in fighting near Quilalí. We attended his funeral the next morning. The man's father was drunk and hurting and wanted no politics, no patriotic speeches or *consignas* at his son's burial. The young militia members, the dead man's *compañeros*, asked us to meet with them, right then, thereby removing us from the cemetery and avoiding a potentially nasty scene with grieving relatives.

"We want to explain to you," they said, "that sometimes our parents don't understand why we have to fight. Or they understand, but it hurts to see us go. Every one of us is willing to die tomorrow to defend our homes, our parents, our Revolution." These young men (fourteen is the minimum enlistment age) are militia members, volunteers who protect the area close to their homes. Nicaragua's army is nothing like large enough to protect every city and town, so local men and women place their names on reserve lists for the militia. When people are needed for defense, they are mobilized, with as little as half-an-hour's notice, often for months at a time. In Limay and Jalapa, in towns all over Nicaragua, so many people are mobilized that only women, children, and old men remain to attend to the vital planting and harvesting which are the heart of Nicaragua's economic life.

I've probably said this before, but I want to reiterate the fact that Nicaragua's military people are nothing other than Nicaragua's people. To my mind, there's nothing less malevolent about killing a *campesina* when she has her green army uniform on. She is still a *campesina* defending her home, the land that is hers for the first time in history.

The next day a number of us hiked about an hour to visit a gold-mining cooperative. Portions of the road to the mine have become a river during the rainy season, and other parts are deep mud or bare boulders. Almost to the mine, we met a woman who called to me, *"¡Hay un muerto más adelante!"* ("There's a dead man up ahead!") He'd been driving a tractor up a hill. The engine had stalled halfway up, and as the tractor rolled back down, it turned over, crushing the driver beneath it. A little stream ran down the middle of the road, and as we walked on we began to see motor oil floating on the water. The smell of oil hung in the air, and for hours I couldn't get it out of my nostrils. We rounded a bend and found the over-turned tractor, its driver, obviously dead, pinned underneath.

It seemed as if we couldn't get away from death in Limay. This death was stupid, accidental. The man was trying to drive a tractor where it couldn't go, up a steep road eroded by rain until it was more a pile of rocks than a road. It's tempting to try to blame this death, too, on the war, on Nicaragua's poverty. Maybe if there were enough money for real roads, enough of the right sort of vehicles, this man would not have died this way.

Then again, maybe he would have. We are all going to die someday, some of us in stupid and accidental ways, and Nicaraguans will always have their share of that sort of death. But they have a right, as well, not to suffer torture and murder, the intentional death sent them by the United States.

The man had been the tractor driver and mechanic at the tobacco farm, and many folks turned out for the wake which we attended that night.

As we returned from the wake to the Maryknoll Sisters' house, a young friend of theirs came by. He'd just gotten a telegram announcing the death in combat of his fifteen-year-old brother—the second in his family to die this year. For many Nicaraguans, a second round of death is beginning; this is not the only family I know of that has lost more than one member in the last year. María Ramos, whose son died in the insurrection, said to me, "Our children died to give us a free Nicaragua. If they kill all our children then we will just have to pick up the guns ourselves, and carry on their struggle."

I have to wonder, what will the U.S. do? Will they begin aerial bombardment? (My Goddess, the *refugios* are still only half-dug in so many places.) Will they encourage a land invasion by Honduran troops? Or will they just slowly drain the blood of Nicaragua away, death by vicious death? Now that Walter Mondale has made clear his position on Nicaragua (a "totalitarian" state which, if he is elected, he will "quarantine"), the temptation to place our hope in a Democratic victory in November shimmers and fades, like the mirage it always was. It seems that people will have to make their case in the streets.

Am I committed to nonviolence? I don't know. But I know I'm committed to making more justice in the world—in part because it is the prerequisite for the peace these arrogant North American activists are clamoring for. And they are right about one thing: the life of the planet dangles from a fraying thread. What they don't see yet is what Alice Walker has said so clearly: *"Only justice can stop a curse."*

In the beginning of October, I'm off to Siuna, a mining town in the middle of the country. I'll be there for two weeks, traveling around with a Sister of Notre Dame to outlying places, listening to stories and learning about the war in Zelaya Norte. There's a good deal of what they call "activity" in that part of the country. Sandy (the Notre Dame Sister) has been ambushed twice in the last six months. The Nicaraguan priest with whom she works receives death threats regularly over the air on Radio Quinze de Septiembre, the contra radio station in Honduras. I don't tell you this to give you the idea I'm brave or a hero—I'm neither, believe me—but to give you an idea of who some of the heroes are.

I hope to be in Puerto Cabezas on the east coast during the Nicaraguan elections the fourth of November. You'll hear all about it.

You folks there have the hard work. I wish you the strength and courage to do it. ◨ *All love*

◨ ◨ ◨

Managua

Tuesday, September 25

Dear friends,

I'm sitting at one of the tables in the central room of the WFP house in Managua, waiting for our long-term team members' retreat to start. We'd originally planned to go down to San Juan del Sur, but there's terrible flooding there, hundreds of people homeless, shortages of everything from eggs to tortillas, so we're going to stay here in Managua.

Meanwhile, eight *campesina* women were killed in an ambush up in Jinotega yesterday. They were traveling the road Joaquín and I took to Bocay, going to visit their sons in the army. I'd like to go up there and hear the story from Juana Centeno, the *responsable* for the Mothers of Heroes and Martyrs whom I met in Matagalpa in August.

On the one hand, it makes sense to me that WFP should interview the survivors of this attack, but on the other hand it seems so arbitrary. These things are happening every day! The war is really heating up, all over the country. Bluefields (on the Atlantic coast) is practically surrounded; people are stuck there and can't return to their homes in the Pearl

Lagoon. Every day people are dying, in combat, in attacks, in ambushes. It's definitely worse than it was two months ago, four months ago. Everyone knows that the contra are planning a major offensive to prevent the November 4th elections here. It is just common knowledge that it is coming—something you live with, knowing it and hoping it won't happen, like nuclear war.

I had a chance last night to see how the war and the U.S. economic blockade are affecting poor and working-class folks here in Managua. I went to a block level CDS meeting called to discuss the problem of transporting basic foods from MICOIN (the agency in charge of food distribution and rationing) distribution points to the people in this barrio. Las Piedrecitas is on the far western edge of Managua, so taxis hate to come here. Not many people have private vehicles, and this exacerbates the difficulties of an already difficult system. In our barrio, there are five *expendios*, individuals empowered to sell the goods distributed by MICOIN. These goods include the basics (rice, corn, beans, milk, soap, oil, etc.) as well as chickens and eggs. The *expendios* are permitted to retail MICOIN goods for a price that covers one trip a week to MICOIN to get the stuff. Problem is that very often, in fact usually, one trip a week is not sufficient. The *expendios* are told, "Come back Wednesday morning, we'll have eggs then." On Wednesday morning they hear, "Try this afternoon." It was clear from the meeting that folks were not blaming MICOIN; they believe that it is the war which causes the shortages and unreliability. In general those present at the meeting seemed inclined to believe that whenever MICOIN has things, the agency makes them available immediately.

So the problem is, the *expendios* don't want, and can't afford to make more than one trip a week to MICOIN, so the barrio has been borrowing private vehicles to make up the difference. Last night's meeting was held in part to come to agreement about how to create a fund to reimburse individuals who use their own cars or pickups to do food runs for the neighborhood.

It was fascinating. At first it was suggested that every household contribute five *cordobas* a week to the fund (about 12 cents, at the current exchange rate). Someone pointed out that not every family could spare five *cordobas* a week; that's how close to the edge people are living. There was general agreement with this observation. The upshot was the creation of a voluntary fund, with a ceiling of five *cordobas* a week and the understanding that no one would be criticized for contributing less.

Next problem: who is to administer the fund? The *responsable* of the CDS who was chairing the meeting explained that it couldn't be the CDS itself, because the anti-Sandinista opposition would print stories in *La Prensa* charging that the CDS is forcing people to pay extra for the transportation of their foodstuffs. It couldn't be the *expendios*, because the prices they charge are set by law and they are not permitted to accept any other money from consumers. It can't be MICOIN itself—for the same reasons. So that leaves the consumers themselves to organize and administer the funds. A woman volunteered to be the bookkeeper and received a grateful round of applause.

Then a few criticisms were aired and the general principles of expressing criticism directly discussed. Several people complained about one *expendio* who they said was charging illegally high prices. "Too often," one woman said, "dissatisfactions hang in the air; everyone talks about them, but the problem doesn't get solved. For example, you're making criticisms of one *expendio* here in the neighborhood. The *compañera responsable* of the CDS is telling us we have the right to replace this man—which is true. But that's a very serious thing to do, to remove someone from his position of responsibility. First we need to try to correct the problems through criticism/self-criticism." This woman clearly had some political education, but what she said didn't seem unfamiliar to the rest of the meeting. All concurred.

One interesting thing about last night's meeting: with the exception of the *expendio* in whose house it was held, and my WFP *compañero* Doug I., everyone present was either a woman or a child. Mary C., another friend from WFP, tells me that in the country, in Jalapa, where the CDS deals largely with matters of defense, most *responsables* are men.

(This doesn't quite tally with my experience; I know two women who are *responsables* in Jalapa, but they may be exceptions.) In Managua, although *vigilancia revolucionaria* was mentioned last night, the main function of the CDS seems to be to serve as a channel for goods and services—the basic things that concern women, such as where they are to get food to feed their families.

The other thing that struck me was just how much the poor and working-class people of Managua do seem willing to put up with, in order to support the Revolution. Of course, I saw a skewed sample last night, because I saw the people who would come to a meeting in the pouring rain. But over 20 per cent participation isn't that bad, I'd say. The *responsable* had visited every house personally yesterday afternoon, explaining that decisions would be made in the meeting which would affect the whole barrio, and that everyone's participation was important.

And during the meeting, she made it clear that even people who weren't present would have the right to raise the same issues again. Nothing in last night's events fits with the U.S. government's representation of Nicaragua as a totalitarian state. In fact, what is surprising to me, given the hardship of these people's lives, is that no one expressed the idea that it would be pleasant not to have the headache of working these things out, or that the government should just take care of them.

In all, a fascinating evening. Over and over in Nicaragua, I've seen people learning to believe they have the right, their community has the right, to analyze and to organize.

A few words here about how goods are distributed in Nicaragua. There are eight basic products whose prices are kept artificially low by the government in order to make them available to even the poorest people. Everyone is entitled to purchase every month a certain amount of each of these eight products (like beans, rice, and cooking oil) at the subsidized price. In addition, people can buy more of these products from private sources at a higher price, if they want to. The distribution of basic products is handled by the government agency, MICOIN, while the paperwork for individual families is handled by the neighborhood CDS's.

Nicaragua is still poor. (Young Cubans who came to help with the literacy campaign were horrified by the poverty of Nicaragua. Nothing in their experience, except museum replicas of pre-revolutionary Cuban homes, had prepared them to see such poverty.) But people here seem to be willing to endure scarcity and inconvenience a while longer. There are rumblings of discontent, though, especially in the small middle class.

How long will the people of Managua, who are not, at the moment, the victims of murders and kidnapping, be willing to put up with scarcity and inconvenience? (For women, this "inconvenience" means hours, days, of their lives consumed in acquiring the basic necessities.) How long? We know which way the U.S. government is betting.

◼ *All good struggles*

◻ ◼ ◻

Subsidies for purchase of basic supplies were one of the greatest achievements of the Nicaraguan revolution. For many poor families they meant the difference between hunger and regular meals. The cost of the war has taken its toll here, too, and in 1985 the government was forced to reduce or eliminate most of these subsidies. As of May 1986, subsidies remained for only five products, and the amount of each product available at subsidized rates had been greatly reduced. These changes, along with the effects of the U.S. embargo on trade with Nicaragua, weigh most heavily on women and children. The embargo has created terrible shortages. It's not uncommon for Nicaraguans to refer to a tractor as a "John Deere." Now a great many "John Deeres" are sitting idle for lack of spare parts. Idle farm machinery means less food and higher prices at the markets.

◼ ◼ ◼

Sunday, September 30
Dear heart,
    The women from Somos Hermanas—a feminist solidarity group—have arrived from the U.S., invited by AMNLAE to

help celebrate their seventh anniversary. Last night I spent a few hours with Teresa and Luisa from San Francisco, which was wonderful. I had not realized how lonely I was for other lesbians until I actually found myself in the presence of two. We talked politics, Nicaragua, and local San Francisco gossip for hours. They'd just been to meet Dora María Tellez, who Teresa says is *clarita*—very clear—about things like feminism, and the dangers of male identification. Teresa was hoping the whole time to get a chance to ask her views on lesbianism, but was never called on. Too bad. That would have been an interesting conversation.

Their group is off to Bluefields today, which surprises me, considering conditions out there. They're not even flying; they're going by road and river, but I guess the women of AMNLAE know what they're doing. I assume they'll have some sort of military escort—not that that necessarily decreases the chances of ambush.

The night before last, I attended the celebration of AMNLAE's seventh anniversary. A good crowd, maybe three thousand. It was wonderful, although not *my* idea of a feminist event. The M.C. (never identified) was male, and of two speakers, one was male. The other was AMNLAE's National Secretary, who is a candidate for National Assembly on the FSLN ticket. It's a sign of how important the event was, however, that the male speaker was Daniel Ortega, the Frente's presidential candidate.

Daniel spoke for over an hour, primarily focusing on the recent ambush near Jinotega in which eight women, who were en route to visit folks in a military base, were killed. He used his speech to respond to the communiqué issued by the Coordinadora Democrática following the ambush (published in *La Prensa*, naturally). In the communiqué they expressed their sorrow at the death of these eight women, a tragic effect of Nicaragua's "civil war." Daniel's point was that Nicaragua is under attack by a foreign power, that it's a lie to speak of U.S. aggression as a civil war. But, he said (in what Sharon says is the strongest statement she's ever heard from him), if the Coordinadora keeps putting out this story, this *"cuenticito,"* about a civil war, they will get a civil war—a class war! Well when Daniel said that, the place went wild, and I have to admit it was pretty stirring. Of course it was probably a tactical error on Daniel's part, as far as the international arena is concerned, but the truth is that *of course* there's a class struggle going on in Nicaragua. That war has already been declared by the class that hopes to benefit from U.S. intervention.

The *acto* finished in the dark with floodlight illumination of the plaza, music, cheers, and *consignas*. All around me, people were building human pyramids—a favorite activity at Nicaraguan demonstrations.

I've certainly wished you were here these last few days to discuss this wretched article for *LesCon* with me. I think it's a case of trying to do too much in too little space, but I wanted to reflect a little on the whole radical feminism vs. socialist feminism debate, in the light of my living next to a real revolution-in-progress for the last few months. And some days when I think about these things, it's clear as clear that no one's going to liberate women from sexism *but* women. Other days, it's all a muddle, and all I can see is that sex oppression will be the last to go, because it is the oppression that lives inside our homes. In that sense, I guess I still believe that feminism holds the potential of being the widest possible lens on the world: I can imagine a society without classes or racism that continues to oppress women. I cannot imagine a truly feminist society that perpetuates class oppression or racism.

But that's all on the theoretical level. On the practical level, I'm not sure women can hope to make revolution, as women, and as we have known revolution in the world. Revolutions are made by classes, it seems, or by national groupings, or by temporary alliances among classes and/or national groupings—not by gender castes. At least they haven't been up till now.

The reason all of this is running around so hard in my head is that I'm coming back from Nicaragua with the conviction that the only hope for the world is a radical shift of power within the United States. I don't imagine this happening until we get squeezed by the Third World a little more, maybe another twenty years, if we have that long.

And, as in Nicaragua, it will have to be a revolution of the spirit as much as anything—which scares me. Can I work in coalition with Christian peace-and-justice groups like Sojourners? I'm not convinced that the world they want to build will have room for me, as a lesbian, as a Jew, as a woman. For one thing, they place a great deal of emphasis on the primacy of the family, and I have an idea that in their view, families are strictly male-run, nuclear phenomena. Well, as Bernice Reagon says, a coalition is not the same thing as a home.

So it goes round and round, gathering force if not direction! ◘ *All love*

P.S. In five days I leave for Siuna. It's been so long now since I was really afraid that I'd forgotten what it felt like. Now I'm remembering. This trip is probably the riskiest one I'll do, and I'm ashamed to find that I'm afraid. Apparently it doesn't show, though. When it really looked as if we were going to die in Jalapa in June, my whole body was convulsing inside. I thought everyone knew I was terrified. Now Mary C. tells me, "I had no idea you were scared. You seemed so cool and organized."

◘ ◘ ◘

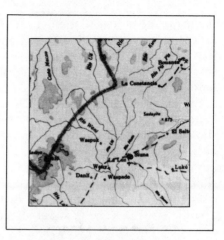

Siuna

Saturday, October 6

Dear Janny,

Following Aeronica's instruction, we arrived at the Managua airport at 6:00 a.m. At noon we finally took off. The flight was short, only an hour, and we stayed low enough to see the terrain pretty clearly. Coming into Siuna, I could see just how dense the forests are around here. It's no wonder the contra can come and go as they please. But the land is so beautiful. Now that we're well into the rainy season, the jungle shows a hundred different greens: pine, banana, coffee and all the shadows between them. Once again I was reminded of how rich this land is, and how much the people love it.

I thought about Arnoldo Vallejo, the mayor of Jalapa, who took me out one day to see his farm. I think he must have shown me every single banana tree. "I fertilized this land with my blood and my sweat," he said. "It's a special thing to love the land."

Barbara, one of the Sisters of Notre Dame, met us at the airport, along with Augustín, the priest from La Rosita. He turns out be a very black man, fluent in English, Spanish and Miskito. (I think he knows how beautiful his skin is; he was wearing a bright red *cotón*—a kind of smock shirt.) Gus invited us to come to La Rosita on the 16th; for five days before then, he's entertaining his bishop.

Barbara took us home to the Sisters' house. Sandy has been called to Puerto Cabezas to do something about her visa, but she's expected today. Their house reminds me of a cross between a boat and your parents' home in Buffalo—not because of its size or shape but because everything is ship-shape. They have a very neat little indoor latrine; rinse water from dishes and washing goes down there, along with a little disinfectant to keep it sweet. Everything is exactly in its place. I'm a little afraid to breathe, just because for me even breathing can be such a messy act!

Siuna is really suffering the effects of the war. Bean rations have been cut to one pound per person per week. Rice is at one-and-a-half pounds. People are pretty upset because there really isn't enough to eat. They don't seem to connect the hardship to the war; they blame it on the government. Transport is the big problem. It's hard to get things in overland because the road is so bad in the rainy season, and the contra make it a pretty dicey proposition. So some stuff comes by air, but it's hard to bring in enough food and supplies for a town of 5,500 in one rickety old DC-3. Newspapers arrive about a week late, but some people have radios.

Siuna does have running water. Electricity used to be available only at night but the government offices need it to run their calculators, so now everyone has *luz* during the day as well. The town's water is pumped from a reservoir about an hour's walk away. Two weeks ago, contra attacked the pump, killing one man. The pump itself escaped damage, but it remains a vulnerable target. During the winter, people might just get by on rainwater (it poured for four hours yesterday), but in summer they'd be out of luck. When the water does run, it's intermittent; today it's running, but cloudy.

(Later) Things move so slowly here. This morning we accomplished the check-in with the local police. The Migración officer scrutinized every inch of our *permisos*—with reason, I guess, since this *is* a war zone, and he doesn't know us from anyone. We have no problem staying in town as long as we like, but before we visit anywhere outside, we have to check in with the police. So it goes.

Sunday, October 7

This morning we attended a *Celebración de la Palabra* in the Catholic church of Siuna. Surprisingly good turnout, considering mass was said yesterday and there will be one tonight as well. I caught my breath when Barbara went up behind the altar to the small cloth house where the Host is kept. I'd never seen a woman offer communion before in a Catholic church. A *campesina* led the celebration, and she and Barbara commented on the texts.

The epistle was from Philippians—about being able to accept abundance and want with equal equanimity. I did find it useful to ruminate on. There's such a temptation here to despair, but no one except us North Americans seems very tempted by it. Every day the war seems to go worse; the contra commit more atrocities. But *siguen adelante*, people keep on. And *cheerfully*.

I brought along some of the magazines you sent me. I see *WomaNews* chose to print your fan letter. What a shock in the middle of Siuna to see your name in print. It was funny because I was thinking as I started to read it, "I should send them a fan letter too; it's such a consistently interesting paper." Then I glanced to the bottom of the letter and saw it was from you.

I thought the article about Nicaragua in this issue was pretty good. What a difference speaking a little Spanish makes, though. No one who did could have made the mistake of thinking *Nuevo Diario* is an opposition paper. The article says Nicaragua has one government and two opposition papers, which is not exactly accurate. There are three papers: *Barricada*, the official organ of the FSLN (but not of the government); *Nuevo Diario*, essentially a pro-Process, but not uncritically pro-government paper; and *La Prensa*, an opposition rag. I suppose "rag" sounds a little biased, but they do use a strategy of outright lies in order to stir up trouble. They create shortages by announcing their existence and encouraging people to hoard goods of which there are actually enough to go around. Most recently they printed a story stating that the land of three people in Matagalpa had been expropriated. They had to eat their words when the three came forward to say that nothing of the sort had happened.

Siuna is actually Siuna-La Luz, two towns built on either side of the La Luz gold mine. After church, Joaquín and I went over the hill to La Luz. We had a pleasant morning talking to the priest there. Then we walked through La Luz, the main street of which looks like the set for an old TV western with horses waiting at hitching posts in front of rough wooden buildings. The town is built on little hills, criss-crossed with foot paths. Everyone seems to have a few flowers growing; what we call houseplants (like coleus) grow wild here.

The architecture is different from that of the Pacific coast. Instead of adobe over poles, most houses have horizontal wooden siding and zinc roofs. Most sit up on posts to let water flow by underneath, and so have real wooden floors, instead of dirt. Although things are hard now, people don't seem as poor here as they do in other places I've been. Even the dogs are less bone and more flesh. Living next to a gold mine makes a big difference.

Monday, October 8

This morning we went to the La Luz side of the hill with Barbara to interview several of the folks living there. They're refugees from a place called Waspuca, about three hours from here on foot. It's the same old story. The contra came in August and kidnapped most of the men. The women and children came down to Siuna, the closest populated area. One man we spoke to had been sick the day they came. They told him that if he'd been well, they would have taken him, too. He's had to sell off his animals at low prices in order to get enough to build a little shack on posts.

We also met a woman who had two children kidnapped, ages four and six. Absurd. What they do when they kidnap children is carry them to Honduras and install them in "refugee" camps, as testimony to the stream of people escaping the Marxist-Leninist regime here. I'd be *very* interested to visit those camps; not that people there would be at liberty to talk, but I'd sure like to know how many of those folks are there voluntarily. What happens when they take whole families is that they hold them in ransom to each other. They force the men to fight with the contra, the women to become "refugees." Each is afraid to escape for fear of reprisals against the other. This particular contra band were five Sumo (an indigenous group), only two of whom spoke Spanish. It's hard for me to believe their presence in the contra represents any kind of informed choice.

Speaking of informed choices, it was worth waiting until I'd been in Nicaragua to read Paolo Freire's *Pedagogy of the Oppressed*. What would have been for me only stirring abstractions if I'd read it in the U.S. seems a live, concrete program in the context of a continuing revolution. Interesting, too, how so much of what Freire wrote has penetrated the average radical's consciousness—to the extent that much of what I'm reading here seems familiar.

One thing that struck me particularly was Freire's insistence that genuine dialogue cannot take place between oppressor and oppressed, and that revolutionaries need not and should not attempt it. For that reason, he believes that even after a popular revolution, the people have no responsibility to dialogue with their former oppressors, who are trying to regain their position. This seems to me a pertinent insight for Nicaragua. Whatever they may say, the Coordinadora Democrática's proposal for a "National Dialogue" that would include the contra leaders is a sham. There cannot be good-faith dialogue between the former owners of Nicaragua and the people, since the former owners' only purpose would be to regain possession of their lost "property."

I also like the way Freire describes identification with the oppressor: as becoming a shell, or a house, for him to live in. Getting rid of the oppressor-within is a genuine exorcism.

All of this actually makes me very hopeful for the possibilities of revolution in the U.S., oddly enough. Freire is also the first radical writer I've come across whose understanding of revolutionary leadership is something I could trust.

Somehow when Christians talk about servant-leaders, I just don't believe them. But I believe Freire when he says that if the leaders don't learn from the people, all they do is perpetuate oppression and retard liberation. Liberation, he says, can never be imposed on someone by force; that's a contradiction in terms. Which should be self-evident, but I can think of a lot of Left sectarians who could benefit from remembering it!

I wish my prose were rich enough to give you La Luz, with its little dirt tracks along the sides of the hills, little wooden houses and gardens of bright hibiscus, coleus, moss roses; Graciela in her sheer gray dress, splitting here and there at the seams so her green underpants show through. The sun is bright, the earth is dark, and the grass and trees glow green.

Sandra arrived today from Puerto Cabezas. It looked for a while as if I were going to be traveling with her and Padré Enrique for a week in the *campo*. But today they've been mobilizing almost all the men, and she says they're not going to let folks travel very far. In any event, I'll go tomorrow to San Pablo, a cooperative quite close to here, for the night. Joaquín's back is acting up, so he'll stay here in town.

Tomorrow we have a meeting with the local CEPAD representative and various Protestant pastors. We're also supposed to meet some men who were kidnapped by the contra and managed to escape.

Sandra just got home from visiting Enrique. Looks as if tomorrow's trip may be off. The contra attacked a cooperative called Labú, quite a ways from here, and he may be going there tomorrow. All day they've been mobilizing the guys here, about 400 in all. Siuna itself seems to be surrounded by contra camps, but about four hours' walk from here. We'll see. You're always with me.

Tuesday, October 9

A good day. We went in the morning to meet with some of the founders of the Misioneras de Jesús, a religious order founded by *campesinas*. Originally these women had hoped to join the order of some U.S. nuns who were working here, but they were First World folks, and although there was good feeling on all sides, the *campesinas* wanted something that was more appropriate to them and their situation. So twelve years ago, they founded their order. The woman who heads the government here, and the FSLN's second-in-command for the whole zone, Dorotea Wilson, are both former members.

All this makes me think of something—absurd but possible. Maybe what the U.S. women's movement needs is a religious order! Seriously, what if there existed some group of women sworn to revolutionary community, bound by some oath of spirit to love each other, the world, the *lucha*, and God? Think about it. (I can hear you now: "First she wants us to start a magazine. Then she wants to go to Nicaragua. Now she wants feminist nuns! What next?") Just think on it; there might be something there.

Tomorrow there's a good chance Sandy and I will go for a few days to Hormiguero, where Sandy is helping to start a women's sewing cooperative. Maybe this "good chance" will really happen.

Thursday, October 11

I'm lying in a hammock in the one-room house of friends of Sandra's at the cooperative "Heroes and Martyrs" in Hormiguero. All the folks living here are refugees; some arrived as long as two years ago and some in the last few months. Here they're growing rice, beans, rubber trees, plantains and bananas. They've built about 90 pre-fab houses up on posts—wood siding, zinc roofs. Most houses have a little flower garden—moss roses, coleus, other local flora. Water is hauled from two wells, or from the river, which is contaminated. The wells are dependable in winter, but in summer they go dry.

Yesterday we slowly worked our way through Hormiguero, letting the women know that there might be a meeting in a day or two to discuss further organization of the sewing co-op. These folks are so poor, but we never left a house without drinking at least a cup of warm, sweet coffee, or a *fresco* (fruit drink). There was one day we ate three breakfasts, so as not to hurt anyone's feelings.

Friday, October 12

Back in Siuna for the moment. We spent two nights at Hormiguero, and left this morning, walking about an hour and a half. At the turnoff for the road to Siuna, we met the one vehicle on the road today and caught a ride the rest of the way home.

I liked walking around the co-op with Sandra, watching her do business. At each house where we stopped, we'd sit awhile, exchange a little news, consume whatever was offered. Then Sandra would rock back on her stool a little. "*Pues* (Well)—oh, by the way, there's going to be a meeting of the sewing cooperative today or tomorrow."

"When?"

"Whenever you say. It's your meeting." She's really learned the Nicaraguan way of introducing the main point of your visit. So many times what is business-like behavior to a North American (e.g., me!) seems really abrupt to a Nicaraguan. And there was so much else to talk about—like what to do about the crazy young man, wild with grief for the father who recently died, who runs around the cooperative with a gun, making threats.

The sun goes down quickly here. Last night we were sitting in full light on someone's porch, talking quietly. The next moment it was black. The co-op had no electricity, and here and there I could see the warm yellow glimmer of a kerosene lamp, but it was *dark*. I walked back by myself to the house where we were staying. Suddenly I slammed into a piece of the dark that was very solid indeed—and extremely surprised, almost as surprised as I was. "Mooo?" she asked. Well, I didn't know the answer to that one in Spanish or English, so I apologized and went on my way. There had been no cow there when I'd come down that path in the daylight!

In what seemed like the middle of the night (about 2:30 a.m.) but is really the *campesino* morning, I heard some noise. By quarter-to-four, the news was out: "There's meat for sale!" I don't know why it should have been so hard for me to eat steak for breakfast, just because I had walked right into it the night before, but it was.

Last night also, the contra came within a half-hour's walk of the co-op. We heard the news that the people in one house could hear their neighbors screaming in the only other nearby house. No one knows any more than that, but they sent a group of 20 from Hormiguero to explore.

I enjoyed my walk back to Siuna with Sandy. We talked, among other things, about God and the Bible—in which she says we still need to uncover both the female part of the godhead and the importance of community to the reign of God. Apparently, the Brazilian theologian Leonardo Boff (who was recently hauled up before the Vatican for an investigation into his liberation theology) has written a book called *The Maternal Face of God*, which I'd like to get hold of.

A distressing thing occurs to me: At this late date in my life, I may be stuck with the Bible as the culturally familiar—albeit sorely adulterated—medium of the Word. What an awful thought.

Dreamed twice of sex last night—once with a man whose attentions I didn't want. In the other dream, I was kissing a woman who was not a lesbian. She was a North American who had lived many years in Nicaragua. As we were kissing (her first kiss from a woman; she was nervous), into the room came a Nicaraguan man. I felt terrible, because I'd led her into a situation in which she risked losing the respect of her Nicaraguan friends. You don't have to dig too deep to understand that one.

Living closeted is *hard*, harder than I'd remembered. I don't want to do it anymore. But it's the agreement I've made with myself, so as not to endanger WFP's church connections here. And it's a small sacrifice, compared to the *entrega de vida* (the gift of one's life) so many are making here.

I can't get out of my head the eight young *maestros populares* (volunteer teachers) who were killed last week in Bocaycito, very near where Joaquín and I were in August. Today *Barricada* carried an interview with some of their *compañeros*, who refuse to stop teaching. One said, "To leave now would be to kidnap *ourselves*, and to rob the children of the right to an education." And these people are little more than children themselves—17, 18 years old. They talked about going on to teach the day the others were killed, struggling not to cry in front of the children. *Qué valor.*

Enough. ◼ *I love you.*

Saturday, October 13, 11:45 p.m.

Dear Jan,

I'm writing this by moonlight, as I keep *vigilancia.* At 9:30 tonight they attacked San Pablo, 45 minutes away from here on foot. There was a good deal of shooting—it seemed much closer by—and we heard the mortars. Just as we decided whatever it was was over, the siren sounded and they got around to shutting off the electricity as well. We dragged our pillows and blankets into the living room and lay huddled on the floor, the four of us, Barbara, Sandy, Joaquín and I, making each other laugh.

At a little after 11:00 p.m., Iliana—Siuna's mayor—and another woman came by, in *compa* greens, AKa's slung over their shoulders. Our household had been scheduled anyway for *vigilancia* from 1:00 a.m. to 5:00 a.m. that night, but they gave us the news about San Pablo and told us everyone was to watch all night. Our house is near the eastern edge of town, facing the hill over which the contra would come from San Pablo. Any attack will probably involve mortars launched from that hill.

"If you don't have your rifle, you'd better get it," Iliana said. We said we didn't have one in the house, and they offered to get us one if we wanted it. Brave women, they're walking the whole town, the two of them, telling everyone what's happening.

A gibbous moon and a recumbent Orion are keeping me company—and the roosters, who crow faithfully on the hour, beginning at 11:00. And my love for you, and the work we've given ourselves to. I think I'm probably terrified somewhere deep, but, at the moment, I'm not afraid. The moon has gone behind the clouds, and now I really can see almost nothing.

It's after midnight now. A horse is walking by in the street. Dogs and coyotes are talking to each other, and I am talking to the light of my life. Although the danger is perhaps more real this time than it was in Jalapa, I don't have that awful wrenching fear of dying without saying goodbye. We've done that. Here comes the horse again, crunching along in the street just like a two-legged beast. I keep my eyes on the hill in front of me, though God knows what I expect to see there.

The air smells of fresh mud, manure and night-blooming jasmine. As the new stars climb over the hill, I'm reminded of the night I sat out on another hill, holding a friend who couldn't stop crying, and waiting for the adults to come back and make it better. The adults who can make it better were an illusion that night and this. Strange to be, to always have been, one of the adults *encargadas*, entrusted, to make it better.

12:45 a.m. All quiet, except for a few dogs and a pig who just began snorting. The horse has ambled away. Zinc roofs pop as they cool, but there's no confusing that sound with gunfire. As the moon rises over the roof of our house the band of light shed on the paper shrinks. Soon there will be nothing. I love you. The horse again. And Orion going beyond the lip of the roof. And I can feel you, have felt you clearly in the last half-hour.

1:00 a.m. I'm going to wake Barbara for the next shift. ◼ *All love*

Sunday, October 14
Dear one,

Well, it wasn't San Pablo; it was a good deal closer, right on the edge of Siuna. Three mortar rounds were fired, all landing close to but not, thank God, on top of houses. Our *compas* chased them away, it seems, although they didn't pursue them, presumably so as not to leave the town unguarded in case of attack from another direction.

Iliana has *vigilancia* again all night. When I saw her this afternoon, she seemed tired but determined. The *vigilancia ocular* (the sitting-and-watching kind) passes to another household tonight, so we'll probably get some sleep, failing another attack. I think another attack is unlikely; they seem to be jumping around, trying to lure the *compas* into leaving someplace completely unguarded.

Tomorrow is the 15th, which is the day Daniel Ortega has told the United Nations that the U.S. would launch a major offensive. I don't think the invasion will materialize, but you never know. The joke going around here is that when Daniel made his announcement, Reagan got really angry and called him a liar. "That lying communist! It's all a hoax. There's no invasion planned for the 15th. It's the *16th*!"

This morning I attended an *acto* for the handing out of land-titles in the town of Coperna. I really liked the way the *responsable* from MIDINRA, the agrarian reform agency, spoke with the *campesinos*. He told them they have the right to push MIDINRA, to insist that the agency keep its promises. He told them about some new pigs and bulls that would be available next year. I could tell he was genuinely excited about these animals, because he knew they were good, and that the *campesinos* would like them.

Barbara and Sandra just came home from visiting the Misioneras de Jesús. Sandra has just learned that the three people the contra took away when she was last in the mountains have never returned. She'd thought at the time that the contra only intended to escort these people back to their houses and leave them. But one is the sister of a militia member they really want, and it seems they're holding her until they can get him. The other two were not connected with anything or anyone, but the contra took them anyway. Sandra's really hurting, because the reason they were caught in the first place was that they were accompanying her to the next village.

Well, dear one, it's quiet so far this evening. I hold you in my heart. ◼ *Soon*

Monday, October 15
Dear friends,

This letter comes to you from Siuna, a mining town in Zelaya Norte, northeastern Nicaragua. Joaquín and I have been here a little over a week, staying with two Sisters of Notre Dame and visiting cooperatives in the *campo*.

Two nights ago, Siuna was attacked. We heard the gunfire begin quite close to our house at about 9:30 p.m., and then, further away, a few mortars.

We took turns keeping watch all night from the darkened porch of our house. I had plenty of time to think out there, staring into the dark hill overlooking our street. I thought about mortars launched from that hill falling through the fragile zinc roofs of people's homes. I thought about how easily bullets slice through plank siding. I thought about the more than 7,000 people who have died at the hands of the contra—more, proportionately, than all the U.S. soldiers who died in Vietnam. What a loss for this tiny country.

Fortunately, the attack on Siuna did little damage, and no one was hurt. Bullets did fly through roofs—I saw the holes today—and mortars fell horribly close to three houses. It seems the contra's objectives may have been more psychological than military, in any immediate sense. An attack like this means mobilization of the few remaining men in town. It means no one sleeps, and work is impeded. It means everyone is a little more afraid.

This is the season for harvesting rice. In the cooperatives all the men have been mobilized for defense and the work of the harvest—vital for all Nicaragua—falls on the women and children. Here, to harvest food is to risk your life. Brigades of students from Siuna are helping with the harvest— machetes in hand and rifles over their shoulders.

So many people have been kidnapped and murdered in this area that I hardly know how to write the reports we do for Witness for Peace anymore. How to keep fresh the horror of torture, of people hacked to death with machetes? Many people continue to work here in the face of direct, personal death threats from the contra.

Siuna sits in the middle of rich land, but people here are hungry. The contra prevent them from harvesting their own food, and they attack and burn trucks carrying supplies from the west. The people who drive those trucks are true heroes, placing their lives at risk every day. Just one story: a truck carrying flour was ambushed at a bridge. The contra threw sack after sack of flour into the water until it looked like a river of milk, a woman told me. "Everyone was crying, because they saw so much food being destroyed," she said.

Do all my stories begin to sound the same after a while? They do to me, too. But the horrid truth is that these things go on happening over and over, and I don't know what else to do but tell you about it.

I spent three days at Hormiguero (the Ant Hill!), a cooperative formed by refugees from the contra. The women there are tough and generous. A *campesina* greeting is a full hug—even for a *gringa* she has never met before. I went with one of the Sisters who is working with women's sewing cooperatives. We spent three days sitting on the porches of people's wooden houses, built on posts to let the rain run by. We heard the news (bad), drank *frescos* (sweet), and admired the latest babies (fat and sleepy). In two years, these folks have done so much, clearing and building on a place that was *pura montaña* (pure wilderness) when they arrived.

One night by kerosene lamp we recorded the history of Hormiguero—which families came first, from which villages abandoned because of contra attacks. "We always knew we would live differently after the Triumph," one woman said. "We knew that we would want to leave our *finca* and live cooperatively, in community with other *campesinos*. Now we have achieved this."

Tomorrow I'm off to Rosita, and to spend some time on Miskito *asentamientos*, if the contra are allowing traffic on the road. Then Joaquín and I will go on to Puerto Cabezas on the Atlantic coast and stay there through the elections. I miss you all and remember every one of you with so much love. *La lucha sigue.* (The struggle goes on.) ◘ *Abrazos*

◙ ◙ ◙

I sent the packet of letters from Siuna out with Barbara. When Jan received them, she wrote, "Your letters from Siuna arrived today. Sorry I am not going to get a phone call, but very glad to hear from you. . . When you were close to being under fire, I was moving; may this be the maximum personal disruption either of us undergo.

"Deb and I were talking today about how I must love you very much; if I didn't I'd have done what she thinks most people would have done, which would be to deaden the pain of your absence by deadening the sense of connection. Instead I live with the pain right at the surface, and it makes me a little strange and crazy. I hope my friends and you will forgive whatever oddities result."

While these months in Nicaragua had given me some new optimism about revolutionary change in my own country, Jan was living in a United States one week away from re-electing Ronald Reagan. Her letter continued, "I spent most of yesterday trying to focus on how very much of my free-floating despair these days, which I tend to associate with you, is actually revolutionary despair. I think that is true; I am having trouble with hope, faced with the impending Reagan landslide, etc. This is something I can work on. In fact, I have realized that what I want in *LesCon* is something for the demoralized and frightened, because that is what we are all going to be in the coming days. Oddly enough, though I am one of the above, I suspect I can write such a thing: it is in the quest for what to say to such a topic that I find Her presence—all the experience and discipline of this lifetime go into being open to whatever there is to hear on this."

As usual, Jan was juggling work, *LesCon* and political commitments. "I am finally getting through with the little termite job I started October 1st. It has been terribly hard. I think the two women who own the house together are fighting—the energy around it is awful. Also, the job consists essentially of destroying a series of thriving termite (and other insect) environments. I have pulled apart sections and have had them seem to 'swarm' as so many creatures scurried around. Will you think me crazy if I tell you that it hurts, that I find myself wondering whether these two lesbians who own a house have the right, through me, to deny millions of insects a place to live and eat? I feel like an imperialist. Pretty strange—and probably exactly as far as my nonviolent impulses go. If I were a critter, I'd bite me—as a number, unidentified, have. I think these reactions are so strong this time because I feel these women are living so luxuriously— when they are not really. But somehow they are using their house as a refuge, an escape from struggle, rather than as the place they live and the place from which they go out to struggle. I suspect having a house for *that* purpose is OK. I think of a number of people I've known with whom I've felt that—including, I hope, us in our big apartment. More and more on this topic when we are together."

Jan wasn't sure she shared my enthusiasm for creating a religious order of revolutionary feminists. "Don't you think they'd have terrific monogamy/nonmonogamy problems?" she asked. "It's no accident that members of religious orders are supposed to be celibate; it keeps the community from being pulled apart by the disruptions and competing loyalties created by private relationships. But I don't think most feminists are going to want to adopt celibacy as a prerequisite for political work!" I had to laugh, but I continued to be impressed by the women religious I encountered in Nicaragua, and by the model for feminist political life some women's orders suggest.

I think it's no accident, for example, that even in the midst of a socialist revolution, some of Zelaya Norte's strongest women leaders have been nourished in an all-female organization like the Misioneras de Jesús. Twelve years before, these *campesina* women had decided they wanted a greater participation in the life of the church than was open to them as laywomen. So they founded their own religious order, to do religious education combined with community organizing. Some of these were older women; some were mothers who had been abandoned or widowed. Even today the Misioneras' house is full of children.

These women do dangerous work, traveling in the mountains from village to tiny village, often the targets of contra threats and ambushes. It is ironic that the U.S. should accuse Nicaragua of repressing the church, when so many church workers have been murdered by the contra. Why do the contra target religious workers? There are a number of reasons, perhaps chief among them being the fact that they represent a genuine popular leadership, which is always a contra target. In addition, many church workers have answered liberation theology's call to make justice for the poor of the earth by cooperating with the revolutionary process in Nicaragua. When those who answer the call are poor themselves, like the Misioneras de Jesús, their capacity for enspiriting the people of their communities is extraordinary. What the Misioneras teach other poor women is that God loves *them*—the poor, tired, grubby *campesinas* who pound their clothes clean on rocks in a muddy river—and that God wants them to be free.

All over Nicaragua I met strong women—North American, Nicaraguan, European, and from other Latin American countries—who have chosen life in a religious order. There is a sense in which women's religious communities are separatist formations; they are groups of women living in community with other women, apart from men. At the same time, women like Sandy Price are deeply involved in the world as it is, filled with all sorts of women and men, but empowered in their work by the backing of a community of women. The experience of women religious working in Nicaragua left me more cheerfully convinced than ever of women's need for autonomous organizations, as bases from which to enter a more general struggle. (This very issue has recently become the subject of hot debate within Nicaragua. In early 1986, Rosario Murillo, the editor of *Ventana*, which is *Barricada*'s literary supplement, published an article questioning women's need to organize, as women, in AMNLAE. Murillo, who is also head of the Sandinista Cultural Workers Union and is married to Daniel Ortega, Nicaragua's president, maintained that in a genuinely revolutionary society like Nicaragua, women's needs will be met as part of the general development of the country. AMNLAE has been quick to respond, and it seems clear that in this case Murillo was expressing an idiosyncratic [though probably not unique] position. Most Nicaraguan feminists are far from prepared to abandon autonomous organizing, even as they continue to encourage women to be as deeply involved as possible in political, economic, and civil life.)

By no means were all the women religious of Nicaragua working for the revolution. Some North American nuns I met seemed to believe they were there to civilize the savage Nicaraguans. One such woman, a sixteen-year veteran, drove Joaquín and me out to visit a Miskito *asentamiento*. On the way back to Rosita, she gave a ride to a Miskito child. As he was climbing out of the jeep she prompted him, "Now what do you say?" When she'd received a disgruntled,

"Thank you," she turned to us and explained, "Sometimes you have to remind these people of their manners."

This woman also worked with a women's sewing co-operative, though her style was very different from Sandy's. She directed everything and showed off "her" cooperative as if she had managed to train some particularly talented wild animals to do something entirely foreign to their nature. Sandy, on the other hand, was at least as interested in the empowerment of the women at Hormiguero as in the clothing they produced. She did not announce, "This is how you set up a cooperative. This is how you decide who gets paid how much. This is how you distribute the products." She sat quietly on someone's porch, and listened to the women discuss their plans. If they had questions, she was glad to try to answer them, but only to provide information the women might not have, never to tell them what to do with that information. Consequently, the cooperative belonged to the women themselves. Their participation also gave them a stronger position within their own community. The project was vital to the whole *asentamiento*, because of the terrible cost and scarcity of clothing. Through the co-op, these women developed skills and self-confidence which made them better able to participate in the political life of the whole community. At the same time, their product was important enough to the community that the work itself was highly respected, by men as well as women.

Not all church workers in Nicaragua are radicals, and not all radical church-people are feminists, either. I remember having a terrific argument with Padre Enrique, Siuna's young and macho priest who had also been threatened many times by the contra. The subject was domestic violence. "You have to understand," Enrique told me, "that many women want to be beaten. They come to me and say, 'My husband doesn't love me.'

" 'How do you know?' I ask them. 'Doesn't he give you money for the children?' They say, Yes. 'Does he run around with other women?' They answer, No. 'Then why do you think he doesn't love you?' I ask them.

" 'He's not jealous of me. He never hits me.' "

Enrique didn't buy my argument that a woman who mistakes being beaten for being loved might be a victim of false consciousness, although he was prepared to acknowledge that wife-beating might be a Bad Thing. Nowhere, though, was there room in his world view for the idea that men's beating up the women they live with might be a *political* issue. And of course Enrique is not the only revolutionary Christian whose ideas about liberation don't quite extend to women. Male supremacists have only to run as far as Paul's letters in the New Testament to find biblical support for their supremacy, which makes the Christian aspect of Nicaragua's revolution a dicey thing for women. It will be interesting to see how the revolutionary church answers women's demands, especially concerning those personal issues U.S. feminists have so rightly named political: domestic relations and reproductive rights.

I have a photograph of the Delegates of the Word (lay church leaders) from the Siuna area: nine or ten people (including a pregnant woman) grouped together in the shade the day of the land-title ceremony in Coperna. At least two of them are dead now, kidnapped, tortured and murdered by the contra. In April of 1985, Sandy was kidnapped for the second time and held for five days. This time, the contra released the Nicaraguans who were with her as well. Two years later, she still has no news of the three who accompanied her the first time she met up with the contra. She continues to live and work in Siuna and the surrounding hills. In June 1986 she wrote me that the contra had burned down the Misioneras de Jesús' house in Siuna. The Misioneras and the war orphans they care for now live at Hormiguero.

When I heard the first *rafagas* (machine-gun fire) the night Siuna was attacked, I was afraid, but it was not the bowel-clenching fear I'd felt in Jalapa in June. Something in me had changed in the intervening months.

I spent my first few weeks in Nicaragua in a state of almost constant fear. Because everything was new to me, I never knew when it made sense to be afraid, and when fear was an unnecessary burden. I remember my first night in Nicaragua. Four of us had laid out our bedrolls on the tile porch of the WFP house in Managua. A jeep roared up in front of the darkened house across the street, cut its engine and sat there, its headlights shining into the night. I was sure this was a team of assassins sent by the CIA to do us in before we even got started. I lay there in a hot sweat for about twenty minutes, until one of the lovers got out of the jeep and went into her house! The other cranked up the engine and roared away.

Living through a full-alert in Jalapa gave me a better idea of when I needed to be afraid. And after awhile it got wearing to carry fear all the time; I just didn't have the strength for it. The first time I took the dirt road from Ocotal to Jalapa, I thought about land mines the whole way—even though I knew the army sent out one of its huge trucks to travel the length of that road early every morning. By the end of my time in Nicaragua, a trip to Jalapa, while it might be a logistical nightmare, was no longer an occasion of terror. The possibility of encountering a mine had not diminished, but my spare energy for worrying about it had.

There was another reason, though, besides emotional exhaustion, that I was not terrified during the attack on Siuna; Nicaragua had helped me make peace with my own death. This peace, surprisingly, is something I learned from young people—some of them sixteen and seventeen years old—who had made a similar peace of their own. The first, I think, was Myrna whom I met in Ocotal. She told me, "If I die, it doesn't really matter. Someone will come after me who will benefit from this Revolution." Myrna has benefited personally from the Revolution: she holds an important position in local defense, a position she could never have achieved under Somoza. She has a lot to lose, she explained, but she is not afraid because she can feel that her life is part of the history of her people, and that history goes on.

I stood beside a lot of graves in Nicaragua, hearing the names of the dead called out, hearing the assembled mourners answering for those dead, *"¡Presente!"* Gradually, I began to see how the dead remain present, not just remembered and honored, but present in the community that they helped to build. Gradually, I began to believe that we in the U.S. can also learn that we are part of history—and that the theft of our history is the theft of our courage as well. I began to be less afraid that my own particular little voice would be squelched before I'd managed to say everything that was on my mind.

When I'd written something about this shift in consciousness to Jan, she wrote back that she felt "a terrific regret that we belong to a movement (the women's movement) that has made it so hard for you to know these truths here in the U.S. Too often feminists in the 1970's concentrated on rediscovering how women have been excluded from and victimized by 'progressive' movements. We have often discounted women who worked *within* those movements as non- or anti-feminists.

"I know that the reason that I personally feel connected to all the movements of struggle in this country is undoubtedly because of Dorothy Day. One of her gifts was to be open to inspiration from all kinds of places, even when she remained critical. That capacity for inspiration made it possible for her to go to Cuba in the early 1960's—and be delighted. It's a great gift, to be able to be inspired while remaining critical. Dorothy could teach me that because, even though she was not a feminist, she was a woman. I've met some pretty heavy, venerable male radicals who never had that effect on me.

"So, yes, the truth is that your part of the struggle counts, and is part of a long continuum of struggling women, even though none of us will probably live to see the victory." To be open to inspiration while remaining critical; that was something else I was learning in Nicaragua.

So the night the contra attacked Siuna, my body was frightened, my teeth did their usual chattering, but the terror just wasn't there. I was part of something bigger than me. Jan and I had said goodbye back in June; I knew she'd forgiven me for leaving, and it was easy to convert fear into the anger I needed to do the work.

■ ■ ■

Rosita and Puerto Cabezas

Siuna is in Zelaya Norte, but culturally it's still part of Western Nicaragua. Most residents are Spanish-speaking *mestizo* people, though some are descendants of Chinese immigrants. Rosita, by contrast, is part of the Atlantic coast. You never know there whether a resident is going to greet you in Spanish, English or Miskito. A few words here about the Atlantic coast of Nicaragua, and Zelaya Norte in particular.

Residents of Zelaya Norte account for roughly 6 per cent of Nicaragua's population, while the region occupies 26 per cent of Nicaraguan territory. Nicaraguan government figures show that most people are either *mestizo* (41 per cent) or Miskito (38 per cent). Creoles—English-speaking descendants of African slaves—and Sumo account for the rest.

Development of Nicaragua's Atlantic coast trails behind that of the western part of the country. Before the Revolution, what infrastructure existed was built by U.S. and Canadian companies to facilitate their exploitation of lumber, minerals and fish. The church provided what education was available, and health care was strictly a free-enterprise proposition.

The coast is isolated from the rest of Nicaragua. Bad roads and contra ambushes make travel between west and east difficult and dangerous. Bluefields, in the south, has a microwave transmitter, but while you can send a telegram from Puerto Cabezas, there is no telephone contact between there and Managua. Newspapers arrive days late in towns that have airports and are rarely seen in the rest of the region. "We live at the ends of the earth," a Rosita shopkeeper said to me.

When my brother heard I was going to Nicaragua, he said to me, "Remember, you're going to a place where they made a revolution on someone else's land." He was referring to the land of the Miskito people, who for centuries have lived on both sides of the Río Coco, which forms the border between Honduras and Nicaragua. For many Miskito, the central event of the last few years was not the Nicaraguan Revolution, but the *Traslado*, the forced evacuation of Miskito in December 1981 from their home on the Río Coco.

The river has an obvious strategic importance for both the contra and the Nicaraguan government. Before the evacuation, contra forces had for some time been attacking communities in the area, employing their usual tactics of kidnapping, torture and murder. On the other hand, some Miskito communities probably also harbored contra collaborators. For strategic reasons, and from concern for civilians caught in the war's crossfire, the Nicaraguan government decided to remove the entire population from the Río Coco.

Not everyone left voluntarily, and it seems clear that many people had little idea of where they were going, for how long, or why. Nor was the evacuation handled well by the government. Spanish-speaking Nicaragua has its share of racism towards indigenous peoples. It's not unusual to hear Nicaraguans say when someone is being stubborn, "That's his Indian coming out."

"They're good people, but they're like little children," a CEPAD official said to me in Puerto Cabezas. "You have to tell a Miskito the same thing a thousand times." I asked whether the Miskito might not wonder why *mestizos* insist on repeating themselves a thousand times, but he didn't get my point.

Miskito have reasons besides *mestizo* cultural insensitivity to mistrust the Nicaraguan government: Zelaya Norte is a rich area, and the Miskito claim much of it as tribal land. Contention for title to traditional communal lands began soon after the Triumph. Negotiations continue today.

Shortly after the Triumph, a pro-Sandinista indigenous peoples' organization—MISURASATA (for Miskito, Sumo, and Rama Sandinistas)—was formed. Its leadership included two men, Brooklyn Rivera and Steadman Fagoth, who today are leaders of contra forces. In 1982 MISURASATA split into two factions, both of which chose to take up war against the government. Fagoth, who commanded MISURA (and now, KISAN) is generally acknowledged to have been a Somoza agent. MISURA, fighting in the north, has been responsible for some of the worst atrocities of the contra war. Rivera, on the other hand, chose to ally with ARDE, Eden Pastora's forces in the south. Rivera has since claimed that the partnership was a temporary alliance, good only as long as it served the interests of the Miskito people.

In July 1984, another indigenous peoples' organization was formed. MISATAN's stance is essentially pro-Process, but the organization does not offer the government uncritical support. It remains to be seen whether MISATAN will emerge as a genuine representative of Miskito interests.

In addition, CEPAD continues to press hard for Miskito rights, particularly as concerns the issue of the military draft. Most Miskito are Moravian Protestants and many of these subscribe to the pacifism which is part of the Moravian tradition.

Since late 1984, the Nicaraguan government has met several times with Brooklyn Rivera, in hopes of negotiating a settlement and developing a model of regional autonomy for the Atlantic coast acceptable to all parties. The issues range from repatriation of Miskito now camped in Honduras and Costa Rica to bilingual education and the disposition of tribal lands.

Before I left Nicaragua, the first Miskito displaced by the *Traslado* were beginning to return to their homes. That return had been greatly accelerated in the first months of 1986, partly because of Nicaraguan Army successes against the contra in Zelaya Norte. Negotiations continue toward regional autonomy for the Miskito.

Meanwhile, in the United States, a concern for these indigenous peoples' rights has been raised in some odd places. The Reagan administration, which has never been distinguished by its concern for, say, the rights of Navajo and Hopi in this country, has made great propaganda use of disputes between the Miskito and the Sandinistas. When outright genocide is practiced by a U.S. ally—for example, Guatemala—our government has no objection.

MISATAN leaders are understandably suspicious of U.S. government interest in their conflicts with the Nicaraguan government. In Puerto Cabezas, Rufino Lucas of MISATAN told me, "We've looked at history, and we've seen how the United States has used indigenous people—like the Hill people of Laos—in the past. We're not going to let ourselves be used that way."

The Native American movement in the U.S. has also split over the issue of Sandinista treatment of the Miskito. Russell Means of the American Indian Movement supports the MISURASATA contra. In 1985 he travelled in eastern Nicaragua with Brooklyn Rivera and has denounced what he calls the Sandinistas' indiscriminate bombing of Miskito villages. (To date there has been no independent substantiation of these charges.)

On the other hand, the International Indian Treaty Council, a national organization with committee standing in the United Nations, has expressed general support for the Nicaraguan government's recent handling of Miskito issues. The Treaty Council points out that Nicaragua's is the first government in America to negotiate genuine autonomy for the indigenous people living within its borders. (Organizations like Americas Watch, which have criticized Sandinista treatment of the Miskito in the past, have in recent reports commended major improvements.)

It's very encouraging to me to know that many of the people I met in the *asentamientos* east of Rosita have now returned to the river they love so much.

◘ ◘ ◘

Wednesday, October 17
Dear one,

This letter comes to you from the restaurant in the downstairs of Hospedaje El Minero (The Miner Inn) in La Rosita. Joaquín and I got in yesterday after a wet, bumpy ride in the back of a little pickup truck. It took about two and a half hours to travel 80 kilometers.

I was sad to leave Siuna; I'd gotten to like the place and the people, especially Sandy Price. It was hard to go, too, knowing they're likely to be attacked again soon, according to all the intelligence they've gotten. But we needed to keep on with our work, so here we are in Rosita.

We'd planned to stay with Augustín but he is still saddled with the Bishop, so we're putting up here at El Minero. Augustín is very friendly, and we had a fascinating talk about his efforts to develop ecumenism in Rosita and in the Miskito *asentamientos*. He says there's a "skin-type" willingness on the part of the Moravian pastor, but that "he's not willing to get down to the meat."

It's true, Gus says, that on the *asentamientos*, people often visit each other's churches, Catholics and Moravians celebrating together. But Gus wants to create a deeper unity, based on whatever they find they share in theology and praxis. He wants an ongoing dialogue with the Moravians in which "we identify what we agree on and move forward with that, while we continue to talk about the things we disagree about." His analysis is that the Moravian pastor finds such a project threatening, because it would mean his having to sit down and identify the tenets of his faith. For Gus, who is well-educated and well-read, that would be no problem, but he suspects that the Moravian is not all that clear about the content of Moravian theology. So he's afraid of looking stupid, and of getting sucked up into Catholicism

somehow. The whole thing is so ironic. A European theological dispute dating to the 16th century, superimposed on
an indigenous American culture.

This morning we were to go with Gus to a nearby Miskito
community but his car battery is dead, so we're doing the
usual Nicaraguan hang-loose shuffle. In a few minutes, I'm
going to do a little laundry. Joaquín's upstairs doing who-
knows-what. It's hard sharing a 6x10 foot cubicle with a
man who needs so much psychic space. We checked in with
the Policía when we got into town. They were very suspicious when they learned we had connections with CEPAD
and that we were members of an even vaguely religious
group. "And what is your connection with
MISURASATA?" the *responsable* asked. (That's the indigenous peoples' organization of which Steadman Fagoth
and Brooklyn Rivera were leaders. What's left of it is a contra
group headed by Brooklyn and operating from Costa Rica.)

"*¡Ninguna!*" ("None!") I said, quite surprised. It didn't
help that he'd never seen a Nicaraguan residency booklet
before. He thought Joaquín's was his U.S. passport without
a visa!

I was talking with Sandra about the revolution of the
spirit that's happening in Latin America. We were saying
that with all the ferment here, we can't believe there's not
something similar going on in other continents. At the same
moment, we both said, "I wonder what's going on in
Africa?"

She'd been telling me about the Virgin of Guadalupe—
the one appearance of the Virgin that Sandy says she
"believes" in, because the story combines so many elements
of the indigenous religion. This appearance, she says, was a
message of liberation to the indigenous Americans who had
been enslaved by the Spanish. ◼ *Such deep love to you*

Thursday, October 18
Dear Janny,

Rosita is turning out to be frustrating for us. The town is
distracted, and not the least bit interested in two well-
meaning North Americans. Augustín, our only contact here,
is too involved in meetings which deal with something

vaguely called the "Special Emergency" to introduce us around as he'd originally offered to do.

In Siuna, we could get a pretty clear idea of what was happening because Sandra had the confidence of the town. She didn't mind sharing her information with us, but Gus is Nicaraguan and has no reason to trust us, nor to confide in us even if he did. So we bumble along, trying to stay out of the way.

This morning we went by the office of CEPAD. The *responsable* is in Puerto Cabezas, leaving Mary Jackson, wife of Milton Hemlock, the Moravian pastor, in charge. She was very nice, but couldn't offer much in the way of introductions outside Rosita itself. She invited us to come round tomorrow morning and meet her husband, however.

Then we went off to the municipal government and talked to the *responsable de finanzas* about Rosita's tax structure— almost non-existent. Fascinating. Stores and restaurants pay a local tax, but the amount is not fixed by law. Since they pay no income tax, they're not required to keep accounts! So the *responsable* is empowered to gauge their business and assess a monthly tax. Five hundred *cordobas* per month (about $12.50) is the highest he's ever charged.

This revenue goes toward maintaining streets, bridges, the electric plant, and street lights and garbage collection for a town of 5500. None of it appears to go to the national government. On the contrary, the local state-owned lumber mill pays a 1 per cent tax on gross revenue to the municipality of Rosita. In general, most government revenue is derived from the export of crops grown on state-owned farms, rather than from taxes.

Our hotel sits right next to the militia command post and there's been a constant stream of military personnel through town for the last two days. For the first time, reservists here are being mobilized. Rosita has been pretty quiet, with not a hint of contra interest in the place. Whether that's about to change, I can't tell. Most people seem pretty calm and care-free, but Gus seems harassed and distracted, so who knows? Apparently Reagan said some god-awful things yesterday about bombing Managua if Nicaragua gets fighter planes.

Someone we know heard it on the radio or I'd have no idea; newspapers rarely reach Rosita.

I spent part of today reading the first book of R.E. Delderfield's *To Serve Them All My Days*. Perfect tripe, but interesting to me because it reminded me just how devastating World War I was to an entire European generation. Sort of puts a tiny country like Nicaragua in perspective. There aren't as many people living in this whole country as died in that war. And yet, something important has happened, is happening here.

Mary Jackson today said that people in Rosita are afraid—afraid of the contra, and a little afraid of the *compas* as well. I think for many people in this part of the country, the Revolution and the war have appeared as an unintelligible blur, as a contention between two forces that have little to do with them. This is in part a failure of the Revolution, but maybe an inevitable one. Every part of Nicaragua's population did not suffer equally under Somoza. And every part did not participate in the same grassroots organizing before the Triumph. On the Atlantic coast, *concientización* (consciousness raising) has been something of a top-down affair, which is, of course, a contradiction in terms. All of this is gross simplification, of course, and there are many folks working for the Revolution here, including many locals. But I don't find the kind of unity here I've seen in western Nicaragua.

This morning when I stepped into the wash house (a little hut with a washtub on a stand inside), I found behind the door one of the biggest spiders I've ever seen. She was lazily spinning a silk-wrapped bundle, the size of a quarter, under her abdomen. I took a quicker bath than I'd intended to, on my side of the tiny hut. Amazing what we phobics can do when we have to!

I've been thinking a lot about my place in revolutionary struggle in the United States. Joaquín and Jean have been talking about using the liberation theology model as a means of consciousness-raising among poor people in the U.S. They talk about "pastoral agents" whose work would be assisting in the formation of Christian base communities, say in poor neighborhoods in U.S. cities. The idea would be a genuine combination of reflection and praxis directed by the people themselves. Middle-class co-workers would offer assistance when asked.

How well would such a model for organizing serve the interests of women? I don't know. I'm not yet convinced, I guess, that the message of liberation really is there in the story of Jesus Christ, that liberation theology is not just a powerful overlay invented by dedicated people struggling for justice. A sort of benevolent idolatry, if such a thing is possible—and I don't really think it is. Ultimately, I guess I do think of God as the liberator, or as offering liberation, but I think the world is due for another incarnation—and female this time. Do I really think that? No. But I do think that the spirit of justice in our time must wear a woman's face. ◼ *All love*

Saturday, October 20
Dear one,

Up and down, up and down. Yesterday was extraordinarily successful. We spent several hours on two occasions talking with Milton Hemlock, Rosita's Moravian pastor. (Here in eastern Nicaragua, many people have English names.) Milton is a good man with a hard job. He was talking about the Miskito who have gone to the mountains with the contra. They don't want to stay there, he says. They want to return to their homes and families. But they are afraid to come down. In spite of the Amnesty, they believe the Sandinistas will kill them or throw them in jail. One the one hand, they're frightened of the contra, and, on the other, of the Sandinistas.

Milton sees their greatest hope in Brooklyn Rivera. "Who else can lead them out? Who else can they trust?" he asks. So everyone is waiting to see whether the rumors of Brooklyn's return from Costa Rica will be true. All of which makes me realize how important a CIA target he will be, if he comes back to Nicaragua and shows any signs of being able to unite the Miskito and bring the people out of the mountains. I have no doubt, in that case, that there would be attempts on his life.

The Miskito seem to be terrified that Mondale will win the election. They think that because the Sandinistas prefer him to Reagan, that he would punish the contra—specifically that he would bomb the mountains where the people are hiding. This is what the contra have told them.

The Miskito live in hope that one day they will return to the Río Coco, which is the spiritual and geographical center of their world. "They don't care," says Milton, "that they don't have shoes. They don't care that there's little to eat, that clothes are too expensive to buy. None of that would matter if they could only go back to the River."

One thing that happens constantly is this: The contra show up in a village and demand food, money, clothing. Some people may help them voluntarily, many others do so at gunpoint. But once they have helped the contra, the people know they are tainted and become terrified that the Sandinistas will kill them as collaborators. This again is part of the contra's propaganda strategy. Milton went four times to one town where this had happened. Only a few people were left, and they were guarding the Moravian church. The rest had fled to the mountains. He managed on his first visit to get 120 out of 800 villagers to come down long enough to kill a cow, eat together and celebrate communion. But when he left, they went back to the mountains. Three times more the Frente begged him to go in to try to bring the people back to their village, but they were too afraid of reprisals to come. I believe that the Sandinistas would keep their word, would not hurt these people, but there's little trust on either side. "The Frente don't trust me completely," Milton says. "They think maybe when I go up in the mountains that I make contact with the contra. It's only natural they should have those doubts."

It came up that Joaquín is going back to the U.S., but will return to Nicaragua next March. Milton said something that I've heard so many people here say: "I'll be dead by then." It's true that every time he leaves for the *asentamientos*, Mary wonders if he'll come back.

In any event, he agreed to take us this morning to Sumubila, the biggest Miskito *asentamiento*. We all would have to find a ride together. But he left this morning without coming by to get us. Evidently, the accompaniment of two *gringos* would have compromised the delicate balance he must keep to maintain the trust of his people and of the Frente. I had a feeling yesterday that he didn't want to take us, but Nicaraguans never say 'No' to your face. So here we are again, stuck in Rosita—which is a lot like Bob Dylan's song about being stuck inside of Mobile with the Memphis blues again!

(Later) Then up again: A truly fine interview with three women and two men who work with the Ministry of Education here. We spent an hour and a half listening to their experiences as teachers here in this forgotten zone. The more I hear, the clearer it is that until the Triumph, this part of Nicaragua really was ignored by Managua. Whatever contact there was with the outside world came through foreigners, from the U.S. or Canada.

Radio Quinze de Septiembre, the contra station in Honduras, broadcasts its death threats every day. At the moment, they're offering $250 in U.S. money for a *técnico de educación* (an "education specialist"). A sub-director of education is worth $300, dead or alive. These people go out to communities and work, knowing they go with a price on their heads. One teacher was kidnapped by the contra and raped repeatedly. Eventually she escaped, but now she is pregnant. Of course, she doesn't even know whose baby it is. But she went back to that same community to teach again.

The most amazing part is how optimistic these people are. Against all odds, they intend to make this Revolution shine. "Sure, we'll tell you about contra atrocities," they said, "but first come and look at the new school we've just finished building here." And they did tell us about atrocities—and about the courage of adult education teachers, who bury their notebooks and pencils in the daytime and dig them up to teach with at night. That way the contra won't catch them with the most damning evidence there is—proof of their willingness to teach other people to read.   ◼ *All love*

Monday, October 22
Dear one,

Well, we've been getting some work done, anyway. Turns out it was all a mix-up with Milton Hemlock. He'd gotten into a canvas-covered truck crammed full with people, assuming we were already inside. By the time he realized we weren't, it was too late; the truck was leaving. However, he told the Moravian pastor in Sumubila to expect us, so we'll be going there tomorrow or Wednesday.

Meantime, we went yesterday to Humbra, a Sumo *asentamiento* about 10 miles from Rosita. These folks are from the only Sumo community that existed on the Río Coco. Everyone else there was Miskito. Other Sumo have lived for years in this area and further south. Humbra was established near three other long-standing Sumo communities. Always interested in these things, I asked about similarities between the two languages. Turns out they are related; cognates exist. But speakers of one do not understand speakers of the other. The government is clearly trying to provide some benefits for these folks. For example, Humbra is the first *asentamiento* I've seen with electricity, provided by a Soviet generating plant. They also have running water, but the pump is out of order at the moment. In the winter—nine months out of the year—rain provides enough water for drinking and washing. (I watched the spill off a zinc roof fill a 55-gallon drum in half an hour.) Actually, rainwater is a great improvement on river water for both purposes.

This morning we interviewed the people at MIDINRA, the land reform agency. Their dream: a future when MIDINRA no longer exists, everyone owns the land she or he works and the people together plan for land use, unmediated by a national agency. I'd like to see the U.S. federal agency whose employees dream of working themselves out of a job!

Meantime, I'm reading Gustavo Gutierrez' *Power of the Poor in History*, eight essays on liberation theology. His approach is so deeply and thoroughly cristological that I find myself constantly bumping up against his hard insistence on the centrality of that one, unique Incarnation. It

sticks in the throat and won't go down. I'm not at all sure
Gutierrez knows there are any women in the world. But
Robert McAfee Brown, who wrote the introduction, not
only knows there are women (he mentioned feminist
theology), he knows there are gays and lesbians, whose contribution to liberation theology in North America he
acknowledges. In spite of these deep doubts, I agree with
Gutierrez' basic position: that liberation theology must be a
mixture of reflection and action, but that it is an asymmetri-
cal mixture, in which action must play the larger part. He
argues this point so emphatically that I wonder if he isn't
talking to Martin Luther as much as to anyone. There's no
question that he's proposing a salvation of works (rather
than Luther's salvation by faith), though not so much a
salvation achieved *through* works, as a salvation that *is* the
works themselves. And the works involved are not the traditional Christian sacraments (though the eucharist remains
important), but rather the Works of Mercy—performed on
the level of social transformation. He talks about
subversion—the saving power of the poor to literally turn
the world over from underneath.

So a picture of liberation in the U.S. begins to emerge for
me: a return to the techniques of consciousness-raising
among women; the institution of neighborhood literacy
campaigns; the possibility of organized religion serving as
contact between feminist and right-wing women; creation of
an order of women dedicated to facilitation of popular subversion in Gutierrez' sense, motivated and sustained by
faith. . . . In short, a feminist, spiritual revolution created by
the poor, especially the poor women, of the United States. Is
this something to work for? I begin to think so.

The women's liberation movement is wandering, and I
think it's wandering because, as radical feminist Brooke has
pointed out in *off our backs*, we've forgotten that the word
"liberation" was once the central term of the expression.

Feminists did not invent consciousness-raising, but we
certainly put it to good use in the early part of this period of
feminism. Lately I think the women's movement has gone
in for a lot more of the top-down brand of politics. Unfortunately, you cannot open up a woman's head and pour in

even the best analysis of her situation. It won't take, in any empowering way.

That doesn't mean I think feminists should stop debating feminist theory or that we should stop trying to change each other's minds. Exactly the opposite, in fact. But it does mean that we should concentrate a lot more on developing literacy among women.

Sounds funny, doesn't it, to be talking about developing literacy in the United States, which is supposed to be a literate country. But literacy is more than the ability to translate squiggles on a page into words. (Although I think we'd be surprised how many people in the U.S. can't do even that.) Literacy is the ability to talk back to what you read, and to use what you read to genuinely understand your situation. And that's an ability which has been denied to so many people in the U.S. ◙ *All love*

Thursday, October 25
Dear Jan,

Twenty-seven days to go. Less than a lunar month. I think we'll make it somehow.

Tuesday we got out to Wasminona, a Miskito *asentamiento* about 12 miles from here. The people have been living there for three years, but it's only in the last year that they've been persuaded to plant anything. They haven't wanted to admit they're not going back to the Río Coco, at least not right away. This year they did plant rice and beans, but they miss their fruit trees, their pigs and cattle, and most of all the sweet fish of the Río Coco.

The nurse's aide who runs the health care center says her grandfather *"murió por la aflicción"*—died of a broken heart—a month after arriving in Wasminona. It's not so bad for the children, she says, but the old people cry every night for their homes. She herself thinks "night and day" of the time when they can return home. I asked her whether she thought the *Traslado*, the evacuation, had been necessary. "This is what I try to figure out all the time," she said. "Why did they do this to us? The contra never came to our town. I never saw them. Were the Frente trying to protect us or were they just being cruel? I don't know."

What do I think about all this? I think the FSLN were in a very difficult position and that they handled it very badly—which is pretty much what they've admitted. The ultimate blame falls on the U.S. shoulders for instigating a military strategy that made use of the Miskito on the Río Coco. There's no question the contra were terrorizing some Miskito towns and using others as staging areas for attacks further inside Nicaragua. From a military standpoint, these towns were in danger, and represented a danger to Nicaragua. Any Miskito I meet who've seen the contra in their towns understand why they had to move. The folks who never saw the contra are less convinced. And everyone wants to go home.

We spent all day yesterday at Rosita's town exit trying to get a ride to Sumubila, half-way to Puerto Cabezas. Eight hours in sun and rain for nothing, I'm afraid. This morning we were up at 4:00 a.m. in hopes of catching the ENABAS (basic grain distribution agency) truck at 5:00 a.m., but here it is 6:00 and no sign of it. We're pretty sure of getting on this one, because the driver is staying at our *hospedaje*. There are so few vehicles in this part of the country. We saw only one in our whole wait yesterday. At least 50 vehicles have been lost to the contra in the last year. And the ones still running also run the risk of ambush.

We've been trying to send a telegram to Managua (there's no phone contact with Siuna, let alone Managua!), but it's an *Alice Through the Looking-Glass* situation. TELCOR's antenna only works in the daytime, but Rosita only has electricity from 6:00 in the evening until 6:00 in the morning. "Jam yesterday, jam tomorrow, but never jam today!" A big new TELCOR building is under construction, so maybe they're planning to upgrade the service. I assume that the restriction of electricity is a conservation measure. There's been no running water in Rosita for the last month; people depend on wells and rainwater. But, believe it or not, garbage collection is regular and dependable!

I've worked my way through most of the Gutierrez book. The last part contains some interesting criticisms of the "Big Three" 20th century Protestant theologians, Bultmann, Barth and Tillich.

Gutierrez says all these guys were dealing with the liberal bourgeois question, "How can we talk about God in a modern world of science?" All very well, he says, but that's not the burning issue for Latin America. In middle-class Europe, the main challenger to the church is the non-*believer*. But in Latin America, the main challenge is posed by non-*persons*: poor, oppressed, submerged human beings whose personhood is denied by their society. So the main question for the church becomes not how to talk about God in light of scientific knowledge, but how to talk about God in a world of poverty and injustice.

I think in a way I knew this back when I was reading Bultmann, Barth and Tillich. Maybe the Enlightenment passed me by, but I always thought the face-off between Science and God was a silly one—probably because I didn't have any strong attachment to biblical authority. I knew that in my classes we weren't getting at the real stuff, but didn't begin to have the language for what the real stuff might be. Gutierrez helps a little, except that his language is so damned allusive that only half the time do I know what he's referring to. I will say it turns out that he does know there are women, and that women are doubly oppressed, but he hasn't—at least in this book—explored the contradictions implied by that oppression.

Well, at 7:00 a.m. the driver seems to have rolled out of bed and has gone off somewhere, presumably to get the truck.

You are always with me. Thank you for listening to my ramblings and ruminations. Love to the cat. Tell her I'm thinking of bringing her a baby pig to play with.

◼ *All love*

Friday, October 26
Querida Janny,

This one is being written at great expense of batteries. The little gas lamp in the INSSBI (social security and welfare agency) office where Joaquín and I are sleeping doesn't give enough light to read or write by.

This is our second night in the Miskito *asentamiento* of Sumubila, half-way between Rosita and Puerto Cabezas. Folks have been living here for three years, since the evacuation from the Río Coco. With about 3,100 inhabitants, Sumubila is a good-sized town. The houses are pre-fab jobs on posts, similar to those at Hormiguero. Here, unlike Wasminona, people have definitely settled in and accepted the idea they're going to be here awhile. Each house has its garden, its bananas or papayas, its flowers.

Sumubila has three churches, five school buildings, a huge *comedor infantíl* and a huge cacao project underway.

The cacao project is especially exciting because of its scope; they eventually plan to cultivate over 1500 square miles. In three years, a *manzana* (1.6 acres) will yield 300 lbs. of cacao. But in six years, when the plants mature, each *manzana* will yield 2000-2200 lbs. of cacao. The plants produce for 30 to 40 years! But the most exciting part, to me, is that they're also going to build a processing plant, either here or in Puerto Cabezas, so Nicaragua can export processed oil, cocoa butter and cocoa itself.

The government is running the program, but they're training local Miskito from Sumubila in all aspects of the work. As the mortgage is paid off on the land and the initial capitalization, a Miskito co-op will take over the project. Right now, folks work in the morning and attend classes in the afternoon, in which they not only study technical aspects of production, but organizing, workers' rights, unionization.

We were taken out to see some of the new plants, riding in a fenced-in trailer pulled behind a tractor. I thought we were going right over when we forded a rocky river, but we made it! I don't know how to express to you the enthusiasm of the guys who took us out to see their cacao. We had to climb just the right hill to get a sense of the breadth of the project. Our guides checked out each individual treelet we passed, making sure it was well-watered, well-rooted, and free from infestation. Rough-skinned fingers brushed over those leaves with such *cariño*, such affection.

The big news here right now is about Brooklyn Rivera's recent visit. It's very sad really. As I wrote you earlier, a lot of people hope Brooklyn will be the person to bring the Miskito back from Honduras and to effect a peace here in Nicaragua. Apparently the first thing he said when he got to

Sumubila was, "I bring you a greeting from the heroes and martyrs fighting in the south," meaning his contra forces. That didn't go down too well with these folks, who suffered a terrible contra attack here in April.

When they tried to tell him what the contra did here, he said, "I'm not here to dialogue with anyone." He refused to tour the place, to see either the achievements or the damage done by the contra.

Brooklyn went on to say that his organization, MISURASATA, should be the only legitimate *"dirigentes"* (directors or leaders) of the Miskito, and that they should especially reject the new indigenous peoples' organization, MISATAN. He talked about the old Miskito empire, and spoke in favor of dividing Nicaragua into a Spanish west and a separate Miskito nation in the east. (What plans he has for the other indigenous people living here, he didn't say.)

I have to give the guy credit for gall. Here he is, at the invitation of the FSLN, profiting from their amnesty. They invite him to dialogue, and he spits in their faces. It would be easier to believe that he cares deeply for his people if he hadn't set Miskito to kidnap, rape and murder their own people. Even here, apparently, he threatened to kill all the Miskito who are participating in the defense of Sumubila— which is most adult men.

I wonder if any of this is interesting to you? I think it must be, but the words on the page seem so far from expressing the reality of Sumubila. For example, I'm lying on a cot in an almost pitch dark room, listening. Nearby a radio has just been shut off. A million frogs are talking; answered by a million crickets. Down the hill the faithful of the Iglesia de Dios, the Church of God, clap and drum and sing in Spanish and Miskito. And children all around speak to each other and to their parents. The roosters, for once, are quiet. So much sound, and yet the total impression is of a quiet night, dark and soft.

Joaquín and I have been getting along well. He's opened up a little and we've had some good conversations about how to make revolutionary changes at home. He turns out to be some sort of revolutionary Christian. Exactly what it means to him, I'm not even sure he knows. I was pleased, though, when he turned out to be eager to do some sort of reflection every day.

Tomorrow, we'll go on to Puerto Cabezas, Goddess willing and the creeks don't rise. That last is to be taken literally, as there are several rivers to cross between here and there, including one attended by a five-vehicle ferry. We hope the Sisters of St. Agnes at the convent there will put us up, as the money's running low. So low, in fact, that we've been buying bread for two meals a day and the cheapest thing on the *comedor* menu for dinner.

Oh, my heart. We've made it so far, so long now. If this space we make for each other's work is marriage, then marriage is good for me. I hope it's good for you as well. I know yours is the harder part, but I feel deeply that they are parts of the same whole piece of work—and that we are blessed in having that work. Sleep well. And the Goddess give us both strength, ferocity and patience. ■ *All love*

■ □ ■

Puerto Cabezas

Sunday, October 28
Dear heart,

I'm feeling a little battered this morning, after a long, hard yesterday. We left Sumubila in the back of an open pickup at about 1:00 in the afternoon. By 2:00 p.m., we'd reached the river Wawa, which can only be crossed on a barge pulled by cables and an electric winch. As we pulled up, we were informed that one of the cables had broken, *"Pero están componiéndolo."* ("But they're fixing it.")

So we stood for four hours in a downpour while they worked on the cable. Finally, they put our truck and four other vehicles aboard the barge and we started across. Halfway over, the cable snapped again. Running a portable welder from a truck's battery, they re-welded the cable, and we began moving towards the other side. Twenty feet from shore, it broke again. Back out to the middle of the river. By this time it was pitch dark, and the rain shone like silver bullets in the blue arc of the welder. Joaquín and I began to wonder whether we'd lose the other cable and just float off downstream—and who would be there to meet us when we came ashore.

Campesina women and children huddled together, soaked and trembling. My fingers and toes had long been numb, and my back ached from carrying my pack; covering it and me with my poncho was the only way to keep my stuff half-dry. At last, we moved again towards the shore and made landfall this time. Another hour in a driving rain brought us to Puerto.

We sought out the convent, because Sandy had said they had lots of room and would put us up. Well, they have lots of room—three stories of it—but not much interest in sheltering two half-drowned North Americans. By then it was 8:00 p.m., so they agreed to give us a room for the night.

In the morning, we had breakfast with them, and attended a mass—a dreary right-wing affair presided over by a North American priest with a terrible Spanish accent. Then one of the three young *aspirantes* (sort of nuns-in-training) took us over to a hotel, where we learned that it would cost us more money than we have to stay the ten days we plan to be here. The young woman was very kind, and quite surprised that the Sisters wouldn't let us stay in their huge, near-empty convent.

In the end, they did let us stay, but I'm hoping that the money we asked WFP to send us by airplane will arrive. One sister, Guadalupe, was very friendly and said that just because they're busy doesn't mean they don't like us, and that we should make ourselves at home. Still, they're reactionary and suspicious of us. They wonder how we got permission to come to Puerto Cabezas, when their own North American Sister, Mary Philippa, has been waiting since June. (We just allowed as how you can never understand a bureaucracy.) I would rather stay in a rat-trap, though, than in a clean, quiet place where I'm not really welcome. The Goddess was good to us and at today's mass the Gospel was from Matthew—the part where Jesus sums up the Law and the Prophets. The priest went on in a not very useful way, about loving one's neighbor—all very abstract with quotes from the Pope about how love is the pre-requisite for social justice and working for social justice isn't enough in itself. Nevertheless, I think the part about loving one's neighbors was sufficient impetus to the Sisters' consciences that they offered us shelter!

I have to admit it was a joy to bathe and wash my stinking clothes. You get so dirty traveling, especially when it's so hot. There's nothing worse than a thoroughly sweat-impregnated pair of pants.

The good news is I saw the ocean today. I began to cry when I got close enough to see a lot of her. There's something about the Atlantic that lumps my throat every time. We couldn't get down to the beach, but there is an access somewhere and we'll find it before we leave.

Puerto is a pleasant town. I like the ocean-side feel of it. There's a little more money here, because it really is a port, than even in Las Minas, the three mining towns of Siuna, Rosita and Bonanza. We sat for an hour in the central park where everyone was out enjoying a break from the rain. We also walked all over town—out to the airport and back—just to get a feel for the place.

The people are an amazing mix—Miskito, *españoles, criollos* (Afro-Caribbeans)—and one hears all three languages, including the Creole English the Black people speak here. Two women were walking all over hand in hand, but I know better than to think anything of *that*, except to notice that they were such different shades of brown. It's hard to imagine in the U.S. two women, one almost white, the other deep black, walking even next to each other in such obvious comfort with their surroundings. What racism there is here—and there is plenty—has as much to do with language and culture, I think, as with color alone.

By now I hope you've gotten the first batch of letters from this trip. All day yesterday in the rain, I kept myself warm with images of you. When I was coldest, I imagined the feel of your long skin along my body. I thought of a dark room, a bed and blanket, and the utter peace of my nakedness touching yours. ▣ *So much love*

Wednesday, October 31
Dear Janny,

My watch calendar tells me it's Halloween. How odd. My body still says it's the beginning of summer. Or maybe it's my mind that says: You didn't go to a Giants game. You didn't watch the kids get loose from school and then be herded in again in September. You didn't watch the conventions on TV. It's ninety degrees out. It's not the 31st of October.

Yesterday we met with ANDEN, the teachers' union. We'd set up the appointment the day before but still we were surprised: the regional coordinator (a woman) had arranged for us to hear from four teachers who'd directly suffered contra violence.

In the afternoon we met with Lloyd Miguel of CEPAD. Among other things, he is the Executive Director of the Ecumenical Council for Peace and Justice (a Nicaraguan organization). We thought we were going to interview him, but he started right in interviewing us—about what these solidarity groups, including WFP, are actually *doing* in the U.S. He said people come and go (including the Third World delegation of WFP), and they never hear anything afterwards about their work in the U.S. I have to say it was refreshing to hear a little frank criticism for a change; people here are usually so polite. At the very least, we'll make sure he's on the mailing list for WFP publications.

Today we have an appointment with Dorotea Wilson, the FSLN's first candidate for National Assembly in this region. She's a good friend of Sandra's and at one time was a member of the *campesina* order Misioneras de Jesús. We're also hoping the packet from Managua arrives, because we are running out of money fast. Even staying in the convent, we're spending a lot on food, although last night we started back on our Rosita regimen of bread for breakfast and dinner with a *comedor* lunch.

The *comedor* in question is a little place in the middle of the market. The woman who runs it keeps the radio on all day, while a procession of people come through to eat. It's common to see soldiers and police in there, along with the general mix of civilians. What's interesting about all this is that the station she plays is Radio Impacto, a contra station from Costa Rica. With the elections so close, we've been treated to repeated messages from Eden Pastora and Adolfo Calero encouraging Nicaraguans to invalidate their ballots—and providing detailed instructions for doing so. Clearly this woman is not afraid of repression. My other favorite detail of the Nicaraguan elections process so far: A full-page ad in the pro-government paper *Nuevo Diario* taken out by the Conservative Party. It reads, in part, "Vote for us, and we'll get rid of this Communist, totalitarian dictatorship!" I'd like to see an ad like that in *Pravda*. (The Conservative Party, by the way, has as its slogan "God, Justice, Order." Charming folks.)

Yesterday evening I sat on a rock on a cliff overlooking the ocean. No rain, fiery sunset behind me, a few sharp stars and a moon, my ocean.

The day before yesterday, Joaquín made an anti-semitic joke. I was so surprised I hit him. Not hard, just a shove on the arm, but not the nonviolent response of a good Witness for Peace, certainly. And it made me wonder whether I was quite in control of myself.

What happened: I was recounting a conversation I'd had with the young Miskito *aspirantes* staying at the convent. One asked me right out, *"¿Cuál es su raza?"* ("What race are you?") I told her I was Jewish, and all three were fascinated. Among other things, they wanted to know what language Jews in the U.S. speak. When I got to this part of the story, Joaquín said, "What did you tell them? 'Discount plus markup equals. . . ?' " I was so surprised that my response was that kind of anger that's half astonished laughter. He immediately made some remark about people talking that way about the Scots, too.

We have gotten loose enough with each other to tease a little once in a while, but he knew immediately that he'd stepped over a line. Unfortunately, his natural stance in the world is so defensive, there wasn't space (or I didn't have the courage) to press it. I think, too, that he's already made the necessary self-criticism, so why rub his nose in it?

Now I must write some articles and wash some articles of clothing. ◼ *Much love*

Saturday, November 3

Dear one,

Well, Nicaragua has made it to one day before the elections. A few last minute rumblings can be heard, from within and without the country.

There's no question that the aggression has increased in the last few weeks. From what I hear, there's heavy fighting still near Siuna, and up north of here, and in the Segovias. The contra have been attacking cooperatives as deep inside the country as Estelí, but it seems as though that offensive has been, as they say in Spanish, *desarticulada*—taken apart. Three days ago, contra forces killed six children in an attack on a cooperative in San Gregorio, a little *comarca* (tiny town) near Jícaro (where the Tupperware Bus stopped for so long on the way to Jalapa). Earlier in October, a WFP delegation stayed at that same cooperative. Five girls and a boy, all under eight years old, were killed by mortar fire. It's hard to know what to do with the outrage over six children's deaths, when I think of the children and adults dying in El Salvador and Guatemala—or the more than a hundred thousand people who have died in the war between Iran and Iraq. But the outrage is still right.

Wednesday (October 31st) a United States SR-71 "Blackbird" spy plane flew the length of Nicaragua, causing sonic booms (which I heard here in Puerto), and presumably collecting all kinds of useful data. This kind of thing makes an invasion feel likely.

On the internal political scene: very interesting stuff. In the last week, Virgilio Godoy, the presidential candidate for the Liberal Independent Party (PLI), has announced he's withdrawing from the elections. At the same time, in the Conservative party, an angry convention decided to remain in the elections, despite individuals' attempts to pull them out.

When Godoy announced his intention to withdraw, PLI exploded. It's clear that the majority of the PLI and most of the candidates, including Constantino Pereia, the vice-presidential candidate, want to go to the polls. Looks as if Godoy has effectively isolated himself from his own party.

Even more interesting, it appears that the clumsy hand of the U.S. Embassy has been revealed to be at work here. Testimony from Conservative Party members (the traditional ruling class party) shows that U.S. Ambassador Bergold was offering $300,000 (cheap!) to any party that would withdraw from the elections. The Conservatives were outraged, but Godoy seems to have taken things in a different spirit.

Meantime, the CIA have made fools of themselves by enlisting one Dr. Horacio Argüello, a lawyer, who unbeknownst to them was also a Nicaraguan counterintelligence agent. Apparently, the CIA is sowing the rumor that he's been taken prisoner in Nicaragua, but the truth is otherwise.

Argüello met four times with the CIA in Miami, once with Adolfo Calero of ARDE. In March of this year, the CIA wanted his opinion of the possibility that Virgilio Godoy might emerge as the one leader of a unified opposition. The CIA got more interested in Argüello when he worked with the commission which revised the electoral law. They hatched a plan whereby Argüello would leave Nicaragua during October and denounce the Nicaraguan elections from Spain. They were to pay him $75,000 for his trouble. Instead, he made the whole plot public.

I think the CIA in both these attempts has really underestimated the Nicaraguan repugnance for U.S. interference in their affairs. Even the Conservative Party—no great fans of the FSLN—objects to direct U.S. involvement in Nicaraguan elections.

I dreamed last night of culture shock, of seeing some big U.S. apartment building and thinking of nothing but how expensive, and hard to come by, concrete is here. Sometimes I'm afraid that when I get back to the U.S., the waters will close in on me, and it will be as if I'd never left. Other times I can't imagine myself sane in a cubicle in the accounting department at Pepsi Cola Co. I'm going to leave, and people here are going to keep on struggling—and keep on dying.

And I'm thinking of you constantly. Hard to believe we'll see each other so soon. Just three weeks. We've survived that before. ◼ *All love to you*

Monday, November 5
Dear friends,

I've spent the last week in the Atlantic coast town of Puerto Cabezas. Yesterday, November 4, marked the first genuine elections in Nicaraguan history. Seven political parties posted candidates for the positions of president, vice-president, and delegates to the National Assembly, which will also serve as a constitutional convention. I don't have to tell you how these elections are being treated in the United States press: either they have been ignored, or routinely referred to as, in Ronald Reagan's words, "Soviet-style sham elections." What follows is an account of the elections process as I observed it, and as it was observed by Europeans and Americans all over Nicaragua.

I visited four different polling places, but I spent most of my time in one—from set-up in the morning, through the closing and ballot counting. One thing struck me particularly: the similarity of these neighborhood polling places to the garage on York Street where I vote in San Francisco. Here, too, voting was facilitated by people's neighbors. Voters and Junta Receptor de Votas (the citizens' committee running the polling place) knew each other, greeted each other. The day was marked by that same self-conscious combination of formality and goodwill I've seen in polling places in the United States.

Voting instructions were given gently, in whatever language—Miskito, Spanish or English—the voter spoke. "Which one am I supposed to mark?" an old man asked. "Whichever one you want—but only one box on each ballot." An old woman came out of the voting booth twice to ask what she was supposed to do. "I can't," she said. She had never made an X in her life, and the task of voting was just too complicated for her. But most people seemed quite clear about why they were voting and for whom.

Procedures: All the ballots were counted before the voting began, one pile for president and vice-president, and a separate pile of the ballots for National Assembly candidates. These numbers were attested to by the president of the Junta Receptor de Votas, and by the three party representatives present—from the FSLN, the Popular Social Christian

Party, and the Communist Party of Nicaragua. The four other parties had no observers in Puerto Cabezas, and indeed had not even bothered to campaign out here, preferring to concentrate scarce resources in the more densely populated western half of the country.

The two ballot boxes—blue top for the blue-striped presidential ballots and grey for the National Assembly ballots—were opened and shown to be empty. These boxes were plywood cubes, about two feet on a side. The party *fiscales* checked the boxes. "Show the *compañera*, too," said a woman, one of the specially deputized Electoral Police. So I looked in and assured myself that the boxes were, indeed, empty. Then the president glued four paper strips over the top, along the edges of each box. The voting began.

Each voter presented a *libreta cívica* (voter registration card) on which could be found the page and line number where the voter's name had been inscribed during July's voter registration in each of two log books. Two local representatives of the *Consejo Supremo Electoral* (Supreme Electoral Council) checked each voter's name off in these logs. The voter received two ballots and an explanation of how to vote, fold the ballots and place them in the appropriate boxes. The voter then retired to vote in private behind a blue curtain strung across the corner of the school room.

Workers were careful to see that the blue-striped ballots went into the blue box and the grey-striped into the grey. After depositing the ballots, each voter dipped a thumb in red ink, to prevent voting, as Chicago Mayor Daley is said to have encouraged his supporters, "early and often." The entrance and exit of voters was orderly. Occasionally a woman would hand a baby to one of the workers or poll-watchers while she went behind the curtain to vote. Fifty-three per cent of registered voters are women, and half those I saw voting were women.

Sale of alcoholic beverages had been suspended at 6:00 p.m. the previous night and no weapons were permitted anywhere near the polling places. Even the electoral police went unarmed.

The law required polling places to remain open until everyone in line at 6:00 p.m. had had a chance to vote, and many places closed much later. At 6:00 p.m. at my polling place it was clear that no one else was coming to vote, so they closed.

At 6:03 p.m., as happens most nights in most parts of Puerto Cabezas, the lights went off. No one had a flashlight, so a couple of people went out and waylaid some passing kids and borrowed one. Someone else went home for a Coleman lantern. By the failing light of the borrowed flashlight, the counting went on.

First, the number of unused ballots was ascertained and attested to by all. Everyone agreed that 225 people had voted. The number of voter registration cards collected was added to the seven *constancias*, papers presented by militia members, proving they had been mobilized during voter registration and so didn't have cards. This also totalled 225. Finally, the two log books were consulted to see whether 218 people had been recorded as voting.

Consternation! One log book showed 220, the other 219. Several people counted, and I was also asked to count, with the poll watcher from the Communist Party (an almost illiterate truck driver) looking over my shoulder. We both agreed on 220 for one book and 221 for the other. Finally, by flashlight, everyone went through the two books together, line by line. Once we found an indentation where the pen had not left any ink and once, a name marked off in one book and not in the other. Everyone present knew the person in question and agreed that she had voted, so her name was checked off in the other book. A final count showed 218 in each book; our earlier counts had been off.

Next the president used his house key to slit the paper bands on the blue-topped ballot box. The ballots spilled out on the table, and the elections workers opened each one out. The ballots were separated into piles for each party, and one for null ballots. A few voters had nullified their ballots intentionally, by marking an X in every box, as the pro-contra Costa Rica station Radio Impacto had been urging for the last week. One voter wrote *"¡Afuera Conquista!"* ("Get out, conquerors!") across the ballot. The rest of the null ballots had more than one party indicated or were blank. On one ballot the voter had marked an X on the

FSLN flag itself, rather than in the circle below the flag. Even though the voter's intention was clear, this ballot, too, was nullified.

Next, each pile was counted. The totals summed, together with the null ballots, to 225. General relief and joy! Final count for president and vice-president: FSLN, 114; Liberal Independent and Conservative—the two traditional opposition parties—followed with a tie at 33 each; Popular Social Christian Party, 20; Communist Party of Nicaragua, 6; Movement for Popular Action (Marxist-Leninist), 3; Socialist Party of Nicaragua, 1. The results for delegates to the National Assembly were similar.

And here is my only criticism of the procedures: When voters asked, they were told they should mark both ballots for the same party, whatever party that might be. When I asked why this was, I heard that people are voting for a party program, not just for candidates. "So why are there two separate ballots?" I wondered. The fact is that here in Zelaya Norte, only three of the seven parties even fielded a slate for National Assembly. At the end of the counting, I pointed out that the people who had voted for the other four parties, because they'd been told to mark the same party on both ballots, lost their votes for Assembly. The president saw my point, and smiled ruefully. My friend the electoral policewoman said, "Look, *compañera*, it was hard enough to get people to understand that they could choose whichever party they wanted—but only one. Can you imagine if we'd had to explain that in the case of the National Assembly, only three parties had candidates? We would have been here all night." In practical terms, she was right, of course, and in future elections the problem will no doubt be corrected. I think this insistence that both ballots be marked for the same party was actually a local phenomenon, the result of a misunderstanding on the part of the president of this particular Junta Receptor de Votas. It was not happening at the other polling places I visited. Nicaragua has trained some 40,000 volunteer elections workers in the last four months.

The results were then recorded in numbers and written out long hand, then signed by the elections workers and party representatives. A final decree was read aloud, recording the formal end of the counting and the names of all those present. I have a tiny place in the written history of Nicaragua; the final words of the decree read, *"y la compañera Rebecca Gordon, como observadora."*

All the ballots were placed in sealed paper bags and put with the rest of the elections materials into one big red plastic sack. Suddenly someone remembered, "María just left, and she still has her pen!" Someone ran after María and retrieved the pen, so that every item they'd received that morning might be returned intact.

Then, as was done all over Nicaragua, the president of the Junta Receptor de Votas went off to TELCOR to telegraph the results to Managua. The election materials were gathered in a central place—the Catholic high school, which is the biggest building in town—for a week of recounting and re-verification.

My overall impression was of a scrupulously honest, serious procedure, beneath which lay a deeply felt sense of pride and elation. One more *logro* (achievement) of the Revolution. ◼ *All good struggles*

◼ ◼ ◼

Managua

Monday, November 12

Dear friends,

I should be pretty discouraged tonight. As you know,
since the day of Reagan's re-election, Nicaragua has had to
respond to one U.S. gesture after another: first, the sonic
booms; then the rumors—later confirmed—of movement in
the 82nd and 101st Airborne Divisions; the appearance of
two U.S. frigates off the coast of Corinto and the full-scale
war "games" going on in the Caribbean. If ever there was
such a thing as state terrorism, Nicaragua certainly has been
its target this last week. In a way, these moves on the part of
the U.S. represent a very familiar contra strategy writ large.
Around Jalapa, for example, all the contra have to do is shift
a column of soldiers from one place to another, and everyone
in town has to stay up all night—because you never know
when this might be the night they really fall on you.

I should be discouraged, but I don't seem to be able to
manage it, any more than I've managed to sleep much in the
last week. A fine ardor—half love, half steady anger—seems
to have taken up residence in my gut. In my barrio in

Managua, people are worried. They're back to work again on the *refugios* they'd left alone for a while in order to concentrate on other problems—like the distribution of food. The government has announced that in the next few days it will arm every adult Managuan who is willing to carry a gun. As they did during the insurrection, Nicaraguans are ready to fight barrio by barrio. I should be discouraged, but I can't quite manage it when no one around me seems ever to have heard of despair.

Will this be the time the U.S. finally falls full-force on Nicaragua? Given the confusion saturating Washington these last few days, I don't think that even the strange assemblage of mutually hostile organizations that directs U.S. military strategy has any idea. I do know that the Nicaraguans have made a decision: they cannot accept further U.S. provocation without responding. Several days ago, Nicaraguan anti-aircraft guns fired on a U.S. cargo plane flying over Corinto. They missed. But these were not warning shots, and next time they may not miss. If the U.S. wants a Gulf of Tonkin incident, they'll get it.

By now, I trust it's abundantly clear to everyone that there are no MiGs, and that no one in the U.S. government ever believed there were. If there were no MiGs (and don't think I haven't wished there were, sometimes, when I've just been with families of people the contra have kidnapped, tortured or killed), then why did the U.S. government pretend there were? Several reasons seem obvious, and because they seem *so* obvious, my disgust with the servile U.S. press is hard to contain. First, the news of impending arrival of Soviet fighter planes in Nicaragua effectively wiped from the U.S. papers and TV any coverage of Nicaragua's first legitimate elections. With so many foreign observers present, it would have been pretty hard to conceal the almost unanimous opinion that what we witnessed here were clean, just and free elections, participated in by a much larger percentage of the population than got out to attend our own dismal affair in the U.S.

Secondly, the recent display of emotional instability on the part of the U.S. government—topped off by Caspar Weinberger's performance in announcing a possible "quarantine" against Nicaragua and the possible recall of the ambassador—serves to unnerve Nicaragua.

If its purpose is to panic the populace, the U.S. has not succeeded. On the other hand, there's now a good chance that Nicaragua will lose much of its desperately needed coffee harvest, as student brigades are diverted from picking coffee to picking up guns to defend the country. My friend Blanca Fonseca still isn't sure to which duty she'll be called, but she's told me she's ready for either—and that in either case, she'll leave her three-year-old son, Leonardo, with her mother.

And the third reason for this flashy wind-up? To test the reactions of the U.S. public to an actual invasion. Will you stand for it? Grumble a little maybe, if it doesn't go well? Cheer and break out the banners if Reagan manages another Grenada? Not likely that he will, though. Daniel Ortega may have exaggerated when he said that the U.S. would have to kill every one of Nicaragua's three million people—but he wasn't exaggerating much. So what you do in the next few days is vital. Please (oh, how tired you must be of hearing this from me!) don't wait until you have an invasion to protest. Congress is in recess. The only thing between Ronald Reagan and the carpet bombing of Managua (which he has threatened) is you.

Meanwhile, I have a little news, not terribly good, I'm afraid. A few days ago, contra attacked Hormiguero, a cooperative near Siuna, where I spent three days in October. Several people died, but who they were I have not been able to discover. Fighting is very fierce right outside Siuna now and I can't help but think of the folks in that dusty town, of Juanita and Iliana stumping along under the waning moon, AKa's slung over their shoulders.

It's important to remember, in the midst of the current crisis, that the contra war goes on. Some days I don't think the U.S. will invade at all; they'll just keep bleeding Nicaragua to death, town by town. It's even more important to remember what the Nicaraguans have known for more than a century: *esa la guerra prolongada* (this is the war that goes on and on). We're in it for the long haul. Which I find oddly cheering these days.

Other news: I got back from Puerto Cabezas a week ago, after spending 33 days in Zelaya Norte. I'm very glad to have had that much time in the Atlantic, as well as an opportunity to visit several Miskito and Sumo communities. In Puerto Cabezas, I met Orlando Wayland, a Miskito teacher who had been kidnapped and held by the contra for six months, while he went through enforced military training. The scars from the beatings he received still glinted on the skin over his ribs. He talked about the many Miskito still living as "refugees" in camps in Honduras and of the men trained under three instructors, a South Korean, a Honduran, and a North American. The training worked in an unexpected way; he was able to escape on his first "operation" inside Nicaragua.

I also met Dorotea Wilson, a Creole woman who is the FSLN's first candidate for National Assembly in Zelaya Norte. I asked her if it were just by chance that all three candidates on the slate from that part of the country were women. She laughed. "Women have always been leaders in this part of Nicaragua," she said.

Later that day, Dorotea appeared in the town square with William Ramírez, the FSLN delegate to the zone, and Hazel Lau, a Miskito woman who was also running for National Assembly. The three had called a town meeting, which they began by explaining why the little radio transmitter outside of town hadn't been functioning for the last two months. Since missing parts made radio transmission impossible, they wanted to get everyone together to let them know about what had happened in the town of Haulover—because rumors were flying.

As the tri-lingual (Spanish, Miskito and English) "newscast" went on, it became clear that what had happened in Haulover was pretty bad: the Health Center destroyed, blood all over the school and no sign of the teachers, and the entire population gone—whether kidnapped, killed or hiding in the jungle, no one knew. Ramírez said, "We wanted you to have the facts, because the people always have the right to know what is happening. The people are the source of all power." And I believe he meant it.

Jan arrives in Managua tomorrow. We decided not to risk getting separated by this war the Reagan administration is threatening. We'll be traveling to Corinto, where Witness for Peace plans to rent a fishing boat in order to challenge the U.S. Navy frigate anchored outside that port in Nicaraguan territorial waters. From there I hope we have some time to travel together to Ocotal and Jalapa, to introduce her to the land and people I've lived with for the last six months.

It's very hard for me to realize that I'll be leaving Nicaragua—assuming we've managed to escape a full-blown invasion—in three weeks. If it was culture shock for me to return to Managua where the houses sit on the ground and not up on stilts as they do in Zelaya Norte, how will it be to return home? For six months, Nicaragua has fed me, body and spirit. Now it's time to keep my part of the bargain, and take up the *lucha* in the U.S. I hope you will all help me move into the work you have been doing all along, while I was permitted to live inside a revolution. ◘ *All love*

◘ ◘ ◘

Joaquín and I flew back to Managua a few days after the elections, in a rickety DC-3. The passenger next to me had to tie his seat belt on—it had no buckle. We arrived in a Managua which, like the rest of Nicaragua, was preparing itself for invasion.

The Pájaro Negro—the Blackbird spy plane—had been cruising the length of the country daily, at a height of 40,000 feet. Most Nicaraguans had never heard a sonic boom and many who lived in the *campo* thought they were listening to the explosion of some new sort of bomb, not very far away. In fact, the Pájaro Negro had been cruising Nicaraguan skies for years, but at an altitude too high to produce these sounds. Even North Americans didn't always recognize what they were hearing. Shortly after arriving in Managua, I was speaking on the phone with one of the Maryknoll women in Ocotal. "Wait a minute!" she shouted. "Something just exploded on the edge of town!" Fifteen minutes before, we'd had a boom in Managua, I told her, but she was certain Ocotal was under attack.

These overflights formed one part of a whole U.S. strategy to convince Nicaragua that invasion was imminent. On the eve of Nicaragua's elections, President Reagan announced that Nicaragua was about to receive a shipment of MiG fighter planes from the Soviet Union. U.S. media participated in his attempts to create a "Nicaraguan MiG Crisis" on the scale of the "Cuban Missile Crisis" over twenty years ago. Reagan swore he would intervene to prevent the arrival of MiGs in the port of Corinto—an absurd threat since these MiGs never existed. A few days later I did see uncrated Soviet imports lining the streets of Corinto—fifty bright red Russian tractors, their tires stamped in English: "Made in the U.S.S.R."

By now Jan had plane reservations for the 21st of November, the day my tour with WFP ended. I called her when I got back to Managua and we agreed she'd wait until then. The next day I devoted to typing reports of the Zelaya trip, all the while wishing I'd had the guts to say, "Don't wait. They may invade; they may impose travel restrictions; you may not get here at all." That evening she called to say she wanted to come earlier, could not risk our being separated by a war. Linda was standing by me while I talked to Jan. When I hung up, she hugged me and said, "She heard you. She knew you needed her to come and she heard you. I know what that feels like, because once my sister heard me call when I needed her that much." Arnold, on the other hand, was annoyed I'd made the "unilateral" decision not to wait another week. Most of my WFP *compañeros* understood our desire not to be separated, if the U.S. were really on the point of invading.

I borrowed the WFP truck to pick Jan up at the airport. Aeronica's Miami flight was late as usual. Following the WFP rule for getting information in Nicaragua ("Ask three people and take an average."), I learned that Jan's flight had either: arrived hours before, been delayed until midnight or been canceled altogether. A woman noticed my evident agitation and asked, "Are you waiting for your husband?" I smiled and said, "No, a friend." Because Spanish conveys the gender of "a friend," she looked a little surprised that the arrival of *una amiga* could occasion such excitement.

Once more the pain of concealment washed over me. I remembered all the times I had lied: "No, I'm not married." "No, I'm not lonely being single." "How could I have left my home to do this work here, if I were married?" A few times I'd said something closer to true: "Since I don't have any children from my own body, I feel a responsibility to many children." But while I had talked often to Chilo of the *compañera* with whom I lived in the United States, I had never told any Nicaraguan that I am a lesbian. I did not turn to the woman at the airport to say, "I am waiting for the star-in-my-heart, the woman whose work sustains mine, the woman whose work I hope I sustain, the woman whose absence I have carried six months like a burning coal in my gut." I kept my eye on the swinging doors of *Aduana* (Customs) and waited.

An hour later, the Miami flight arrived and she was through the swinging doors, and we were out together in the warm Managua night. In ten minutes we were talking as fast as always.

"I'm going to open you up and shake you out for information, you know," she said. "Do you mind?"

"I'm going to try to tell you everything I know all at once," I said. "Do you mind?"

We didn't have much time for reunions. WFP had a short-term delegation in town, who were more than a little nervous at the possibility of getting stuck in a real war. Meanwhile, WFP had decided to do something about the warship sitting outside Corinto, well within Nicaraguan territorial waters. We were going to rent a fishing boat and go out to have a word or two with the crew. In addition, we would declare a vigil on the sandy spit of land at the edge of Corinto, set up tents and remain for two weeks. Jan and I left for Corinto the next day with the rest of the long-termers.

I thought sailing out to talk to a warship through a megaphone was a silly action, but I was surprised at how it captured the imagination of the Nicaraguans. The boat, its crew of WFP people, Sixto Ulloa of CEPAD and about twenty members of the press did in fact get within hailing distance of the warship, which promptly upped anchor and steamed away. Stuart, our silver-tongued preacher, had been delegated spokesman. For once, the power of persuasion deserted him; his message to the U.S. Navy had its own truth, if not eloquence. "Go away!" he shouted. "You're not wanted here!"

And the "fragile fishing boat" made the front page of *Barricada* and *Nuevo Diario* for four days running. Months later in the U.S., I met a man recently arrived from El Salvador. When I told him I'd been in Nicaragua with Acción Permanente Cristiana por la Paz, he grinned. "Oh, you're the people with the fishing boat! That came out really big in El Salvador." From the Nicaraguan point of view, WFP was doing something extraordinarily brave. We knew perfectly well that the U.S. Navy was not about to sink a boatload of U.S. religious pacifists, especially pacifists so well accompanied by members of the press. But Nicaraguans remembered perfectly well living under Somoza, who had no such compunctions.

This issue had arisen for WFP before. Many Nicaraguans wanted to know whether our government wouldn't punish us for opposition to its policies. How to answer a question like that truthfully? Joaquín used to talk about the velvet gloves our government wears when dealing with its own people. Often I responded by saying that how the repressive power of our state in the U.S. treats its enemies depends a good deal on their color and degree of power in the world. People wanted to know if we would be sent to prison for showing solidarity with Nicaragua. The truth is that some of us will probably serve time in prison, as right-wing power grows in this country—but that white citizens opposing the U.S. government have never faced repression on the scale that was daily life for Nicaragua under Somoza. The difference is that in the U.S., state violence has yet to be unleashed against the *majority*.

WFP spent several days in Corinto, camped out on the beach. During that time, we had a meeting with local women, some of whom had worked to set up a collective of women who had been prostitutes. One woman, Teresa, talked to us about the experience. "We went into the project very proudly. We thought we were going to rescue these poor, exploited women and teach them a better way. In the end, we learned more from them than they did from us. We learned that their way of making a living wasn't that different from our own marriages." She talked, also, about her husband's opposition to her work in the church and to her political work.

From Corinto, Jan and I went north, planning to stop in Ocotal on the way to Jalapa. I wanted to say goodbye to Chilo and to show Jan Nueva Segovia. Once again, the war intervened. Pastora, a Nicaraguan lay missioner who lives with the Maryknollers in Ocotal, opened the door to the Sisters' house. A big smile split her face; she had been alone for some days now, and was glad for some company. Joan was in Managua; Rachel was spending a few months in the U.S. Would we stay with her until Joan got back from Managua? I knew that the Sisters had received telephone threats, and that they sometimes felt the isolation of living behind the big Iglesia San José, so I called WFP in Managua. We'd been going straight on to Jalapa, because no one was at our house there, since we'd all landed in Corinto, but Arnold agreed that a request for company from a real person took precedence over babysitting a house.

That night we lived through one of those strange, never quite explained incidents that happen in this war. Jan, Pastora and some friends, and I were chatting in the *sala* (living room) when suddenly we heard automatic weapons fire. Through the screen door and windows, I could see the red trails of tracer bullets, very close to the house. I leaped up and slammed shut the big wooden door. We held one of those conversations I'd gotten so used to in the past months: Is it the contra? Well, it's Saturday night. Maybe it's only *bolos* (drunks). We never did find out who was shooting right outside the doors that night, but since no attack was reported, I assume it was *bolos*.

We stayed a few days with Pastora. Jan and I hiked all over Ocotal. I took her to see the twisted remains of the granaries, destroyed in the June 1st attack. We walked around the barrios. On one road a group of folks were digging trenches to lay pipe for running water. They talked with us for a while, describing how hard it was to get everyone involved in the project, even though everyone would eventually benefit from it. Pastora worked at the Child Development Center and gave us a tour, including the *refugio* out back, still unfinished after many months. It turns out that the earth is too sandy in Ocotal to form vertical walls. Failing concrete, the project will probably never be completed.

Joan arrived from Managua, bringing Peter from WFP. She sent the three of us out to scour Ocotal for candies, cigarettes and *novelas* (comic books) to wrap as Christmas gifts for the soldiers who guard the bridges on the road between Honduras and Ocotal. We had a good time selecting the few comics that were neither too sweetly religious to interest the *compas* nor too sexist to allow our consciences to buy them. In one little store we found something I'd never seen in Nicaragua—a block of plain old U.S.-style cream cheese. Eighty *cordobas* later it was ours, and we headed back to the Sisters' house to make cheesecake.

Next morning, Jan and I took the bus to Jalapa. Mary D. had returned from Corinto and was glad to have company in the WFP house. We only had a couple of days in Jalapa before we had to get back to Managua to confirm our reservations, so we went off right away to Chilo's house. She was home, by great luck, and fed us coffee and cookies. We talked for a while, until she had to go to school. She promised to come by that evening with a friend.

That night we made *palomitas*—the Nicaraguan word for popcorn, which means "little doves"—and Chilo told us the story of her life.

"I wasn't born in Jalapa. My family used to live far away from here, near Waslala. My father is a carpenter, but he also was interested in cooperatives. When I was very little, we had to move several times, because the Guardia were after him. Eventually we ended up here in Nueva Segovia.

"I first went to work when I was about eight or nine years old. I worked on the tobacco farm down the road, La Mía. You know the story about La Mía: One day Somoza was driving down the road between Ocotal and Jalapa, with a friend of his in the car. He looked out the window at the land on either side of the road. I guess he was in a generous mood, because he pointed to the land on one side of the road and said to his friend, 'All that land is mine—La Mía—and all the land on the other side of the road is yours now—La Tuya. Never mind who might have owned it before. La Mía is a cooperative now, and you've been with me to La Tuya;' now it's the *asentamiento* called Santa Cruz.

"But in those days, La Mía belonged to Somoza, and I went to work there in the tobacco fields. It was very hard work, many hours every day, and tobacco plants have a juice inside that can burn your skin. The pay was very low.

"I was young, but there were even littler children working there. One day, one of the bosses started to beat up on a little boy, seven years old, because he wasn't working fast enough. I got really mad and told the boss to stop hitting this little boy. Even while I was screaming at him, I knew it was a terrible mistake. I knew I was going to lose my job, but I couldn't help it, because I was so angry.

"When I got home that night and told my mother what had happened, she was furious. 'I guess now you're going to have to sell tortillas on the street,' she told me. I hated selling my mother's tortillas worse than working in the tobacco fields, because I was so ashamed.

"After a year or so of that, I got a job working in a bakery. I would go in the middle of the night to make the bread for the next day. The bakery paid better than selling tortillas, and I got to be proud of how well I made the loaves of bread. The bakery job had another benefit as well, because about that time I started to do political work.

"I became involved with a group called the Holy Spirit, a youth group, organized by my parish priest. We did the ordinary things a church group would do, but we were also secretly working against the dictatorship. We organized discussion groups in town and among the *campesinos* out in the countryside. We would go to the mountains for a week or two at a time, visiting tiny settlements. Of course we did Bible study with the people there, but we also talked about how they could organize to overthrow Somoza. My job at the bakery was good cover because it gave me a reason to be out at all hours of the night.

"Often I would meet with different groups all night, then show up for work, just before dawn. I remember one morning I was coming from a meeting, when the Guardia stopped me. 'We know you,' they said, 'and we know what you're up to.' I told them I wasn't up to anything, that I was on my way to work at the bakery. They said they didn't believe me, and that I'd better be careful because they had their eyes on me. I guess they were just trying to frighten me, because they never did anything more to me than that.

"I began to work more directly with the Frente, running messages and that kind of thing. There was a lot of fighting right here in Jalapa during the summer of 1979. My best friend, Janet López, was killed then. She was sixteen years old. Now the barrio where I live is named after her.

"Since the Triumph, I've worked with the Juventud Sandinista (Sandinista Youth), and of course in health care. You know I'm a regional representative for my union, FET-SALUD (Federation of Health Care Workers)."

Chilo went on to tell us her news: she'd been awarded a six-month scholarship to study community organizing in Cuba. She hoped to spend a month first in Mexico visiting a relative. She was embarrassed about admitting she might be taking a vacation. "I hope you understand," she said, "but I really need to take a rest for a little bit. The pressure of the war is affecting my health."

In the end, Chilo didn't get either her vacation or her community organizing class. Soon after I left Nicaragua, the government began implementing a much more aggressive military strategy against the contra. The November 1984 elections gave the Sandinistas the mandate they needed to fight all-out, employing a strategy that involved displacing many civilians from the zones of conflict. In the Jalapa region, several new *asentamientos* were set up to receive these new *desplazados*, and Chilo went to work in one of these, named El Portillo. In May of 1985 she wrote me that she had married and was going to have a baby. Of her husband she wrote, "He's committed to the revolution, and our struggles are the same struggle."

Before Jan and I left Jalapa, Chilo brought me a couple of new poems, one of them about the Pájaro Negro:

"It booms out, it booms out
and the ground shakes

and the rifles shake
and the fields all shake
the people are astonished at
the enormous thunder
of the Pájaro Negro.
The children run
the birds leave off singing
and it booms, and it booms
the Pájaro Negro.
There is no silence.

The other poem I treasure, because in it she called me a revolutionary, "even though the enemy might not like to hear it." One verse describes the qualities of human solidarity as being, "Lovely, simple, humble—and attainable." Chilo's—and Nicaragua's—gift to me is a faith that the last of those words is true.

Jan and I left Jalapa the next day, and a few days later Sharon, Peter and Joaquín dropped us at the Managua airport. We nearly missed the plane, however, because I'd made a mistake filling out my exit papers.

"What year were you born?" asked the man in the *caja* (little booth).

"In 1952," I answered.

"Well, that's what it says on your passport. But that's not what you put down here." I looked at the paper I'd just filled out. Sure enough, I'd written '1954.'

I laughed. "It's because I don't want to leave Nicaragua."

The official laughed, too. "Be sure you come back, then," he said, and waved us through.

◼ ◼ ◼

San Francisco

Sunday, December 16

Dear friends,

I guess this is my last letter to you. I've been back in the United States for a week now—long enough for the first strangeness of well-stocked store shelves and traffic jams to wear off. But not long enough to forget the warmth and beauty of Nicaragua.

Sandra Price came through Managua the day before I left, with some news about Zelaya Norte. Hormiguero, the cooperative where she and I spent three days in October, was attacked recently. Back in October three little girls led us down the steep river bank to their secret washing hole one afternoon. As a hard Zelaya rain began, Sandra and I dipped water over our bodies, washing away days of dust. We scrubbed our clothes on the rocks, rinsing them in the river. The five of us climbed giggling back up the muddy bank, holding huge wide banana leaves over our heads in a futile attempt to keep some portion of ourselves dry. Sandra tells me that the father of these girls died in the attack.

She had some news, too, about the attack on Siuna during the time Joaquín and I were there. Seems we were all pretty lucky. The *campesino* grapevine says that two contra bands were supposed to squeeze Siuna from opposite directions. When we heard the first *rafagas* (machine gun bursts) we were hearing the first band's signal to the second band. It's probably because the second band never showed up that I'm able to write this letter to you today! All of which seems not quite real to me in San Francisco, so far away from where any of this is happening.

Thank you all for being with me during these last six months. I know that the strength I was able to find on occasions when I needed it arose in part from the love and hope you sent me.

Over and over, people wrote to me sentences like, "I know you can't possibly be interested in the trivial details of my life, when you are in Nicaragua doing something *real*." Oh, folks, if the details of our lives aren't important, I don't know what a revolution is for. Please let me hear about your lives, which are as real as life gets.

The WFP Hotline tells me that ten kilometers away from Limay there were four separate ambushes one morning last week. I begin to realize just how hard the work is here. I've been sending you information like this for months now, expecting you to know what to do with it. Sometimes all there is to do is mourn. And sometimes you just have to get out on the street with your rage. It's deeply encouraging to have returned to a country exploding over the issue of apartheid. South Africa is very far from Nicaragua, but Goddess knows I don't begrudge the energy—and neither would the Nicaraguans.

So, while there is an ache in me from the bones out for the people I've left behind in a danger *I* was able to leave, I'm also able to believe I've come home. This is the place where I live. Jan says she thinks we have to be able to love the United States in some way in order to change it. I know that the people who made a revolution in Nicaragua loved that country. A popular song goes, "Nicaragua, little Nicaragua, my most beautiful, best-loved flower. Ah, but now that you're free, Nicaragua, I love you so much more." How would it feel to be able to sing that way about our own home? ■ *All good struggles, Rebecca*

Afterword

A great deal has changed in Nicaragua, since I left in December of 1984. The war against the contra has gone much better. The economy has gotten much worse. In October 1985, the State of Emergency—which had been in effect much of the time I was in Nicaragua—was reimposed. In March 1986, the National Assembly produced the first draft of the new Constitution, which will now be discussed in hundreds of town meetings throughout Nicaragua. Through all these changes, women have continued the struggle for their own *reinvindicaciones* within the new Nicaragua. And the issue of gay rights has surfaced publicly for the first time.

THE WAR

When Joaquín and I were in Zelaya Norte, I remember feeling frustrated that it seemed the contra could, with a small number of soldiers, so completely dictate the life of the area. It sometimes seemed that all the Army could do was to chase them back and forth across the wide jungle expanse of Zelaya. The contra managed to attack Siuna in relative safety, because raids on neighboring settlements had pulled militia members out of the town. After the attack on Siuna, the militia returned and the contra attacked the *asentamientos* at Hormiguero and Ulí.

A number of Nicaraguans told me that the government was waiting until after the elections to begin an all-out assault on the contra. They wanted to have the mandate of the Nicaraguan people, before they undertook the measures necessary to drive the contra back to the borders of Honduras and Costa Rica. Subsequent events bear out this contention.

The first few months after I left were some of Nicaragua's bloodiest. The contra staged a series of raids along the road to Limay. Julie, one of the WFP long-termers who arrived in August, spent days preparing tortured and mutilated corpses for burial. Nancy Donovan, the Maryknoll Sister who often entertained WFP in Limay, was kidnapped for several hours. Not the kind to be easily intimidated, Nancy was released, after telling her young captors exactly what she thought of these goings-on.

In April 1985 I got a letter from Sandy Price, saying that she, too, had been kidnapped and held by the contra—this time for five days. There were Nicaraguans with her, whom the contra had threatened over Radio Quinze de Septiembre, but they escaped harm by giving false names.

The Río San Juan, which forms much of the border between Costa Rica and Nicaragua, was impassable because of the operations of ARDE contra. There are many little towns and villages spread along both sides of the river, but for two years the San Juan had been too dangerous to travel. In August 1985, WFP decided to take a short-term delegation along the San Juan, in order to make the point that both Nicaraguans and Costa Ricans ought to be free to use the river in safety. They rented a fishing boat and cruised up the river toward the town of El Castillo.

Eden Pastora, the maverick leader of the ARDE contra, issued a series of public threats against WFP, promising to attack the "Communists' " boat if it dared to sail the San Juan. Sure enough, on the way, ARDE attacked. The boat's occupants were ordered off and marched through the Costa Rican jungle, where they were held for 29 hours. Along with

WFP, ARDE had captured a film crew from NBC television, so the event was extremely well publicized.

The Reagan administration tried to suggest that the boat had been stopped by the Sandinistas, and not by the contra. When that story didn't fly, they suggested that the kidnappers might indeed be contra, but that they were members of a heretofore unknown contra group, and not of Eden Pastora's ARDE. From WFP's point of view this was particularly amusing, since their captors had spent a good deal of time bragging about their connections with ARDE. Just as WFP was to be released, a new contra *comandante* came running into camp, in time to inform the delegation that they had been seized, not by ARDE, but by another, heretofore unknown, group.

The event proved an embarrassment to the Reagan administration, and fortunately no one was hurt. Had the boat's occupants been Nicaraguans, rather than U.S. churchpeople and a film crew from NBC, they very likely would have been killed.

In spite of some bloody successes, in 1985 the war began to go very badly for the contra. The Nicaraguan government began to clear civilians out of the mountainous northern regions, in order to be able to fight all-out, without fear of injuring non-combatants. Many new *asentamientos* have been established, to house the more than 200,000 people displaced by the war. My friend Chilo Herrera is now working in one of these, El Portillo, outside Jalapa. Although the Reagan administration has tried to make political points from the plight of the *desplazados* of Nicaragua, the international community—and the Nicaraguan people—have largely supported the Nicaraguan government's actions, which are entirely within the international rules of war.

Militarily, the strategy has worked. By early 1986, the contra had been contained almost entirely within Honduras and Costa Rica. Although occasional attacks continue, for the most part Nicaraguans in rural areas are much safer than they were when I was there. David McMichael, the ex-CIA agent who was working with WFP, visited Nicaragua in March 1985. On his return he reported traveling in perfect safety to places he would never have considered going when he was there in 1984. An example? San José del Bocay, from which Joaquín and I had just returned the first time I met David. I was very happy to hear that somewhere so isolated as Bocay is now safe from contra attacks.

It seems the contra are suffering from attrition as well as military defeat. Contra forces have shrunk from a high of fifteen to twenty thousand, to six or seven thousand. The United States continues to supply and train them, however. In June 1985, Congress appropriated $27 million in so-called humanitarian aid, much of which was spent for planes and helicopters, and $7 million of which seems, according to the Government Accounting Office, to have disappeared altogether.

In early 1986, President Reagan requested $100 million in direct military aid to the contra. The House of Representatives at first rejected any aid, while the Senate passed a "compromise" bill, dividing the aid into two parts. A quarter of the aid was to be administered immediately, again as "humanitarian" aid, and the other three quarters were to sit in escrow for ninety days, during which time, the Nicaraguans were expected to negotiate with the contra. In June of 1986, the House rescinded its earlier decision, appropriating the full $100 million requested by the President. Many observers, including the Nicaraguan government, consider this move tantamount to a declaration of war.

REGIONAL PEACE EFFORTS

Changes in the rest of Latin America have affected the efforts of the Contadora group. Originally consisting of Mexico, Panama, Venezuela and Colombia, the group gained four new supporters in early 1986: Peru, Brazil, Uruguay and Argentina. Election of civilian governments in Argentina and Brazil have undoubtedly contributed to the capacity of those nations to participate in Contadora.

The Contadora group (named after the island in Panama where delegates of the original four countries first met) seeks a regional solution to the problems of Central America. By "regional" solution, they mean one which does not depend on military intervention by forces outside of Central America, and which does not seek to recast regional conflicts in cold war terms. In September 1984, Contadora produced a draft agreement which provided for:

- Free elections in all Central American countries.
- Prohibition of international military maneuvers in the region.
- A moratorium on arms purchases by Central American nations.
- Elimination of foreign military bases or schools.
- Withdrawal of foreign military advisors.
- Cessation of attempts by military groups to overthrow or destabilize governments in the region.

In September 1984, it appeared that the Central American nations were all prepared to sign the Contadora document. The only question mark was Nicaragua, which the United States judged to be unwilling to give up its Soviet and Cuban advisors. When Nicaragua announced it would sign unconditionally, the United States immediately pressured its clients in the region to refuse, citing difficulties of verification. Although Guatemala at first resisted, it eventually joined Honduras, Costa Rica and El Salvador in rejecting the accords.

Since that time, the Contadora nations have continued the search for a negotiated, regional settlement to conflicts in Central America. Most recently, all eight countries requested the Reagan administration to delay making its request for further contra aid until after the Spring 1986 Contadora meetings. This the administration refused to do.

Meanwhile, Nicaragua and Costa Rica have been pursuing bilateral talks. In March 1986, the two countries signed an historic agreement to establish an international peace-keeping force—administered by Contadora—on the border between the two countries. This is very good news, for two reasons. First, such a force may provide Nicaraguans some protection from contra raids across the Costa Rican border. Second, and perhaps even more important, a peace-keeping force will help prevent border incidents from either side escalating into war, or providing the United States with an excuse to invade Nicaragua. Once again, changes inside Costa Rica—in spite of that country's rightward drift during the last few years—made this agreement possible. Of two hard-nosed centrist presidential candidates, the one who most favored negotiations over war with Nicaragua, Oscar Arias, was elected in 1986. At this writing, the Costa Rican congress has still to ratify the accord, but it remains an embarrassment to the United States, and an example of what can be accomplished through negotiation in Central America. President-elect Arias has also announced that when he assumes power in May 1986, ARDE will no longer be welcome in Costa Rica.

The election of Vinicio Cerezo to the presidency in Guatemala may also affect the balance of power in Central America. Cerezo is Guatemala's first civilian president in many years. A Christian Democrat, he is no revolutionary, but he has pledged to end the military's violent repression of his people. Given the military's stranglehold on the nation, it's unclear what success Cerezo will have in altering the realities of power inside Guatemala. On the other hand, Cerezo is a genuine nationalist who has already indicated that Guatemala will not necessarily follow the direction of the United States in its dealings with Nicaragua.

CHANGES IN THE NICARAGUAN ECONOMY

As might be expected, the war doesn't make the economic life of Nicaragua any easier. The contra have destroyed many schools and health care centers, and the money for new ones will not be forthcoming for a long while. Because up to 50 per cent of Nicaragua's budget is now going to defense, domestic spending has had to be cut. Nicaragua's poor experience these cuts most directly in the loss of subsidies for basic foods and other products, and in shortages of items like cooking oil or sugar.

In 1985, the government decided to let the *cordoba* float, rather than continuing to peg it at the artificially low rate of 28, and later 40, to the dollar. At this writing, the legal exchange rate hovers around 1600 to one. Allowing its currency to float against the dollar has helped the government to combat speculation on the black market.

The United States' trade embargo on Nicaragua has had its effects, not all of them obvious. Often the scarcity of a particular product in Nicaragua can be traced only indirectly to the embargo. For example, some regions of the country can't get powdered milk. It's not that the milk itself is unavailable, but that the milk packages used to be made in the U.S. and a new supplier has not yet been found.

There are a few positive economic signs, however. During the 1984-85 coffee harvest, a number of people died in contra attacks, and only about three quarters of the crop was brought in. The following year, military success against the contra made it possible to bring in almost the entire crop, with no loss of life. Because of a coffee blight in Brazil, prices have soared world-wide, which makes the Nicaraguan crop even more valuable.

Apart from various manufactured articles, Nicaragua's most important import is oil. "You pay in cordobas," the Managua billboard reads. "Nicaragua pays in dollars. Conserve energy." Recent difficulties within OPEC (Organization of Oil Producing and Exporting Countries) have driven the per barrel price of oil down to around $10, and the price may go even lower. This is very good news for Nicaragua, which suffers chronic shortages of gasoline and diesel fuel.

THE STATE OF EMERGENCY

Half the time I lived in Nicaragua, the country was living under a State of Emergency, declared by the FSLN, because of the contra war. Emergency measures included restrictions on anti-government demonstrations (though not on religious demonstrations, which, when organized by the church hierarchy, often had an anti-government flavor); prohibition of strikes in government-run industries; some press censorship; and some restrictions on travel to the war zones. Except perhaps for the prohibition of some strikes, the restrictions of the State of Emergency did not affect the daily life of most Nicaraguans. On July 19, 1984, many of these restrictions were lifted, primarily to permit free campaigning by opposition parties before the elections.

In October 1985, President Ortega announced the reestablishment of the State of Emergency, in view of the continued war and of attempts at subversion from within the country. Many in the United States, including some of those opposed to U.S. intervention in Nicaragua, responded harshly to this announcement, in part because the U.S. press described it in terms of the suspension of all civil liberties in Nicaragua. In fact, life under the current State of Emergency is no different from what it was during my first few months in the country.

One of the biggest issues raised by the State of Emergency is that of press censorship. Joaquín and I used to argue about this all the time. He maintained the Nicaraguans ought to shut down *La Prensa* and be done with it, since the paper insisted on printing fraudulent articles about food shortages and land confiscations. I held out for what has largely been the Nicaraguan government's position: that people have to be trusted to make up their own minds. Both of us agreed, however, that *La Prensa* should have to print at least one missing truth in every issue: a line reading, "Published with funds from the United States Central Intelligence Agency."

World War II was not fought within our borders. U.S. civilians were never threatened the way the contra threaten Nicaraguans. Nonetheless, press censorship—along with the censorship of soldiers' private mail—flourished here throughout that war. How would the U.S. government have responded to attempts to undermine the war effort and to create economic panic on the part of a major newspaper funded in part by the Nazis?

A look at recent history will show that the United States has no qualms about using manipulations of another country's press, its economy or existing differences among its people to overthrow a government the U.S. doesn't like. All these measures were employed in Allende's Chile, for example. To think that the U.S. refrains from such activities in Nicaragua would be gross naiveté in U.S. citizens and culpable ignorance in Nicaraguan officials.

President Ortega responded to criticism of the State of Emergency from the U.S. left by reminding us of the grief we felt at Allende's murder. Nicaragua, he said, would rather offer the world a live revolution to criticize than a dead one to mourn. Re-imposition of the State of Emergency is not a happy decision. Who is to say whether it was the right one?

ADDRESSING WOMEN'S CONCERNS

At the end of September 1985, AMNLAE presented to the Special Constitutional Commission of the National Assembly its proposals for constitutional guarantees of women's rights. These proposals represent a major shift for AMNLAE, not only in terms of their content but because they represent a new emphasis on issues of particular concern to women. Since the beginning of the contra war, and with the deepening of the country's economic crisis, AMNLAE had focused its attention almost exclusively on the integration of women in the tasks of defense and production. AMNLAE's new position is that, in spite of the war, women's needs must be addressed in the new Constitution. In an interview with *Barricada Internacional* (the FSLN's international weekly), María Lourdes Bolaños, an attorney and former magistrate of the Supreme Court, asked, "If we wait until the war is over, when will we begin to solve women's problems?"

In the same interview, Bolaños went on to describe those problems: domestic violence—including rape by husbands, brothers or fathers; sexual harassment on the job; inequalities in the existing laws governing divorce (under which only a woman can commit adultery!); unequal access for women to training and employment; and *la doble jornada laboral* (the double work day) with which women in the rest of the world are all too familiar.

AMNLAE put forward the position that in order to establish genuine equality for women, Nicaragua will have to, in fact, give women preferential treatment to correct past inequalities. Principles AMNLAE would like to see incorporated in the new Constitution include:

- Proportional representation for women at all levels of government.
- Equal employment opportunity for women, with preference for women with dependents.
- Preferential access to education and technical training for women.
- Equal rights for women within couples, whether

married or not.
- Equal sharing between men and women of rights and responsibilities within the home, including responsibility for children and housework.
- Guarantee of the right of a woman, whether head of a household or not, to own land and other property.
- Legalization of abortion.

As might be expected in a Catholic country, the call to legalize abortion has opened a major debate. In November 1985, a series of articles about abortion appeared in *Barricada*, beginning with a report of the discussion which took place during an annual Nicaraguan-North American health conference. At the conference a team from Bertha Calderón Maternity Hospital in Managua discussed the results of a two year-study on abortion. They reported an average of ten admissions per *day* for medical problems arising from illegal abortions. Ten per cent of the women studied had died and another 26 per cent became sterile as a result of septic abortions. Complications arising from abortions are the single greatest cause of maternal death in Nicaragua.

Existing Nicaraguan law permits only "therapeutic" abortions, and only with a doctor's consent, upon request of the *husband* of the pregnant woman. Requiring a husband's permission for abortion automatically excludes any unmarried woman from obtaining one. In spite of the suffering it causes women, changing the abortion law will not be easy.

Barricada continued the abortion debate with a center-page spread on November 25, 1985. This roundtable discussion involved women doctors from Bertha Calderón, representatives of the Ministry of Health and of the Women's Legal Assistance Office of AMNLAE. While all participants agreed on the eventual need to legalize abortion, they disagreed about how soon it must happen. One of the doctors summed up her position this way: "A discussion like this is no good. Sex education is a long-term solution. Contraceptives just aren't available. There must be an immediate solution so that women do not continue to die." The issue continues to be discussed, both in *Barricada* and on government-sponsored television.

It's exciting that discussions of women's rights in Nicaragua are being framed in specifically feminist terms. It also seems there's been some genuine cross-fertilization between the U.S. and Nicaraguan women's movements. While Nicaraguan feminists make it clear that their priorities are often quite different from ours, they have also adopted positions based on the best principles of U.S. and European feminism: the idea that personal relations are political relations (especially between women and men!); the idea that women must control our own reproductive capacities; and the idea that women have a right to safety from sexual assault, and, perhaps more surprisingly, a right to sexual pleasure.

Nicaraguan feminists have even adopted some of the language of the U.S. women's movement. For example, in the *Barricada* article quoted above, the author referred to racism, sexism and classism as forces deforming Nicaraguan society. Spanish speakers don't usually use the word "classist" to mean "furthering class stratification" or "favoring the upper classes." It's an expression that originated in the women's movement of the United States.

While *Barricada* was considering abortion rights, in the pro-government paper *Nuevo Diario*, the issue was gay rights. The debate began almost by accident, when Adolpho Miranda Saenz, a regular columnist, published an article about littering, in which he wrote, "The (Nicaraguan) levels of drug addiction and homosexuality are low compared to those in nearby decadent societies. That's something to be proud of. But it doesn't justify the other kind of trash." By "the other kind of trash," Miranda Saenz meant litter in the streets of Managua, but it turned out that *Nuevo Diario* readers were much more interested in the first kind. In subsequent articles, Miranda Saenz advanced the thesis that homosexuality is unnatural and that any other view on the subject is "unscientific" because "the purpose" of sexuality is reproduction.

Among other readers, Pablo Juarez Calvo responded that while reproduction is certainly one purpose of sexuality, "that it is the only purpose, is not so clear." He went on to argue that Nicaragua is in the process of leaving behind an old society that had "great sexual sensitivity and little social sensitivity." In the old Nicaragua, the only sins recognized either by the Church or by society were sexual sins. In fact, wrote Juarez Calvo, a number of perfectly natural acts are social evils, for example, "abandoning a woman you've gotten pregnant, or not supporting the children you've pro-created in the most natural way possible—sins which don't seem to bother many Nicaraguan men."

This discussion of gay rights in the pages of *Nuevo Diario* represents something new under the sun. To my knowledge, such a discussion has not happened within any other revolu-tionary society. And although most of the participants were men, it was clearly framed, at least for some, in feminist terms.

In this vein, the monthly *Pensamiento Propio* (published by a Nicaraguan government agency) printed a fascinating and very sophisticated summary of both the abortion and gay rights discussions. The connection between the two issues, writes Isabel Laboy, is that they concern the power to control one's own sexuality. In her conclusion entitled "Sexuality and Democracy," she points out that the issue of abortion rights, in particular, places AMNLAE in a difficult position. As has happened before, AMNLAE will have to work to reconcile the larger interests of the Revolution with the urgent demands of a problem that pertains *specifically* to women. Laboy clearly believes those interests must be recon-cilable in a just and democratic society.

Laboy's final paragraph reads, "(Winning abortion rights) is a long-term project, and possibly as it develops, other themes will arise, which have hardly even been sug-gested yet. Themes like relations within couples, the power of the concept of 'family' as it affects Nicaraguan reality, etc. At the same time, it's to be hoped that in this process of democratization, discussions *about* (her emphasis) women and homosexuals will disappear, and both groups will finally be free to create—and control—their own discus-sions, and their own sexuality."

Lesbians in the U.S. women's movement did not have an easy time convincing other feminists that our concerns were anything more than, in Betty Freidan's words, a "lavender herring". It appears that in Nicaragua, at least some feminists are willing to skip that debate and place gay rights where they belong: within a larger analysis of sex oppression and sexual freedom.

THE NEW CONSTITUTION

The new Nicaraguan National Assembly was elected in 1984 to serve both as a legislature and as a constitutional convention. Clearly, this second function will have far reaching effects on Nicaragua. Drafters of the new constitution have consulted with experts on constitutional law from around the world, including many from the United States. Perhaps more importantly, they've consulted with people from all over Nicaragua. In March 1986, the National Assembly released a million copies of their first draft of the new constitution. Nicaraguans will now discuss and criticize the draft in hundreds of town meetings scheduled around the country in the next few months.

Most of the major political parties have taken part in writing the draft. Exceptions include the members of the Coordinadora Democrática, none of which participated in the 1984 elections, either. In addition, the Liberal Independent Party has withdrawn support, although negotiations are still in process to secure its participation. Several of the parties continue to have major reservations in two areas: the amount of power vested in the executive branch of government and the interpenetration of the FSLN and the Nicaraguan army.

From a U.S. point of view, the draft is nevertheless an extraordinary document, codifying the right of the people of Nicaragua to decent housing, food, education and work. It promises freedom of religion and defines Nicaragua as a secular state with no official religion. It guarantees the right to strike and the right to organize politically.

How many of AMNLAE's demands are addressed in the draft? Abortion rights are not mentioned. On the other hand, it does decree "absolute equality of rights and responsibilities between women and men" within the family; it guarantees childcare to all working parents and paid maternity leave to all mothers. One of the contested articles also guarantees the right of all Nicaraguans to create a family, whether through matrimony or simply through cohabitation. The implications of women's right to form relationships without the blessing of the state, and yet to maintain rights within those relationships, are far-reaching.

FEMINISM AND REVOLUTION: LEARNING FROM NICARAGUA

Nicaragua is not the United States. It would be absurd to lift the experience of Nicaraguan women out of its context and attempt to apply it unchanged to the issues facing women in this country. But we can still learn a great deal from that experience.

Early in the current wave of U.S. feminism, women rightly rejected martyrdom as a lifestyle. For centuries, women had devoted their whole lives to the interests of husbands and families. Feminists were not going to ask of each other the same kind of self-sacrifice. The ethic of the Nicaraguan revolution, on the other hand, profoundly embraces personal sacrifice. Yet, though many Nicaraguans give up sleep, food, time with loved ones, and their very lives, theirs is not the sacrifice of *personhood* demanded of women by patriarchal society. In a real sense, these *"héroes y mártires"* of the Revolution are moved by what I believe to be the best, most dependable motive for political action: self-interest.

Over and over I met people in Nicaragua who were prepared to die to defend something in which they had a very personal stake. A fifteen-year-old soldier recuperating in a military hospital in Jinotega told me, "Before the Revolution, my family had nothing. Now my parents have a little farm in Chinandega and a land title that says no one can take it away from us. That is what I am fighting to defend." Freedom is a very tangible thing in Nicaragua—a piece of land, paper and pencil, participation with the rest of the community in decisions affecting daily life.

But what good is freedom if you personally are too dead to enjoy it? This is the paradox of the Nicaraguan revolution: that it is made by and for people motivated by self-interest, yet who are willing to sacrifice their own lives to achieve its benefits.

The key to this riddle lies in how one defines both freedom and self-interest. The dominant culture of the United States presents everywhere—from political speeches to movies to television ads—an image of freedom as something pertaining to and experienced by *individuals*, those lonely, but noble and self-actualizing beings who wander the world, creating their own reality as they go. I'm certainly not the first observer to point out that this understanding of freedom serves very well the needs of a capitalist economic system, in which each individual must compete with every other to sell her or his labor. Capitalism turns freedom into a commodity, repackages it as individuality and then sells it back to us, as the consumers of the beer or make-up or deodorant that will make us special and unique. Freedom, the legitimate right to exercise power over the direction of one's life, is debased to mean the opportunity to choose from among competing products.

This belief that freedom is a property of individuals, rather than something pertaining to a community of people, makes united political action very difficult to achieve. Anyone who has worked, for example, in the women's movement in the United States will have observed how processes originally intended to empower more women— like consensus decision-making—often produce, instead, an experience of frustration and disempowerment. How many of us have sat through four-hour meetings trying to accomplish business that could be done in a quarter of the time? Because many women bring to our political work this individualist understanding of what power is, we often feel we need to have—and to express—an opinion on every issue, no matter how tiny. If we don't have an opinion, we'll manufacture one—and cling to it. Otherwise, how can we be sure we haven't given away our power?

I'm not arguing here against consensus as a means of making group decisions. Oddly enough the Junta de Reconstrucción Nacional, the ruling body in Nicaragua until the 1984 elections, was a politically diverse group that made all its decisions by consensus! I'm trying to show that an exaggerated individualism perverts the process, making it difficult or impossible to act. This perception, by the way, accords with criticisms some feminists of color have made of white groups operating through consensus—that they're all talk and no action.

I think this kind of individualism disguised as empowerment damages the work of political groups in another way. By personalizing all conflicts, individualism makes it very difficult to distinguish between private conflicts and genuine political differences. Every issue within a group comes to carry the same weight. Class and race issues, which by their nature concern large numbers of people, are reduced to struggles between individuals.

So what's the alternative? Maybe we missed a step when we threw out the bad old ethic of martyrdom for the oppressor's benefit and replaced it with a concentration on defining and meeting individual, personal needs. We might have done better by substituting something understood very well by that soldier I met in Jinotega, an ethic based on our needs as members of something larger than ourselves: the community of women. When we identify with a community—or communities—in struggle, it is not altruism. The benefits are great, because such a consciousness reflects the truth of our shared interests.

"If I die," a young woman soldier told me, "it doesn't matter. Someone will come after me who will benefit from this Revolution." Feminism for the long haul requires the consciousness that we are part of something that began long before we were born, and will continue long after we die. When we experience ourselves as part of a history of struggle, as many Nicaraguans do, sacrifice takes on new meaning and death becomes a little less terrifying. We remember that giving of ourselves to the women's movement means giving not only to other women but to something that belongs to us, too.

THINKING ABOUT WEALTH

People in Nicaragua—and in the rest of the Third World, as well as in parts of the Third World transplanted inside the United States—are poor. That poverty is not accidental. It is the inevitable result of an economic system that makes the majority of the people in the United States rich by comparison to the rest of the world. We did not make all that wealth by ourselves. Not even the labor of all the working people in the United States made that wealth. It also came from labor and raw materials taken by U.S. and multi-national corporations from other, poorer, countries.

If I'm trying to build a feminist ethic of genuine self-interest, based on my membership in a community of women, what does it mean to me as a feminist that my wealth depends on other women's poverty? If I really believe that my own liberation depends on the liberation of women everywhere, am I going to have to sacrifice some of my material comfort so that other women will have running water, health care, education and decent food?

I'm afraid of becoming too attached to a status quo which I need desperately to change. In the last few years, at least in my part of the country, getting ahead financially, making a few investments, maybe acquiring rental property, have become acceptable expressions of feminism—the kind of feminism that says it's revolutionary for women to put themselves first. I guess I'm saying something pretty hard here: that kind of feminism is not revolutionary. In the long run it will not benefit women, not even women who "get ahead" financially but are emotionally and spiritually diminished by locating themselves outside the wider struggle for freedom.

Everyone in the world has the right to have food to eat, a decent place to live, an education, and meaningful work to do. Many women in the United States have been denied those rights through the systematic operation of class stratification, racism and male domination. I would not presume to tell these women that "The Revolution" requires that they continue to be so deprived, or to define for anyone else what is an "ethical" standard of consumption. That would be the height of arrogance coming from someone like me, a woman who has received the benefits of 33 years of what, by global standards, is staggering wealth.

But I do think that U.S. feminists need to struggle together through the implications of the extent to which we share the stolen wealth of this country. We won't be alone in the struggle. For at least 40 years the U.S. left has confronted the problem of creating revolution in a country the majority of whose working class has enjoyed a relatively high standard of living. And anti-imperialist activists face the knotty task of convincing the U.S. public to oppose foreign policies that actually benefit them materially.

One way out of this dilemma lies in a re-interpretation of self-interest to include something beyond material wealth. The forces of power in this country have fed our people's hunger for justice with a surfeit of *things*. A labor movement whose original goal was worker *control* has been bought off with high wages instead. I think that those people in the United States today who do have enough to eat are hungry for something of the spirit. The forces of the Right have already recognized that hunger and have rushed to assuage it with the combination of authoritarianism, racism and misogyny that is the Specialty of the House of fundamentalist Christianity. That way lies genuine fascism. Feminists had damned well better have something more wholesome to offer, if we're to survive the next few years.

CONCLUSIONS

I took a lot of questions to Nicaragua, and many of them I brought home with me again. I took a number of convictions with me as well, and none of these was too badly shaken up. I still wonder about the capacity of a revolution that calls itself "Christian" to address the rights of women, as women. And I am more convinced than ever that liberation can only happen from the bottom up. If there's one thing I learned from Nicaragua's revolution, it's to have faith in the power and vision of those who are awakening from oppression.

The most important question I had is one that feminists have debated in the United States for at least the last twenty years. It's been phrased in many ways: "Can women's oppression be explained strictly in terms of contradictions between economic classes?" Or, "Do women need an autonomous movement or should feminists work for the socialist revolution which alone can achieve justice for women?" Or, most simply, "Does socialism liberate women?"

What I saw in Nicaragua is that a genuine revolution turns traditional power relations upside down, and throws traditional beliefs about the nature of the world and human beings open to question. When a whole society is awakening, anything can happen. I can certainly imagine no more promising time for women to demand justice in Nicaragua than now, in the context of the political, economic and social revolution Nicaragua is making.

That is not to say that women's *reinvindicaciones* are the automatic results of a left revolution, or that with Somoza gone, Nicaraguan women have only to sit back and watch their new equality roll in. Vida Luz, a woman poet visiting from Nicaragua, said to me one evening recently, "I know many men, brave men, who are ready to die tomorrow for Nicaragua. Yet for them, the Revolution stops at the doors to their own homes." During the insurrection, the song *"La Consigna"* offered an underground invitation to join the struggle against Somoza. One line goes, *"Esa es la guerra prolongada."* "This is the war that goes on and on." That same evening, someone said to Vida Luz that the struggle for women's rights looks to her like *la guerra prolongada*. The poet threw back her head and laughed her agreement.

In the U.S. as well as in Nicaragua, real feminism must want more than change which creates parity between women and men within each class, but which leaves relations between those classes untouched. It's not enough that women of one class should have equal access to the board room of General Motors, while women of another have equal access to the Food Stamp office.

On the other hand, I'm not suggesting that women in the United States should postpone agitation for our own *reinvindicaciones* until some future "Revolution" throws power relations in our own country open to the same kind of radical scrutiny as has occurred in Nicaragua. Only that if such a time of ferment ever does come in the United States, women should be ready to take advantage of the opening it will create.

So, does socialism liberate women in Nicaragua? The answer has to be yes—*and* no, at least not without a struggle.

In Nicaragua as in the rest of the world, women working in liberation movements live with a special kind of pain. There comes a moment when you realize that for your *compañeros*, liberation of "the people" was somehow never meant to include liberation of the women within that people. You find yourself forced to defend justice to the very people beside whom you've been struggling for justice. Inevitably, you're accused, at best, of irrelevance; at worst, of betrayal. And you begin to wonder if maybe the accusations are true. That's the time when you draw on the work of those who've gone before you.

History is long and, famous maxims to the contrary, does not repeat itself. Each time women face these contradictions, the situation is a little different, and maybe even a little easier, because it's been faced before somewhere else, by someone else. The struggles of my Nicaraguan *compañeras* make my struggle a little easier, and a good deal more hopeful. I may not live to see a just world. But someone will.

◼ ◼ ◼

Index

Resources

Literally hundreds of groups exist today to support Nicaragua or to oppose U.S. intervention in Central America. Besides the national organizations listed below, in most large cities and in many smaller ones, grassroots groups have sprung up which focus on special interests or special projects. (In the San Joaquin Valley of California, for instance, a group of dispossessed farmers plans to take up the Nicaraguan government's offer of land to farm in Nicaragua. Other farmers have sent tractors and dairy cattle to their Nicaraguan counterparts.) If you're unsure how to get in touch with the right group for your area and interests, one of the organizations below can probably get you connected. Many of these groups also publish newsletters and other resource materials.

Witness for Peace
1414 Woodland Dr.
Durham, N.C. 27701
(919) 286-0248

Newsletter address
2124 Kittredge, #94
Berkeley, CA 94704

Hotline (current information from Nicaragua, updated weekly)
(202) 332-9230

Caribbean Basin Information Project
1826 18th Street N.W.
Washington, DC 20009
(202) 462-8333

Central American Historial Institute Intercultural Center
Georgetown University
Washington, DC 20057
(202) 625-8246

Chicago Religious Taskforce on Central America
407 S. Dearborn, Room 370
Chicago, IL 60605
(312) 427-2533

Coalition for a New Foreign and Military Policy
120 Maryland Avenue NE
Washington, DC 20002
(202) 546-8400

Central Americal Legislative Hotline (3 minute message, 24 hours a day; it is changed at least once a week)
(202) 483-3391

Council on Hemispheric Affairs (COHA)
1612 20th St., NW
Washington, DC 20009
(202) 745-7000

Ecumenical Program for Inter-American Communication and Action (EPICA)
1470 Irving Street, NW
Washington, DC 20020
(202) 332-0292

Institute for Food and Development Policy
1885 Mission Street
San Francisco, CA 94103-3584
(415) 864-8555

Inter-Religious Task Force on
Central America
475 Riverside Drive, Room 633
New York, NY 10115
(212) 870-3383

Michigan Interchurch Com-
mittee on Central American
Human Rights (MICAH)
4220 W. Vernor
Detroit, MI 48209
(313) 841-4320

National Network in Solidarity
with the Nicaraguan People
2025 "I" St. NW, Suite #1117
Washington, DC 20006
(202) 223-2328

NETWORK
806 Rhode Island Ave., NE
Washington, DC 20018
(202) 526-4070

Nicaragua Interfaith Committee
for Action (N.I.C.A.)
942 Market Street, 7th Floor
San Francisco, CA 94102
(415) 433-6057

Nicaraguan Information Center
P.O. Box 1004
Berkeley, CA 94701
(415) 549-1387

North American Congress on
Latin America (NACLA)
151 West 19th Street
New York, NY 10011
(212) 989-8890

Quixote Center
P.O. Box 5206
Hyattsville, MD 20782
(301) 699-0042

Religious Taskforce on Central America
1747 Connecticut Avenue,
NW
Washington, DC 20009
(202) 387-7652

Washington Office on Latin
America
110 Maryland Avenue, NE
Washington, DC 20002
(202) 544-8045

Women's Coalition Against
U.S. Intervention in Cen-
tral America and the
Caribbean
475 Riverside Drive
New York, NY 10115
(212) 870-2347

The Quixote Center in Baltimore publishes an excellent 16 page tab-
loid called "Nicaragua: a Look at the Reality," which includes the above
list. They also coordinate "Quest for Peace," a national project to tally all
the material aid North Americans have sent to Nicaragua.

The Nicaragua Information Center in Berkeley publishes "Nicaraguan
Perspectives," a nationally distributed magazine, which gained instant (if
fleeting) fame when President Reagan attacked it as "slick propaganda for
them and against us." They also publish pamphlets and a bi-monthly
"Bulletin."

Rebecca Gordon is a bookkeeper living in San Francisco. A long-time feminist activist, she and three other women publish the quarterly, *Lesbian Contradiction: a Journal of Irreverent Feminism*. She is also the author of several plays, and a collection of poems, *By Her Hands*.

A Jew who received little religious training in her own tradition, she absorbed the Christianity of the dominant culture. Acquaintance with marxism and feminism gave her new lenses with which to view the world. Now thoroughly confused, she lives for the day when it all finally makes sense to her. In the meantime, she keeps on balancing the books and producing as many puns as those who love her will permit.

Photo: Sharon Hallas

▨spinsters | *aunt lute* ▣

Spinsters/Aunt Lute Book Company was founded in 1986 through the merger of two successful feminist publishing businesses. Aunt Lute Book Company moved from Iowa City to San Francisco in 1986 to join with Spinsters Ink. A consolidation in the best sense of the word, our recent merger strengthens our ability to produce vital books for diverse women's communities in the years to come.

Our commitment is to publishing works that are beyond the scope of mainstream commercial publishers: books that don't just name crucial issues in women's lives, but go on to encourage change and growth, to make all of our lives more possible.

We also want to thank you, our readers, for your commitment. Whether you support us by buying our books or choosing one of the many other ways to invest in Spinsters/Aunt Lute, you enable us to bring out new books. Write to us for a free catalog of our 26 titles and our women's art notecards. Or let us know of your interest in an investors' brochure.

Spinsters/Aunt Lute
P.O. Box 410687
San Francisco, CA 94141